BRITISH MAPS
OF THE AMERICAN
REVOLUTION

by Peter J. Guthorn

PHILIP FRENEAU PRESS

Monmouth Beach, N.J.

1972

Other titles in the Philip Freneau Press
Bicentennial Series on The American Revolution

AMERICAN MAPS AND MAP MAKERS OF
THE REVOLUTION
Peter J. Guthorn
LC No. 66-30330/ISBN 0-912480-02-5

THE HESSIAN VIEW OF AMERICA 1776-1783
Ernst Kipping
LC No. 72-161384/ISBN 0-912480-06-8

VALLEY FORGE CRUCIBLE OF VICTORY
John F. Reed
LC No. 70-76769/ISBN 0-912480-04-1

THE BATTLE OF TRENTON
Samuel S. Smith
LC No. 65-28860/ISBN 0-912480-01-7

THE BATTLE OF PRINCETON
Samuel S. Smith
LC No. 67-31149/ISBN 0-912480-03-3

FIGHT FOR THE DELAWARE 1777
Samuel S. Smith
LC No. 74-130878/ISBN 0-912480-05-X

THE BATTLE OF MONMOUTH
Samuel S. Smith
LC No. 64-56379/ISBN 0-912480-00-9

This Bicentennial Series
on the American Revolution
has been designed throughout by Paul R. Smith

Photography by Daniel I. Hennessey.

Copyright 1972 by Philip Freneau Press
Library of Congress No. 72-79889
International Standard Book No. 0-912480-07-6

TABLE OF CONTENTS

PREFACE

INTRODUCTION

MANUSCRIPT AND PRINTED MAPS By Maker

FOREWORD

Cartographic history has, until recent years, invited the interest of but a small number of researchers in the United States. The select group of map historians and cartobibliographers includes not only professional geographers, historians and librarians, but also a scattering of individuals from various non-cartographic professions. Among the latter are lawyers, brokers, military leaders, physicians, college professors, clergymen, merchants, and industrialists. In collecting and perusing maps they find relaxation, enjoyment, and release from the tensions and pressures of their primary endeavors. Some among them, such as the author of this volume, have become authorities in their particular specializations and made significant contributions to the history of American cartography.

Dr. Peter J. Guthorn, a New Jersey surgeon, has, for more than a decade, been concerned with maps of the American Revolution. In pursuing this interest he has researched the major map collections and archives in Great Britain and the United States. In 1966 Philip Freneau Press published his *American Maps and Map Makers of the Revolution,* which described several hundred maps and presented brief sketches of their makers.

The volume in hand features the cartographic contributions of British military engineers and map makers to the war for American independence. Thanks to a concerted mapping effort prior to and during the French and Indian War, British commanders had more and better maps at their disposal than did General Washington and his associates. This is evident in Dr. Guthorn's second compilation which includes the maps and biographical sketches for some 130 map makers, with descriptions of their cartographic works.

The bicentennial of the American Revolution will, undoubtedly, stimulate scholarly and popular studies on various aspects of the origins of our nation. Contemporary maps are among the source materials basic to such research. Dr. Guthorn's two publications are essential guides to the contemporary cartographic resources of the period. The compiler emphasizes that both lists are preliminary efforts which may contain errors and omissions. They do, nonetheless, introduce us to the maps and map makers of the American Revolution.

Walter W. Ristow
Chief, Geography and Map Division
Library of Congress

INTRODUCTION

History and geography are joined in the maps of the American Revolutionary War. The maps form a rich resource for students of history and cartography, separately and collectively.

Because extant maps are so widely dispersed, it has been difficult to make more than a piecemeal study. My previous preliminary study attempted to identify maps and to study the various aspects of the scope, background and accomplishments of the American map makers of the Revolution. This compilation, also a preliminary study, is concerned with the same aspects of the accomplishments of the British.

This volume is organized to emphasize the dominant role played by the individual map makers. Biographical sketches are presented as broad profiles of background and training, and therefore some index of the reliability and value of the man's work. The individual accuracy, care, methods, drafting techniques, and number of maps produced vary widely. The organization, background, training and attitudes of each nation are reflected in their collective accomplishments.

During the early part of the 18th. century, mapping activity in the American Colonies was sporadic, and was carried out with little official sponsorship or interest. The maps of Henry Popple, Lewis Evans and John Mitchell were published in 1733, 1749 and 1755, the latter with initial official support. Evans' original map, and later extensions, were important in first demonstrating the increasing expansion and influence of France on the western frontier. This was reemphasized and confirmed by Mitchell's map. The westward movement of settlers from Pennsylvania, Virginia, and other states, brought them into increasing conflict with the French, soon to culminate in the North American part of the Seven Years War. The excellence of the earlier work of Evans and Mitchell continued to be recognized, editions of their maps being produced during the Revolution.

British and American colonial military activity caused a sudden increase in surveying and mapping, and brought some attendant official concern and recognition. It was evident that the central seaboard portions of the colonies were reasonably well delineated, but that the northern, southern, and western areas were only casually surveyed; also, that coastal charting was too inaccurate for Naval operations. Surveyors General of the Northern and Southern Districts were appointed to fill the void. Samuel Holland was selected to supervise the Northern, and William deBrahm the Southern District. Other surveyors were appointed, some in conjunction with the Military or Admiralty, under sponsorships and orders, which are not now entirely evident.

The years covered in this volume are "The Revolutionary War Period," ending with the close of hostilities. The rather loose date of the beginning permits inclusion of the important contributions of some whose work preceded the formal outbreak of hostilities, although not the roots of the disagreements leading to the war. Reproduction of these maps did not occur until after hostilities began. Also included are revised and reedited versions of earlier printed maps, produced during the war years, some in numerous editions or issues. Some of these were based upon surveys made twenty or more years before, and were among the more outstanding and valuable maps employed during the war.

The primary interest of this study is in the manuscript maps and their makers. A number of these were never reproduced in printed form or were so altered that the relationship is not recognizable. Printed maps and their compilers, engravers, editors, and proprietors are an interesting study in themselves. These are, however, of secondary interest to the current study, although they made their own important contribution. In a number of printed maps, the origin is obscure, or they were eclectic inventions based upon other secondary sources. Careful analysis of the possible relationships is not merited here.

Military cartography is dictated by its purposes: to provide data for the movement of troops and trains, to provide protection and cover, to provide subsistance, and to note features of terrain lending themselves to offense or defense. The military map is perhaps the most valuable tool available to the soldier on foreign ground. The maps under study fall into six broad categories: military geographical surveys, surveys of encampments and fortifications, casual offhand sketch maps, public information news maps, formal documentary battle or campaign maps, and finely finished artistic renderings to serve as personal souvenirs for public or private exhibition.

The first, military geographical surveys, may indicate a great deal of data about the countryside and community including the locations and size of streams, marshes, rivers, bridges, fords, hills, farms, forage, local industries, and even the names of local residents. Field officers were particularly aware of the need for data. Lord Rawdon complained about the inaccuracies of maps in a letter to Tarleton, October 23, 1779. Frederick Mackenzie noted the need for officers capable of taking sketches of the country. Simcoe recorded the places of origin and residence of his men so they could be employed as guides.

The surveys of fortifications and encampments are usually carefully finished renderings done by trained and experienced engineers and draughtsmen. In some cases, a series of surveys, over several months or years, demonstrate the development or fate of a fort or fortified town or encampment. Surveys of this type are proportionally more numerous due to contemporary emphasis on establishments of this type, and the presence of a static situation immediately at hand, and easy to survey.

The casual offhand sketch maps were generally the first to depict an area, operation or campaign. They are particularly interesting as they may represent a first view or evaluation of a military situation. They are worthy of study for their omissions and errors, as well as their accuracy. Generally, scale cannot be determined, and occasionally, the geographical area cannot be located. Many of the maps fail to indicate authorship, and some represent the estimate of a situation by a local but loyal resident, who was possibly poorly educated.

The public information news maps were occasionally of high quality, and were reproduced in a surprisingly short time, considering the speed of travel, and plate production. Some were regional or area renderings with little of current military importance, employed to illustrate a military account. The best and most informative were in *The Universal Magazine* and *The Political Magazine*.

The documentary battle and campaign maps were records of troop dispositions and movements. These were studied and careful renderings, which could be studied and used to praise or condemn the actions of the commanders. Careful analysis demonstrates

some occasional interesting discrepancies.

The last type, fine and artistic renderings, presumably as personal souvenirs, were not encountered among the American maps. These excellent, usually fully colored and carefully rendered creations, may have been prepared by the map maker as a mark of esteem for the commander. They could be retained in his private collection, or used for exhibit by him, or by the department or bureau wishing credit for an undertaking or mission. Some of the maps obviously fall into more than one of the broad categories.

An interesting feature is noted in a number of maps. This is inclusion of soundings, shoals and obstructions to navigation. They are sea and harbor charts as much as land maps. They indicate the awareness of British military map makers of the importance of seaborne supplies, and of the troop mobility supplied by the merchant marine and navy. As an extension, manuscript surveys of the shores and harbors have been included in this study. Notably, some are essentially land maps, making a distinction occasionally difficult.

The area covered is the present United States. Adjacent areas have been included if the objective of an American expedition, or if they served as a base for major British invasion efforts. Maps on exotic materials, unrelated eclectic maps, and maps produced after the cessation of hostilities have been omitted. Some produced following the war, but based on earlier manuscripts, have been included. It is occasionally difficult to make this distinction, so that some material meriting inclusion may have been omitted.

Some of the engraved maps in the Faden Collection of the Library of Congress have been discussed in conjunction with, and in the section on, manuscript maps. This applies particularly to those maps which are incomplete engravers proofs with added manuscript additions and corrections. Some engravers' fair copies are particularly difficult to distinguish.

Initially a discussion of contemporary surveying methods, a description of instruments and methods of map plotting and construction had been planned in the volume on American map makers, but had been omitted. Montresor's biographical sketch notes some aspects of these matters.

The political and military aspects of the war present conflicting and anomalous facets, increasingly evident with an increasing perspective. Horace Walpole referred to it as the war in which England saved a rock and lost a continent. Britain faced an increasingly difficult task in coping with the political and economic, and later military aspects, in the progressively more rebellious American colonies. The larger population centers were along the coast, within easy reach on navigable waters. However, road connections between major cities, and with the developing frontier, were poor and largely unmapped in detail. In England, there was less than widespread political support for an extensive, expensive and distant campaign against the colonials who were generally well liked and respected.

Fortune favored the colonies. The Revolution occurred in the command hiatus between Marlborough and Wellington. Clear cut, well defined, long term military objectives and alternatives were generally lacking; as was a coordinated central command. The general officers of the British Army were drawn from families of wealth, position and influence. Many were active in politics, Burgoyne, Clinton, Cornwallis, Howe, and Gage holding seats in the House of Commons during the war years, in the company of many other officers.

The hard professionalism, dedication and discipline of some continental armies was not evident in many of the general and field grade officers. While frequently resourceful, courageous and perceptive, they often refused to serve with others they did not like, and refused duties they did not relish, particularly in the distant and unpopular war in North America. They also were conservative in the development of new weapons and tactics.

Although the British Government generally failed to correctly evaluate the temper, perseverance and ability of the enemy, the ability of the British commanders was good. Burgoyne, Howe, Clinton, Cornwallis and Grey were able officers before and after the Revolution, and occasionally during its course. Many younger officers, Campbell, Ferguson, Rawdon, Simcoe, André and Tarleton, for example, were able, aggressive, resourceful field leaders.

The Loyalists were a large and potentially valuable military resource, including a large proportion of men in the professions. They were principally utilized in irregular legions, and as guides and pioneers, where their local knowledge was particularly valuable. The British chose not to formalize their inclusion into the regular, or provincial establishment during the early years of the war. Their motives were mixed, fearing reprisals of the Loyalists against their former neighbors, and seeking to avoid the financial responsibilities of addition to the establishment. Sabin estimates that 25,000 Loyalists served the Crown. Utilization was piecemeal and delayed. They remained of potential value and promise, rather than achievement.

One important common experience shared by British and American officers was their service during the French and Indian War. Many of the future antagonists became acquainted, and mutually well disposed, as comrades in arms. A large number of the officers of greater age and higher rank, in the opposing forces, were well known to each other. The military lessons were comparatively better learned and remembered by the Americans. The common experience was further extended by the long residence and service of British officers in North America. Many had firm friendships, and some had married into colonial families. Conversely, some future American officers formerly had been regular officers in the British establishment before being won to the colonial cause.

The maps under study were made by members of the Engineers, the Artillery, by the Surveyors of the Northern and Southern Districts and their deputies, by regimental officers, by draughtsmen variously employed, and a few men employed in or by several of the preceding. The talents and abilities of the British military cartographers were of a very high order indeed, which largely escaped contemporary recognition and reward. A number were Scots, German, French or Dutch, who had previous training in military engineering, and often experience on foreign fields. Some had university training, private tutoring, or apprenticeship. A few map makers, whose surveys or reproductions were used by the British, were American sympathizers or officers. These included Hutchins, Mouzon, Scull and Romans.

The officers of the Royal Engineers, Artillery and Navy were unique in the British armed forces in having a professional education. The Royal Military Academy at Woolwich trained students in all the current military technical fields, including mathematics, surveying, and military engineering. Other student engineers may have received instruction as map copyists, under supervision. Prior to 1757, posts were held by warrant from the Board of Ordnance. The officers had no regular military status. Often, they held commissions in regular line regiments as well. Occasionally, an officer had to relinquish his engineering status, when called to rejoin his regiment. A mark of the low esteem and secondary status was the omission of their names from the annual printed army lists. In 1757, they received regular commissions, due to the influence of the Duke of Cumberland; and their names were included in the regular army lists the following year.

In 1759, events in North American were reflected by increasing demand for the services of engineers. The corps increased from 49 to 61, a number of men of future importance and stature being commissioned then. A large number of names suggest Scots origin.

The officers of the line regiments, and higher command, continued to view the Engineers as necessary workmen, decidedly of lower rank than fighting men. Promotions were slow, and life often less than pleasant. The complaints voiced by Montresor in his Journals are typical and characteristic.

By contrast, French military engineering had a superb reputation, was highly regarded by the French officer corps and command, and had a proud tradition inherited from deVille, Pagan and Vauban. The school of military engineering at Mézieres, and France's eminence in science and engineering, were widely acclaimed.

The technical training of officers of the Royal Navy started with instruction in seamanship and navigation, as cadets in the Royal Naval Academy. Occasionally, formal training was carried out aboard major vessels at sea. Promotion depended upon the decision of the master of a vessel, competition leading to hard work and development of a sense of responsibility. The professional and technical aspects were relatively important, although family and influence were still a major consideration.

The 60th. Regiment included a number of skilled and often prolific map makers. The Royal American Regiment of Foot, initially designated the 62nd., was formed in 1756, in North America, following Braddock's defeat. The men were chiefly German and Swiss Protestants, recently settled on the American frontier, many in Maryland and Pennsylvania. They were considered particularly suitable potential opponents to the French, in race, language and religion. At first they were required to serve only in North America, but were later incorporated into the regular army. European officers of similar background were recruited as a nucleus.

The 60th. garrisoned many of the frontier posts, engaging in successful and effective forays against the Indians under the colorful leadership of Henry Bouquet and others. The explorers and map makers carried out extensive mapping of the frontier, posts and fortifications, waterways, portages, and other means of communication and transport. Other map makers were assigned or attached, and the mapping of other areas detailed to them. Sometimes, members of the regiment were reassigned to similar duties with other organizations. Among the map makers and surveyors were Des Barres, Demler, de Diemer, Burrard, Gordon, Holland, Hutchins, Pfister, Pauli and Ratzer. The successor of the regiment is still in existence.

The remaining map makers were attached to line regiments, were members of the Guides and Pioneers, were civilian employees of the Admiralty, or were otherwise employed under terms of service, which are not now entirely clear.

A number of maps were produced by teams. Holland supervised the work of Wheeler, Grant, Sproule, Blaskowitz, and probably others. They accomplished a vast amount of surveying, including the Atlantic coast north of New York, New England, New York State, and New Jersey. DeBrahm supervised the work of Purcell, Romans, and probably others. They explored the greater part of the East Coast of Florida and the Keys between 1765 and 1767, although work continued until 1774. John Stuart, Indian Superintendent for the Southern District, supervised the work of, or employed, Gauld, Taitt and Romans. Taylor and Skinner, and Grant and Wheeler, are examples of two-man teams. Each of the individual surveyors was capable of independent work, and in fact produced individual work. In the team efforts, it is difficult to assign primary responsibility at this great distance. The initial survey by one individual may have been incorporated into a preliminary sketch by a second, finally drafted by a third, and copied by a fourth in different versions, styles and scales. Although serving the British, the work of de Diemer and Wintersmith will more appropriately be included in the study on Hessian map makers.

The major collections of Revolutionary War maps are in the Geography and Map Division of the Library of Congress, the William L. Clements Library of the University of Michigan, the Map Room of the British Museum, and the Public Record Office in London. Smaller but important collections are in the Huntington Library in San Marino, the Newberry Library in Chicago, the Library of the Duke of Northumberland at Alnwick, the New York Historical Society, the New York Public Library, and the Library of the Hydrographic Department of the Ministry of Defense at Taunton.

The core of the Library of Congress' Revolutionary War holdings are the Force and Faden Collections. Peter Force, prosperous printer, publisher and archival compiler, amassed a large number of maps, including a number of manuscripts of the war, prior to his death in 1868. The Faden Collection consists of manuscript maps, manuscript fair copies, and proofs, of many War maps published by William Faden. The entire group is included in the manuscript map section. These were acquired by purchase from British governmental sources by the Reverend Mr. Cannse of New Haven, between 1835 and 1840. The 100 maps were used as security for a loan made to Cannse by the father of E.E. Hale of Boston. They came into Hale's hands about 1860, were initially studied and described by him, and were purchased by the Library about 1862.

The Clements Library Collection consists basically of the manuscript collections of Lord George Germaine, Generals Thomas Gage, Sir Henry Clinton, and Josiah Harmar. The material purchased by Mr. William L. Clements, a distinguished and informed Michigan collector, from the descendants of Sir Henry Clinton in 1926, was augmented by purchase of the related material. The Library and much additional material was a later gift to the University. Where applicable, reference is made to *The Guide to the Manuscript Maps in the William L. Clements Library* by Christian Brun.

The basic part of the Revolutionary War collection of the Map Room of the British Museum was the library of George III. It was the finest geographical collection of its day, consisting of 50,000 maps and charts, including many manuscript surveys of North America. It was presented in 1828, eight years after the King's death.

The Public Record Office, equivalent to the United States National Archives, houses Revolutionary War maps, correspondence, and related material, formerly in the files of the War Office, Colonial Office, and other bureaus and administrative bodies.

The Library of the Hydrographic Department of the Ministry of Defense, at Taunton, is the repository of a number of manuscript surveys of North America, particularly of the coastline of New England, Florida and the Gulf Coast. Many are by Samuel Holland, his deputies, George Gauld, and others. A number are on a monumental scale, and are of superb quality and historical interest. Many were employed for the engraving of DesBarres *The Atlantic Neptune*, first published in 1777. Of great interest, but beyond the scope of this volume, are manuscript surveys of Eastern Canadian areas by Captain James Cook. A future study of Revolutionary War marine charts and atlases, including *The Atlantic Neptune*, is planned.

The small collection of superb and unique manuscript maps in the collection of the Duke of Northumberland at Alnwick contains those used by General Hugh Percy, and relate particularly to Concord and Lexington, Long Island and New York, his areas of military activity or command. A preliminary study of these has been carried on by Mr. R.A. Skelton of the British Museum, and Professor W.P. Cumming of Davidson College.

The other collections contain maps of importance and interest, but without constituting a separate and distinct historical corpus meriting specific description.

The acquisition of biographical data has been occasionally difficult, often confusing, and on rare occasions, impossible. Some biographical sketches never developed beyond the name. Reliable data is often not recorded if the individual was unimportant politically, economically, or was not a member of a distinguished family. Minor baronets in Britain, and undistinguished American political figures in the United States, may rate a large amount of coverage, while an important map maker or technical contributor remains obscure. Also, the lives of contemporaries with the same or similar names may never be untwined. Individual records of officers were not instituted by the War Office until 1829. Parentage and background were occasionally indicated in applications for commissions directed to the Commanders-in-Chief, after 1793. These may be of occasional indirect or retrospective value.

Some geographical areas were proportionally more extensively mapped, representing a longer period of occupation, presumed greater military or strategic importance, the development of extensive fixed fortifications, or the chance higher concentration of a larger proportion of map makers without other assignment. The areas most completely covered were Boston, Rhode Island, Lake Champlain, New York City, New Jersey, Yorktown, Charlestown, Savannah, and Florida. A unique manuscript atlas of the Province of New Jersey was produced by John Hills for Sir Henry Clinton. It is particularly worthy of note.

Each map entry in this study is described in the briefest possible terms to conserve space. The approximate size in inches, within borders, and location, is noted. In a few cases, only photocopies were available for study. Rarely, the location of the original could not be determined, or may have disappeared. Not infrequently, photocopies failed to identify the location or their origin. Generally, illustrations and data from dealers catalogs have not been employed.

In reviewing the material, I note that some descriptions are inconsistent and not uniform. These have been corrected in retrospect, but some undoubtedly persist, perhaps due to changes in my enthusiasm over the span of years employed in carrying out the study. Lastly, the omissions, inconsistencies and errors are entirely the author's.

Substantial aid, suggestions and advice on the general resources and location of material have been made by Mr. Gerard L. Alexander of the New York Public Library; Mr. Howard C. Rice, Jr. of the Princeton University Library; Mr. Walter W. Ristow, Chief of the Geography and Map Division of the Library of Congress; and Mr. Alexander O. Vietor of the Yale University Library. Similar aid, suggestions and advice on resources and collections in Britain were made by Mr. R. A. Skelton and Miss Helen Wallis, respectively former and current Superintendent of the Map Room of the British Museum. I acknowledge with appreciation the help of Mr. Richard W. Stephenson of the Geography and Map Division of the Library of Congress for bibliographical and historical material.

The use of the resources of the William L. Clements Library was aided and guided by Mr. Howard C. Peckham, Mr. William S. Ewing, Mr. Nathaniel Shipton, and Mr. Douglas W. Marshall. Substantial aid, and guidance through the collections of the Public Record Office was made possible through the friendly interest and experience of Mr. Peter A. Penfold; similarly, to Miss Margaret Perry, Librarian of the Hydrographic Department of the Ministry of Defense at Taunton, to Miss Jeanette D. Black of the John Carter Brown Library, to Mr. Wilson G. Duprey of the New York Historical Society, and to Mr. David Woodward, Curator of Maps at the Newberry Library.

Also, my gratitude is expressed to Sir Hugh Algernon Percy, the Duke of Northumberland, for access to his private library at Alnwick, and to Mr. Graham, his Librarian, for his aid and courtesy; to Mrs. John Nicholas Brown for data on British Regimental History, to Mr. W. E. May of London, and to Mr. John F. Reed of King-of-Prussia, Pennsylvania, for additional data, and historical aid.

Proportional dividers, 18th century, employed in altering the scale of a map. The Adler Planetarium and Astronomical Museum.

MANUSCRIPT AND PRINTED MAPS

Arranged by Map Maker

1. ADAM ALLEN

Adam Allen, a Loyalist, was born in 1757, probably in Pennsylvania. He served as a lieutenant in the Queens Rangers, under command of John Graves Simcoe. The maps in Simcoe's *A Journal of the Operations of the Queen's Rangers* were made mainly by George Spencer, another Loyalist. Allen was responsible for a single map. The original rough drafts were at least partly the work of the commander of the Rangers himself. Jointly, Simcoe, Spencer, and Allen were able to perpetuate the military history of the Queen's Rangers by the well illustrated and early publication of the Journal.

Following the Revolution, Allen went to St. Johns, New Brunswick, on half-pay status. In 1798, he commanded the post at Grand Falls, on the St. Johns River. He died in York County, New Brunswick in 1823.

1. *Skirmish at Richmond Jan. 5th. 1781*. A careful manuscript rendering, 8⅛ by 6⅝. In the lower left, outside the border, is "from a sketch of Lt. Allen of the Queens Rangers," indicating that Spencer may have done the rendering. Colonial Williamsburg. Simcoe Papers (63-23c).

2. *[Skirmish at Richmond.]* A rough, unlabeled manuscript, 11 by 6¾. In the lower left, outside the border is, "From a rough draft of Lt. Allen Q.R." Colonial Williamsburg. Simcoe Papers (63-37a).

3. *Skirmish at Richmond 5th Jan. 1781*. A careful manuscript in color, 8 by 7. The title and references A through F are contained in a square cartouche in the lower left. There is also a notation "by Lt. Allen Q. R. copied." Huntington Library.

2. JOHN ANDRÉ

André was born in London in 1751 of Genevese parents. He was employed by his father, a wealthy merchant, for a short time, making a business tour of the continent as his agent. Bored after his return to London, he obtained a commission in the 7th., or Royal Fusileers in March 1771, which he joined in Canada in 1774. His talents were soon recognized, and he was rapidly promoted. He was captured by the Americans at the capitulation of St. Johns in November 1775, and exchanged in December 1776.

His administrative abilities led to his appointment as Adjutant-General on 23 October 1779, after service as aide to Generals Grey and Clinton. His activities and influence are obvious on any brief survey of contemporary correspondence and reports. He was a talented, industrious, adroit and able planner and executive, as evidenced by his military journals and correspondence. His part in the Benedict Arnold betrayal was of prime importance. He was captured in civilian clothes, tried and finally executed 2 October 1780.

1. *[Fort Lee, N.J.]* Rough manuscript 7⅜ by 9. Clements Library. Brun 481.

2. *First Position at Middlebush, June 14, 1777 [N.J.]* Manuscript 7⅜ by 5⅝ in André Journal. Huntington Library. HM626.

3. *Second Position at Middlebush June 15, 1777 [N.J.]* Manuscript 7¼ by 5⅝ in André Journal. Huntington Library. HM626.

4. *Course of the Rariton at Brunswick with the Disposition of the Br. Army encamped there 21 June 1777 [N.J.]* Manuscript 14½ by 5⅝ in André Journal. Huntington Library. HM626.

5. *Encampment of the Army on Landing the 26 Aug. 1777 [Md.]* Manuscript 7 by 5⅝ in André Journal. Huntington Library. HM626.

6. *Encampment of the Division under Lt. Gen. Knyphausen 29 August 1777 [Md.]* Manuscript 7 by 5⅝ in André Journal. Huntington Library. HM626.

7. *Position of the Division under Lt. Gen. Knyphausen at Cecil Church 1 Sep. 1777. [Md.]* Manuscript 7 by 5¾ in André Journal. Huntington Library. HM626.

8. *Camp near Carsons Tavern [Buck Tavern] 2 Sept. 1777 [Md.]* Manuscript 7 by 5⅝ in André Journal. Huntington Library. HM626.

9. *Position of the Army near Aiken's [Rikin's] Tavern 5 Sep. 1777*. Manuscript 7 by 5⅝ in André Journal. Huntington Library. HM626.

10. *Position of the Army at New Garden 8 Sep. 1777*. Manuscript 7⅛ by 5⅝ in André Journal. Huntington Library. HM626.

11. *Position of the Army near Iron Hill [Del. & Md.]* Manuscript 208 by 260 mm. in 11½ page journal of the campaign from August 25 to November 20, 1777. Sothby Sale Catalog 6 January 1961.

12. *Battle of Brandewyne on the 11th. September 1777. This plan is intended to show chiefly the operations on the left, by tracing the general course each corps took. The yellow parts are the places near which the Rebels made most opposition.* Detailed manuscript 7¼ by 11½. Huntington Library.

13. *Position of part of the Army at Brandewyne 12 Sept. 1777. [Pa.]* Manuscript 7 by 5¾ in André Journal. Huntington Library. HM626.

14. *Position of the Army at Truduffrin 19 Sept. 1777. [Pa.]* Manuscript 7⅛ by 5¾ in André Journal. Huntington Library. HM626.

15. *Surprise of a Rebel Corps in the Great Valley 21 Sept. 1777. [Pa.]* Manuscript 7⅛ by 5⅝ in André Journal. Huntington Library. HM626.

16. *Position of the Army at Charlestown 21 Sept. 1778.* Manuscript 7⅛ by 5¾ in André Journal. Huntington Library. HM626.

17. *Position of the Army at Norrington 25 Sept. 1777. [Pa.]* Manuscript 7⅛ by 5¾ in André Journal. Huntington Library. HM626.

18. *Battle of German Town the 4th. October 1778. [Pa.]* Detailed manuscript and wash 20¼ by 22½, segment missing. Huntington Library.

19. *Position of the Army after the Battle of German Town Oct. the 6th. [1777.]* Manuscript 6¾ by 5⅜ in André Journal. Huntington Library. HM626.

20. *[Chestnut Hill] 4th. Decem. 1777.* Manuscript 8 by 5½ in André Journal. Huntington Library. HM626.

21. *Attack of an advanced Corps of the Rebels the 6th. Dec. 1777.* Detailed manuscript and wash 6½ by 11¼. Huntington Library.

22. *Marches of the British Army from the 4th. to the 7th. December 1777.* Manuscript 6½ by 3½ in André Journal. Huntington Library. HM626.

23. *Position of part of the Army near Derby 22 Decem. 1777.* Manuscript 7¼ by 5⅝ in André Journal. Huntington Library. HM626.

24. *Position taken by the Detachment under M. Gen. Grant the 25 Dec. [1777.]* Manuscript 7¼ by 5¾ in André Journal. Huntington Library. HM626.

25. *Position taken by Maj. Gen. Grey the 26th. Dec.* Manuscript 7 by 5½ in André Journal. Huntington Library. HM626.

26. *Second Position of part of the Army near Derby 27 Dec. [1777.]* Manuscript 7¼ by 5⅝ in André Journal. Huntington Library. HM626.

27. *Redouts near Philadelphia.* Manuscript 11 by 7¼. Huntington Library.

28. *A Map of the Operations on the Delaware River.* Detailed manuscript 310 by 380 mm. Sothby Sale Catalog 6 June 1961.

29. *Mud Island with the Operations for reducing it 15th. Nov. 1777.* Detailed manuscript 9½ by 14¾ with profiles. A finished version of the preceding. Huntington Library.

30. *Progress of the British Army from the landing in Elk River to the taking possession of Philadelphia anno 1777.* Manuscript 10¾ by 10 summarizing all the operations. Huntington Library.

31. *A General Map of the Campaign.* Manuscript, routes in color, 189 by 230 mm. Note by André "This is not given as an accurate map, but only to afford some idea of the progress of the Army from the landing at Elk to the taking of possession of Philadelphia." Sothby Sale Catalog 6 June 1961.

32. *Evesham June 19th.* [*1778, N.J.*] Manuscript 6¾ by 5 in André Journal. Huntington Library. HM626.

33. *Mount Holly 20 & 21 June* [*1778, N.J.*] Manuscript 7¼ by 5½ in André Journal. Huntington Library. HM626.

34. *Black Horse 22 June 1778* [*N.J.*] Manuscript 6½ by 5⅜ in André Journal. Huntington Library. HM 626.

35. *Crosswicks 23 June 1778* [*N.J.*] Manuscript 6⅜ by 5½ in André Journal. Huntington Library. HM626.

36. *Upper Freehold 24 & 25 June 1778* [*N.J.*] Manuscript 13 by 5½ in André Journal. Huntington Library. HM626.

37. *Field of Battle 26 to 28 June.* [*Battle of Monmouth, N.J.*] Manuscript 6⅝ by 5 ½ in André Journal. Huntington Library. HM 626.

38. *Battle of Freehold 28 June 1778.* Manuscript and wash 19¾ by 10¾. Huntington Library.

39. *Middletown 29 & 30, 1778* [*N.J.*] Manuscript 13⅞ by 4⅞ in André Journal. Huntington Library. HM626.

40. *Progress of the British Army thro the Jerseys Anno 1778.* Manuscript and wash 16 by 10¾. Huntington Library.

41. [*Present Union, Middlesex and Somerset Counties, N.J. and Staten Island, N.Y.*] Manuscript 8¾ by 14½. Clements Library. Brun 517.

42. [*Present Union, Middlesex and Somerset Counties, N.J. and Staten Island, N.Y.*] Manuscript, partly colored, 12 by 16. A more complete version of the preceding. Clements Library. Brun 516.

43. [*Present Bergen County, N.J.*] Manuscript and wash 10½ by 17¾. Huntington Library.

44. *Plan of Forts Clinton & Montgomery Stormed Oct. 6th. 1777 by the troops under Sir Hen. Clinton.* Detailed manuscript and wash 19½ by 10. Accompanied by a detailed descriptive sheet. Huntington Library.

45. [*Fort Lafayette and Verplanks Point.*] Manuscript 7⅜ by 12½. Clements Library. Brun 344.

46. *Plan of The Island of New York From Horn's Hook to the Advanced Posts in Front of Kingsbridge from a Survey in July 1778 by Jno. Wilson Ens. 71st. Regt. and assistant Engineer.* Detailed manuscript 41 by 19½. Huntington Library.

47. [*Disposition of British Troops on Manhattan, Staten Island and Long Island in 1776.*] Manuscript in outline 12¾ by 15¾. Clements Library. Brun 338.

48. [*Long Island Sound and New England Shore from New York City to Nantucket and Cape Cod.*] Manuscript and wash 39½ by 11¾. Huntington Library.

49. [*New Bedford and Fair Haven, Mass.*] Finished, colored manuscript 9½ by 14. Clements Library. Brun 175.

50. [*New Bedford and Fair Haven, Mass.*] Manuscript and wash 8½ by 10½. Huntington Library.

51. [*Atlantic coast from Long Island to Cape Henry.*] Manuscript 8¼ by 13¾ with a plan for subjugation of the middle colonies. Huntington Library.

52. [*Modern Suffolk County, N.Y.*] Manuscript 11 by 16¾. Clements Library. Brun 338.

53. [*West Point, N.Y.*] Manuscript sketch map 12½ by 7⅞. Clements Library. Brun 458.

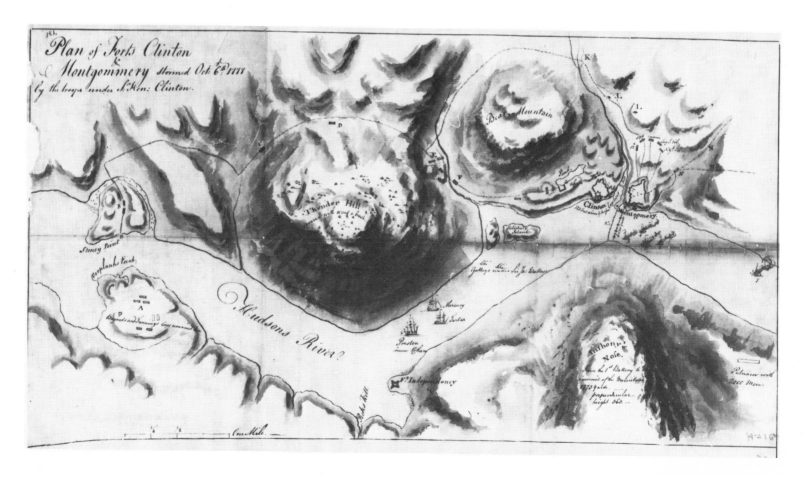

John André's map of Forts Clinton and Montgomery October 6, 1777, descriptive sheet separate. See 2/44.

3. BENEDICT ARNOLD

Arnold was born in Norwich, Connecticut in 1741, of a distinguished and long resident family. He served as a volunteer during the Seven Years War but proved restless under the restraints of military discipline. A successful merchant, he was an early volunteer following Lexington. He was an active, imaginative and aggressive leader, serving in a number of areas, but was frequently in conflict with his superiors.

His most notable act was his treason, in conjunction with André. His one map was made after he had been commissioned a Brigadier General in the British Army. He led expeditions against Richmond, Virginia and New London, Connecticut. Scorned by the British, he lived in St. John, New Brunswick for a period, and died in London in 1801. Five of his seven sons eventually served in the British Army.

1. *Road from Sleepy Hole by which Colo. Simcoe marched to Portsmouth. By Brig. General Benedict Arnold 1781*. A rough manuscript of the roads between Nansemond River and Portsmouth, 8¼ by 9⅜. Clements Library. Brun 582.

4. THEOPHYLACT BACHE

Bache was born in England in 1729, and came to New York about 1755, establishing himself as a merchant. His principal trade was with the West Indies and Newfoundland. Later he was an agent for packets sailing between Falmouth and New York. Bache, who resided in Flatbush, was sufficiently respected to be elected President of the Chamber of Commerce in 1773. He was a supporter of the Crown, and remained an ardent Loyalist throughout the Revolution.

Bache and another Loyalist, Colonel James Moncrieffe, were captured by one of Capt. Marriner's whaleboat raiding parties in 1778. Bache was permitted to return to New York following the Revolution, dying there in 1807. A brother, Richard, married Sarah, the daughter of Benjamin Franklin. He was a determined Whig. Theophylact may have had Whig sympathies in the early years when he was associated with John Jay in the Committee of Correspondence. The seizure of a cargo belonging to Bache, by the Sons of Liberty, on 23 April 1766, possibly altered his attitude.

1. *[Flatbush]* A manuscript of the roads about Flatbush, 14¼ by 12⅞. Clements Library. Brun 341.

5. GERARD BANCKER

Bancker was a descendant of early Dutch settlers, born in New York. In 1762, he made a manuscript copy of the 1745 *Road from Trenton to Amboy....* publication of which had been planned, but never carried out. He was appointed as a public surveyor, with Francis Marshalk, by the Common Council of New York in 1763. His name appears frequently as a surveyor, at committee meetings, and as a recipient of fees for his work.

When the Revolution started, Peter VanBrugh Livingston was appointed as Treasurer to handle all funds for defense for the Provincial Congress. Bancker was appointed assistant treasurer, and succeeded Livingston in 1778. Bancker, with his iron money chest, financed the Revolution in New York, moving between Rochester, Hurley, Kingston and Albany.

He was appointed Treasurer of the State of New York in 1784, and a commissioner to settle property claims in New York City arising from the great fire of 1776. In addition to numerous property surveys, he was joint author of Faden's map of New Jersey. His part had been the surveys for the Earl of Dunmore, Governor of New York, from 1770 to 1771, later Governor of Virginia, then the Bahamas.

1. *A Plan of Fort George in the City of New York, Made at the Request of the Honorable John Crugar Esquire, and of the rest of the Committee appointed to fix on a suitable place for building a Government House.* Careful, colored manuscript 13⅝ by 18⅛. New York Historical Society.

2. *Plan of the Fort Made at the Request of Mr. Speaker & the Committee appointed to fix on a Suitable Plan to Build a Govt. House.* Careful manuscript 19¼ by 14⅝. Dated April 12, 1774. British Museum. Royal United Services Institution Collection.

6. THOMAS GEORGE LEONARD BARRETTE

Barrette formerly resided near Blackheath, Kent, son of a prosperous landowner who had fathered ten children. Barrette, who occasionally appears in records as Barrett, arrived in America in February 1779, having previously resigned a commission as Lieutenant in the Marines. He had previously served for 12 years. In America, he was a Captain of Provincials and Aide-de-Camp to General Browne. He was detached from engineering duties to return to his unit, the 23rd., or Royal Welch Fusileers, before the southern expedition. His service in the regiment lasted from 23 August 1779 to 1785.

The map of the Battle of Camden was forwarded to Sir Henry Clinton in a letter dated 26 August 1780, with a detailed account of the action. Barrette served as a Captain on half-pay in the 100th. Regiment of Foot from 1786 to 1795, even though the unit had been disbanded in 1783. He served as Captain in the 41st. Foot from 1795, and was promoted to Lieutenant Colonel in 1798.

1. *Plan of the battle of Gum Swamp alias Sutton Wood, on the 16th. August 1780 [Camden, South Carolina.]* A careful, finished manuscript 7¾ by 9½. Clements Library. Brun 625.

7. EDWARD BARRON

Barron was a Lieutenant in the 4th. or King's Own Regiment, in 1776 with rank from 25 October. He was promoted to Captain in 1779.

1. *Plan of the Peninsula of Charlestown.* Careful, finished manuscript in full color, 18⅛ by 13¼. A flag shaped cartouche is in the lower left. Duke of Northumberland Collection, Alnwick.

2. *Line of March of the First Brigade, from the Right by Sub Divisions.* Careful, finished manuscript in colored wash, 17⅛ by 11. Rectangular cartouche in lower right. Expedition to Concord and Lexington. Duke of Northumberland Collection, Alnwick.

3. *Arrangement of the Army, Commanded by General Howe Agreeable to his Orders of the 15th. May 1776.* Careful, artistic manuscript in full color, in an oval 13 by 9¾. Duke of Northumberland Collection, Alnwick.

4. *Plan of the Town and Environs of Halifax...Presented to...Earl Percy...1779.* Careful, colored manuscript, 27⅛ by 16¾. Flag shaped cartouche in upper center and table of references on right. Duke of Northumberland Collection, Alnwick.

5. *Map of Nova-Scotia Drawn From The Original in the Office of the Surveyor General Of The Province and Humbly Presented To the Right Honourable Earl Percy By His Lordship's Most Devoted Humble Servant Edwd. Barron Captn. Kings Own Regiment.* Careful, colored manuscript 34¼ by 21¾. Descriptive title in upper left. Duke of Northumberland Collection, Alnwick.

6. *Plan of Fort Edward at Windsor Nova Scotia in 1779 E. Barron fecit.* Careful, wash colored manuscript 17⅜ by 10¼. Title in flag shaped cartouche in upper right and references A through H in lower right. Duke of Northumberland Collection, Alnwick.

7. *Plan of Fort Cumberland On the Isthmus of Nova Scotia 1779.* Careful, colored manuscript. References in upper right. Duke of Northumberland Collection, Alnwick.

8. *Plan and sections of the intrenchment of the Citadel Hill Halifax. Halifax 5 March 1779 W. Spry commandg: engineer E. B.* Manuscript plan and sections 24 by 13. Clements Library. Brun 20.

9. *Plan of Fort Edward in Nova Scotia. E.B. Spry Commandg: engineer. Halifax 5 March 1779.* Colored manuscript plan 13½ by 20. Clements Library. Brun 23.

10. *Plan of Fort Howe on the River St. John Nova Scotia E.B. 1779 W. Spry commandg. engr: Halifax 5 March 1779.* Colored manuscript plan 13½ by 20½. Clements Library. Brun 24.

11. *Plan of the Fort of Annapolis Nova Scotia in its present state 1779. E. Barron ft. W. Spry commandg. engineer. Halifax 5 March 1779.* Colored manuscript plan 22 by 17½. Clements Library. Brun 30.

12. *Sketch of the Disposition and Commencement of the Action near Camden in South-Carolina 16th. August 1780 as described in the Letters of the Right Honble. Earl Cornwallis to the Secretary of State and the Rebel General Gates to Congress. Most respectfully inscribed to the Right Honb. Earl Percy by his Lordships most humble servant Ed. Barron.* Careful, artistic manuscript in full color, in an oval 9⅛ by 6⅞. Duke of Northumberland Collection, Alnwick.

8. PATRICK BELLEW

Bellew was commissioned an Ensign in the 1st. Regiment of Foot Guards 21 August 1765. He was promoted Lieutenant and Captain in 1773 and Captain and Lt. Colonel 9 December 1778.

1. [*New York Harbor*] A rough, unfinished pencil sketch of the harbor to accompany four water color, and one uncolored, views of Staten Island, New York Bay, Neversink Hills etc. British Museum. Crown Collection CXXII29.

9. RICHARD BENDYSHE

Bendyshe was commissioned a Practitioner Engineer and Ensign, dating from 13 March 1772. He served during the New York campaign of 1776.

1. *A Plan of...Part of Long Island....* See Wheeler map 7.

10. BIDDLE

Cited as source of data for Hills map 5.

11. CHARLES BLASKOWITZ

Between 24 March 1764 and 24 December 1775, Blaskowitz was employed as a surveyor under Samuel Holland, being rated successively as a volunteer, volunteer surveyor, assistant surveyor, and finally deputy surveyor during this period, possibly of apprenticeship. During 1774 he was allowed extra expenses in surveying the road from Newbury to Charlestown, Massachusetts.

Blaskowitz was appointed Captain in the Guides and Pioneers on 3 May 1777, a rank he retained to 1783. He was on the half-pay list of the Colonial Corps from 25 October 1783 to 1796, then on the half-pay list of the Guides and Pioneers. His name does not appear for 1801. He is presumed to have passed away in 1835.

Blaskowitz' notable cartographic contributions were the surveys of Rhode Island. The work probably was initiated during the summer of 1764 to illustrate Newport's potential as a naval base. The Honorable Robert Melville, Governor of Grenada, had been ordered by the Admiralty Board to visit Newport to study its suitability at first hand. He sent back a "large map" and commended Blaskowitz as an able surveyor. The map was later engraved for Faden's North American Atlas in 1777, with new place names added. It was reissued unrevised in 1794, and copied in reduced size in 1778 for inclusion in the *Pilote Américain Septentrional....* and the *Neptune Americo-Septentrional....* for the French Naval Service.

Blaskowitz made a number of Canadian surveys including one of Bonaventure in the Bay of Chaleurs in 1765, and of Halifax in 1784. He produced a talented water color sketch of a floating battery reputed to have been used by the Americans, including representations of different spears used by the Rebels. These are in the Print and Photo Collection of the Library of Congress.

1. *A Survey of Lake Champlain Including Crown Point and St. John's On which is fixed The Line of Forty Five Degrees North Lattit. Terminating the Border between The Provinces of Quebec and New York Agreeable to his Majestys Proclamation Done by Order and Instruction Of the Honourable James Murray Esqr. Governor of the Province of Quebec And the Honourable his Majestys Council By John Collins Dep. Sur. Genl. May 21st. 1765.* Careful, colored manuscript 17⅝ by 49. "Charles Blaskowitz, Draughtsman" in lower right. Library of Congress.

2. *A Plan of the Sea Coast from Gouldsborough Harbor to the West Passage of Passamaquody Bay including the Harbors, Bays and Islands in that Extent. Surveyed agreeably to the Orders and Instructions of the Right Honorable the Lords Commissioners for Trade and Plantations to Samuel Holland Esqr. His Majesty's Surveyor General of Lands for the Northern District of North America by Mr. Charles Blaskowitz a Deputy of the Said District.* Careful colored manuscript 75 by 28. Title in upper left and "Drawn by Charles Blaskowitz" in lower right. Soundings are shown. Hydrographic Department Library, Taunton. A9449.

3. [*Piscataqua Harbour*] *The River Mouth Showing New Castle, Portsmouth, adjoining creeks and islands.* Finished, colored manuscript 23 by 18½. Public Record Office. C.O. 700 N.H. No. 6.

4. *A Plan of the Sea Coast from Little Rocks Near Hampton to Normans Woe near Cape Anne Including Cape Anne, Ipswich, Newbury and Hampton Harbors. Surveyed by James Grant & Thos. Wheeler under the Directions of Samuel Holland Esqr. Surveyor General. Drawn by Charles Blaskowitz.* Finished, colored manuscript 25¼ by 36. Public Record Office. C.O. 700 Mass. Bay No. 13.

5. *A Map of the Bay of Narragansett with the Islands therein and Part of the Country Adjacent.* Careful colored manuscript 13¼ by 16⅜, title in upper right, many additions to the map in red ink. Library of Congress. Faden Collection 87.

6. [*Rhode Island and Narragansett Bay*] Careful colored manuscript 13¼ by 16½ showing soundings. "Charles Blaskowitz, Del." in right lower corner. Library of Congress. Faden Collection 89.

7. *A Plan of Rhode Island with the Country and Islands adjacent.* Careful colored manuscript 46¾ by 37¾. Title is in the upper right with "Surveys by Charles Blaskowitz," many references on the left. Hydrographic Department Library, Taunton. A9456.

8. *A Map of New York & Staten Island and Part of Long Island Drawn by Charles Blaskowitz, Capt. Guides & P[ioneers.]* Careful colored manuscript 58 by 40, soundings around Sandy Hook, descriptive table of forts around New York. Very similar to that of Taylor and Skinner. Public Record Office. MR954.

9. *A Map of New York & Staten Islds and Part of Long Island Drawn by Charles Blaskowitz, Capt. Guides & P. with soundings around Sandy Hook taken in July 1782.* Careful, colored manuscript 58¼ by 40½. References to the campaign of 1776, and to refugee posts on the New Jersey shore of the Hudson River in W.O. 78/3745, is very similar to MR 954, see under Taylor and Skinner map 3. Public Record Office. PRO 1137.

10. [*North-western part of Long Island*] Careful colored unlabeled manuscript 47 by 47 endorsed "Blaskowitz's Plan." Public Record Office. MR1193.

11. *A Survey of Frog's Neck and the Rout of the British Army to the 24th. of October 1776 under the Command of His Excellency the Honorable William Howe, General and Commander in Chief of His Majesty's Forces &c &c &c By Charles Blaskowitz.* Careful colored manuscript 16½ by 29 with much data on the operation. Library of Congress. Faden Collection 57.

12. *Sketch of the White Plains by Captain Blaskowitz.* Careful colored manuscript 22¼ by 18⅜. Library of Congress. G3701 S3219 1776 B5.

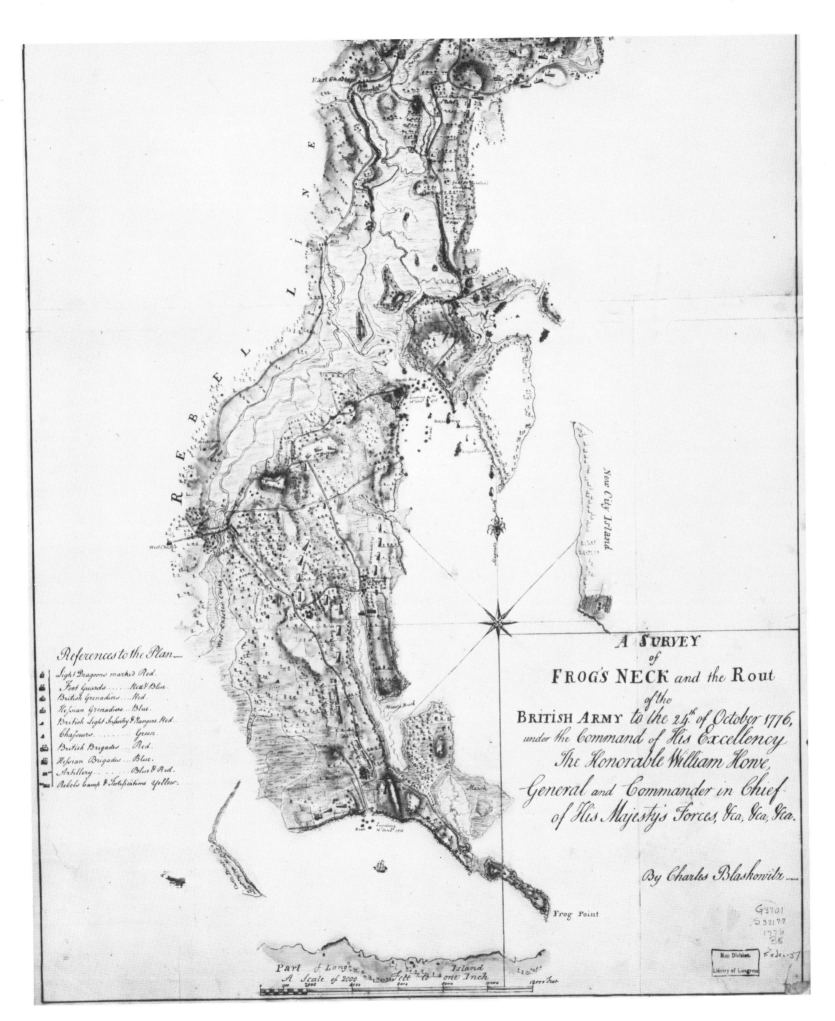

Charles Blaskowitz' 1776 map (section) of British action at Throg's Neck, Bronx, New York. See 11/11.

13. *A Plan of the Narrows of Hells-gate in the East River near which Batteries of Cannon and Morters were Erected on Long Island with a view to take off the Defences and Make Breaches in the Rebel Fort on the Opposite Shore to facilitate a landing of Troops on New York Island.* Careful colored manuscript 23 by 17½. Library of Congress. G3701 S32142 1776 B5.

14. *A Plan of Mud Island and Fort Mifflin with the Siege thereof and its Evacuations the 15th. of November 1777... Also Red Bank with the Shoals, Banks, Islands & Flats in that Extent...with Explanation. Drawn by Charles Blaskowitz, Captain of Guides & Pioneers.* Colored manuscript 20 by 19¼. Sales Catalog January 1970.

15. *A Plan of the Siege & Surrender of Charlestown South Carolina to His Majesty's Fleet and Army. Commanded by their Excellencies Sir Henry Clinton Knight of the Bath, General and Commander in Chief, And Mariot Arbuthnot, Esqr. Vice Admiral of the White, and Commander-in-Chief of His Majesty's Ships and Vessels in North America &c &c &c May 12th. 1780 Surveyed during & after the Siege by Charles Blaskowitz Capt. Guides & Pioneers.* Careful colored manuscript 26½ by 29. A portion of the upper center is missing. Lettering somewhat shaky. Public Record Office. MPH 666.

12. WILLIAM BRASIER

Brasier was a draughtsman and surveyor for the engineering establishment from 1758 to 1774. During 1758 and 1759, he was actively employed by James Montresor in the Lake Champlain area and in western New York. He made at least one original survey, that of Crown Point in 1759, but was more commonly a draughtsman for Breheam, Ratzer and Sowers. He also drafted a map of the Falls of the Ohio River from Thomas Hutchins' surveys, of the Mississippi from Pittman's surveys, and of Pensacola and St. Augustine. The maps are in the Clements Library, the Royal United Services Institution Collection in the British Museum, and in the Public Record Office.

1. *Project for taking Post at Crown Point 13th. May 1774.* Careful, colored manuscript 13½ by 20. In lower right corner "copy W. Brasier Delt 29th. May 1774." Bears signature of John Montresor. Public Record Office. MPG 355.

2. *A Survey of Lake Champlain including Crown Point and St. John's surveyed by order of His Excellency Major Genl: Sir Jeffery Amherst, Knight of the most honorable order of the bath, Commander in Chief of His Majesty's forces in North America &c &c &c. By Wm: Brasier draughtsman. 1762. William Test. delt: 1776.* Careful, finished manuscript 102 by 28¼. Clements Library. Brun 446.

3. *A Survey of Lake Champlain from Crown Point to Windmill Point, and from thence to St. John's. Surveyed by order of His Excellency Major-Gen. Amherst, Commander-in-Chief of his Majestys Forces in North America. Anno 1762. By William Brasier, Deputy Draughtsman in the office of Ordnance.* Careful, finished manuscript 15 by 51¼. Library of Congress. Faden Collection 20½.

4. *A Survey of Lake Champlain Including Lake George, Crown Point And St. John's Surveyed by Order of His Excellency Major General Sr. Jeffery Amherst Knight of the most Honble. Order of the Bath, Commander in Chief of His Majesty's Forces in North America (now Lord Amherst) by William Brasier Draughtsman 1762.* In the lower right, an inset "A Particular Plan of Lake George Surveyed in 1756 By Capt. Jackson." Printed map 17¾ by 25¾ by R. Sayer and Jno. Bennett dated August 5, 1776. See under Jefferys.

5. *Plan of the Fort at Saint Augustine.* Finished, colored manuscript 26 by 22⅞. In lower left "Phillip Pittman Lieut. 15th. Regt. Wm. Brasier Delt." British Museum. Royal United Services Institution Collection A 30/22. See also Hutchins and Pittman. Surveys of the Fort Ticonderoga area in the British Museum, Crown Collection CXXI, 24 and 25 Brasier drew or copied.

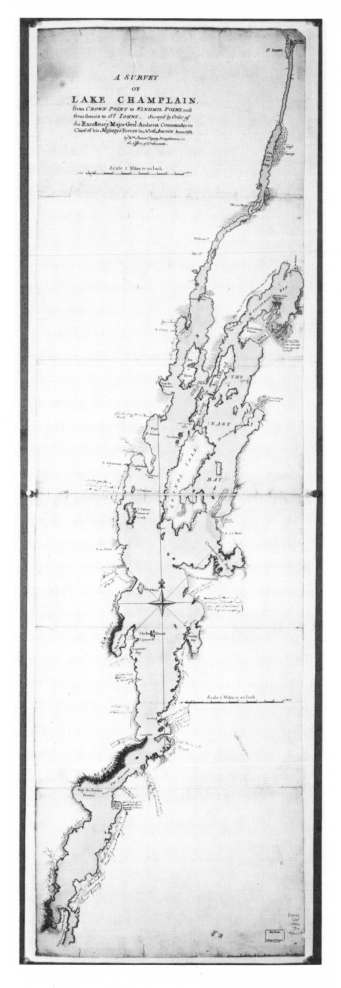

William Brasier's 1762 map of Lake Champlain, scale two miles to the inch. See 12/3.

13. JOHN BROWN

Brown was a Second Lieutenant in the 23rd. Regiment, or Royal Welch Fusileers, dating from 1 March 1775. While on duty in Boston on the eve of the Revolution, he and De Berniere reconnoitered the surrounding country. The latter was probably mainly responsible for the execution of the sketch maps. Brown is referred to as a Captain in Gage's instructions.

1. see De Berniere 1.
2. see De Berniere 2.
3. see De Berniere 3.

14. HARRY BURRARD

Burrard was born at Walhampton, Hampshire in 1755. He was commissioned an Ensign in the Coldstream Guards in 1772. Promoted Lieutenant then Captain, he transferred into the 60th. Regiment in 1777, returning to England after service in America under Sir William Howe and Cornwallis. His later military career was distinguished, with Burrard becoming Lieutenant General in 1805 and commanding the expedition in 1807 against Copenhagen under Lord Cathcart. He died at Calshot Castle in 1813.

1. *Sketch of St. Augustine and its environs. By H. Burrard 60 rt.* Crude sketch map 17½ by 13¾. Clements Library. Brun 659.

15. JOHN CALEF

Calef, a Massachusetts Loyalist, was born in 1725, grandson of Robert Calef who was the principal antagonist of Cotton Mather during the Salem witch conflict. John memorialized the unsuccessful American attack upon the present Castine, Maine. Calef died in 1812. A collection of his papers are in the Clements Library.

Calef, a surgeon, served with the regiment of Colonel Ichabod Plaisted at Crown Point in 1756. He was discharged in January 1757, serving at the Albany hospital for a time. He returned to Massachusetts where he served in the state general court. He is said to have written an account of the capture of Louisbourg, since lost. He was active in the Penobscot expedition as a surgeon, acting chaplain, and as commissary for the inhabitants of Lincoln. He went to England in 1780 as the unsuccessful agent for the Penobscot Loyalists who wished to establish the area as a new province.

1. *To The Right Honourable Lord George Germaine One of His Majesty's principal Secretaries of State &c This Chart of Penobscot Representing the Situation of about 700 of His Majestys Troups under the Command of Brigr. General Francis Mcbean and Three of His Majesty's Sloops of War Commanded by Captn. Henry Mowat Senr. Officer, when Beseiged by more than 3300 Rebels July 1779 Commanded by Brigr. Genl Lovell, and Seventeen Vessels of War Commanded by Commodore Saltenstall is most Humbly Inscribed by His Lordship's most Obedient humble Servant John Calef agent for the Inhabitants of the District of Penobscot.* Detailed printed map 17½ by 22⅛. Engraved by Jno. Neele, Russell Court. In *The Siege of Penobscot by the Rebels....* by Calef, and published in London in 1781.

16. DOUGALD (DOUGAL, DUGALD) CAMPBELL

A Dougal Campbell of the Engineers is mentioned in 1744, 1745 and 1747. Dugald Campbell is recorded as dying before 5 September 1757. Other men of the same name are noted in returns of 1777-8 from America as serving in the 42nd. Regiment, in the 71st. Regiment, and promoted to the South Carolina Royalists.

1. *Plan of Fort George and the Battery On the South West end of New York Island From a Survey by Dug'd Campbell, Lieut. &* *Assist. Engr.* Manuscript plan 28 by 23. Public Record Office. MPH570.

2. *Plan of Fort George and the Battery at New York From an actual Survey by Lieut. Dugd. Campbell Asst. Engr. 1782.* Manuscript plan 14⅛ by 8¾. Public Record Office. MPH570.

3. *Plan of Sandy Hook and the Shoals from an Actual Survey Shewing the Breadth and Soundings of the Channel from the Entrance of the Bar to the S.W. part of the E. Bank.* Manuscript 23⅛ by 22¾. Public Record Office. MPH567. See also under Hammons.

17. JOHN CAMPBELL (CAMBEL)

Campbell (if indeed the identical man) was an engineer at Pensacola in 1772, when the post was commanded by Sowers, as chief engineer. He was in command of the rag-tag group from 1778 to capitulation on 9 May 1781 to Galvez. He (or another of the same name) made two maps of Charleston in 1776 and was in a somewhat huffy exchange of correspondence with Major Moncrief, 16 July 1780.

1. *Charleston and the British Attack of June, 1776. By: John Campbell.* Finished, colored manuscript 24½ by 38¾. Clements Library. Brun 607.

2. *Plan of the scene of action at Charleston in the Province of South Carolina the 28th. June 1776. John Campbell.* Finished, colored manuscript 23⅜ by 36½. Clements Library. Brun 627.

3. *A Sketch of St. Augustin Harbour &c. 28th. Febey. 1780.* Somewhat rough, colored manuscript 17½ by 13¾, signed "Jno. Cambel Commandg Engineer." Clements Library. Brun 658.

4. *[Pensacola and Surrounding Area]* Careful, detailed manuscript in color 21 by 18⅜. Detail of one of the block-houses, and descriptive data. In lower right "A.D. 1774 I.C. Lieut. of Engrs." British Museum. Royal United Services Institution Collection A 30/59.

5. *[Gulf Coast and Mississippi Delta]* Careful, colored manuscript 27 by 36½, from Sabine River to Santa Rosa Bay, Pensacola, Mobile, Spanish settlements on the river. In lower right "I.C. Lieut of Engrs A.D. 1774." British Museum. Royal United Services Institution Collection A 30/87.

18. JONATHAN CARVER

Carver was born in New England in 1732. He served in the Provincial Troops during the French and Indian War from 1756 to 1763, his highest rank being captain. A pioneer English explorer west of the Mississippi, he traveled in the North West territory, the present Minnesota, Wisconsin, Illinois, and adjacent between 1766 and 1768, going to England a year later.

Carver was associated with Richard Whitworth, Member of Parliament for Stafford, in a plan to explore the west flowing "Oregon" River. This was dropped because of the war. He was encouraged and aided in the publication of *Travels Through the Interior Parts of North America....* by Sir Joseph Banks, president of the Royal Society, and later John Coakley Lettsom, his physician. The first edition was published in London in 1778, and again in 1779 and 1781. An unauthorized edition was published in Dublin in 1779. The account contained two maps. In addition, he is cited as a source for two other printed maps by Sayer and Bennett, and for DeCosta's map of Boston. Carver died in London in 1780.

A definitive study, *Jonathan Carver's Map of His Travels,* was published by John Parker, Curator of the James Ford Bell Library of the University of Minnesota about 1964.

1. *[North America between 39°51' and 50°20' north, and 80° to 108° west.]* Rough but detailed manuscript 29 by 21. British Museum. Add. Ms. 8449 fol. 41.

2. *[North America]* Careful, finished manuscript 14 by 10½,

based upon preceding. Appears to be an engraver's fair copy. British Museum. Add. Ms. 8950 fol. 102.

3. *A Plan of Captain Carvers Travels in the interior Parts of North America in 1766 and 1767.* Printed map 13 by 10, in editions of his "Travels."

4. *A New Map of North America from the Latest Discoveries 1778.* Engraved for Carver's "Travels." Printed map 13¾ by 12½, in editions of his "Travels."

5. *A New Map of the Province of Quebec according to The Royal Proclamation of the 7th. of October 1763 from the French Surveys connected with those made after the War By Captain Carver and Other Officers in His Majestys Service.* Printed map 24¾ by 18 with insets "Isles of Montreal," "Plan of Montreal," and "City of Quebec." London, Sayer and Bennett, 1776. Other issues in 1788 and 1794. Included in Faden's *The North American Atlas* of 1777.

6. *A Map of the British Empire in North America, By Samuel Dunn, Improved from the Surveys of Capt. Carver.* Printed map, London 1776, Sayer and Bennett. In Sayer and Bennett's *The American Atlas* of 1776 and 1782.

7. See DeCosta no. 1.

19. WILLIAM CHAMBERS

Chambers flourished between 1758 and 1816, ending his career in the Royal Navy with the rank of rear admiral. He commanded the British naval armament on Lake Champlain between 1779 and 1782, with the rank of captain.

1. *Plan of Lake Champlain from Fort St. John to Ticonderoga including part of Lake George. The particular Surveys and Plans of the Principal Anchoring places, together with the Rocks, Shoals, Sands, and Soundings, as taken in the Years 1779, 1780, 1781, and 1782 by Captain William Chambers of His Majestys Royal Navy Commanding the Naval Armament employed on the said Lake.* Careful detailed manuscript 126 by 38¾. Hydrographic Department, Taunton. X24 87.

2. *The Rocks and Soundings between Rocky Point and Pointe de St. Amont taken by Capt. Wm. Chambers in August 1780.* Careful manuscript 16¼ by 10¼. Hydrographic Department, Taunton. 282/1.

3. *The Soundings and Rocks that lie between Id. Point and the North end of the Isle à Motte between the 20th. May 1779 by Capt. William Chambers.* Careful manuscript 19¼ by 15. Hydrographic Department, Taunton. 282/2.

4. *Isle a Motte Channel.* Careful manuscript 15¼ by 9½. Hydrographic Department, Taunton. 282/3.

5. *Western Entrance to Channel South of N. Hero.* Careful manuscript 13 by 9½. Hydrographic Department, Taunton. 282/4.

6. *The two Brothers and Soundings round them taken in Aug't 1779 by Capt. Wm. Chambers.* Careful manuscript 12½ by 9. Hydrographic Department, Taunton. 282/5.

7. *Baye du Roches Fendu and the Soundings taken in August 1780 by Cpt. Willm. Chambers.* Careful manuscript 12 by 6⅞. Hydrographic Department, Taunton. 282/6.

8. *Bouquet R. coast about. These Soundings taken June 1779 by Capt. Wm. Chambers.* Careful manuscript 15¾ by 9⅛. Hydrographic Department, Taunton. 282/7.

9. *Ligonier Pt. Southward.* Careful manuscript 15¾ by 9¼. Hydrographic Department, Taunton. 282/8.

10. *The Soundings and Rocks that lie between Id. Point and the North end of the Isle à Motte, the 20th. May 1779, by Capt. William Chambers.* Careful manuscript 20½ by 16¼. Hydrographic Department, Taunton. 282/9.

11. *Willsborough Pt. to Ligonier Pt.* Careful manuscript 15 by 8¾. Hydrographic Department, Taunton. 282/10.

12. *Four Brothers [The Four Islands]* Careful manuscript 9⅛ by 7⅝. Hydrographic Department, Taunton. 282/11.

13. *Schuylers Island and the Soundings round it taken by Capt.* *Wm. Chambers, June 30th. 1779.* Careful manuscript 11⅝ by 9¼. Hydrographic Department, Taunton. 282/12.

14. *Valcour Island.* Careful manuscript 14 by 9. Hydrographic Department, Taunton. 282/13.

15. *Shoals about Sable Pt.* Careful manuscript 15⅝ by 9½. Hydrographic Department, Taunton. 282/14.

16. *Sable Pt. and R Kent.* Careful manuscript 14½ by 8. Hydrographic Department, Taunton. 282/15.

17. *Treadwell B. to Valcour I.* Careful manuscript 14⅞ by 9½. Hydrographic Department, Taunton. 282/16.

18. *Cumberland B.* Careful manuscript 15¾ by 9⅞. Hydrographic Department, Taunton. 282/17.

19. *Treadwell's B.* Careful manuscript 15¼ by 9¼. Hydrographic Department, Taunton. 282/18.

20. *Schuylers Pt.* Careful manuscript 11 by 7. Hydrographic Department, Taunton. 282/19.

21. *Valcour I. to Four Brothers Is.* Careful manuscript 16⅝ by 13. Hydrographic Department, Taunton. 282/20.

22. *Providence I. to Hogback I.* Careful manuscript 11½ by 7¾. Hydrographic Department, Taunton. 282/21.

23. *Colchester Pt. to Appletree Pt.* Careful manuscript 12 by 7⅝. Hydrographic Department, Taunton. 282/22.

24. *Burlington B.* Careful manuscript 10¾ by 6⅞. Hydrographic Department, Taunton. 282/23.

25. *Shelburne Pt.* Careful manuscript 15⅞ by 14¼. Hydrographic Department, Taunton. 282/24.

26. *Juniper I. to Shelburne Pt.* Careful manuscript 14½ by 9¾. Hydrographic Department, Taunton. 282/25.

27. *Shelburne B.* Careful manuscript 7 by 4⅜. Hydrographic Department, Taunton. 282/26.

28. *Split Rk. Pt. to Kingsland B.* Careful manuscript 13¾ by 9⅜. Hydrographic Department, Taunton. 282/27.

29. *Mill Bay.* Careful manuscript 15 by 9¾. Hydrographic Department, Taunton. 282/28.

30. *Bloods Bay and the Soundings taken in July 1779.* Careful manuscript 14 by 9½. Hydrographic Department, Taunton. 282/29.

31. *New Road and the Soundings taken in August 1779 by Captain William Chambers.* Careful manuscript 9⅞ by 7¾. Hydrographic Department, Taunton. 282/30.

32. *The Soundings Between Lee Point and Parson's Point taken in July 1779 By Capt. Wm. Chambers.* Hydrographic Department, Taunton. 282/31.

33. *Fylers Bay.* Careful manuscript 15½ by 9½. Hydrographic Department, Taunton. 282/32.

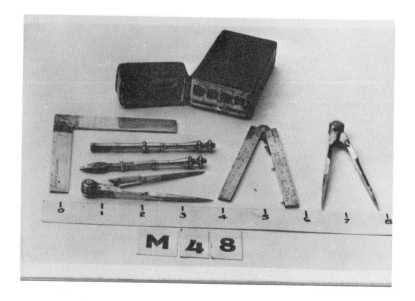

Draughting instruments in field case 17th-18th century. The Adler Planetarium and Astronomical Museum.

20. CLINTON

"Clinton" is cited as a source of data on Hills' map 5, and "G. Clinton" is cited on Hills' map 21. Charles Clinton, a surveyor, was involved in viewing lands near the disputed New York-New Jersey border in 1742. He had previously protracted a property division in northwest New Jersey in 1719. Clinton had also surveyed the Walkill River area in New Jersey in 1741, which included the New Jersey-New York line as protracted by Wells and Robinson.

This data was probably at hand in the Office of the Proprietors of East Jersey in Perth Amboy, and easily accessible to Hills, during its occupation by the British. George Clinton, father of Sir Henry, had been a Colonial Royal Governor of New York. He had been involved in the border dispute with New Jersey, was a correspondent, and may have had pertinent maps in his possession, which later came into the possession of Sir Henry.

21. SIR HENRY CLINTON

Henry, son of Admiral George Clinton, Governor of New-foundland and later New York, was probably born in 1738. He served in the New York Militia and later joined the Coldstream Guards. His military career was distinguished. He served as aide to Ferdinand of Brunswick during the Seven Years War, was promoted to colonel in 1762 and major general ten years later. Clinton was elected to Parliament in 1772 due to the influence of the 2nd. Duke of Newcastle, his cousin.

During the Revolution Clinton took part in the battles of Bunker Hill and Long Island, succeeding Howe as commander in 1778. He then concentrated the British troops in New York, as a base for expeditions. He directed the invasion of North Carolina in 1779 and the capture of Charleston in 1780. His command was characterized by friction with his second in command, Cornwallis. His North American command was given to Carleton after York-town. Manuscript notes in Clinton's hand are found on a number of the manuscripts and printed maps among his papers in the Clements Library. These are of the Long Island and New York campaigns, New Jersey, the Philadelphia campaign, Yorktown and Charlestown, South Carolina. Many appear to have been made retrospectively, possibly in defense of his earlier military judgements. Clinton again served in Parliament and was appointed Governor of Gibraltar in 1794, where he died the following year.
1. *British camp on west bank of the Schuylkill River at Philadelphia. By: Sir Henry Clinton.* Manuscript sketch, showing pontoon bridge, 7¼ by 8⅞. Clements Library. Brun 523.

22. SIR WILLIAM HENRY CLINTON

Son of Sir Henry, he was born in 1769 and entered the army in 1784. His career was brilliant, serving in the Low Countries in 1793 and as aide to the Duke of York in 1796. He was promoted colonel in 1801, served in increasingly important missions and posts, and was promoted to full general in 1830. He died in 1846.
1. *A Plan of the attack of Fort Sulivan near Charles Town in South Carolina by a squadron of His Majesty's Ships on the 28th. of June 1776 with the disposition of the King's land forces and the encampments and entrenchments of the Rebels. W.C. delint Brunswick.* Careful, colored manuscript 11⅛ by 14¾, with inset. Clements Library. Brun 621.
2. *A Plan of the attack of Fort Sulivan, near Charles Town in South Carolina, by a squadron of His Majesty's Ships, on the 29th. of June 1776. with the dispositions of the Kings Land Forces and the encampments and intrenchments of the Rebels. W H C: delint: Sepbr: 1791.* Careful, colored manuscript 20¾ by 29⅜, with inset. Clements Library. Brun 622. Both are copies of the map of the attack on Fort Sulivan by Lt. Colonel Thomas James.

23. ABRAHAM CLOSE

Close was one of a family of Loyalists from Salem, Westchester County, New York. He served in the Corps of Guides and Pioneers, first as Ensign then as Lieutenant. A Lieutenant Close of the Queen's American Rangers was wounded in the Battle of Brandywine, and resigned on 17 Sept. 1777, less than a week later. Benjamin Close of Salem abandoned property and family in 1776 to join the British Army, while Davis Close was a Tory prisoner at Fort Montgomery in May 1776.
1. [*Part of the present Litchfield and Fairfield Counties in Connecticut and Westchester and Putnam Counties in New York*] On verso "The within is a rough draugh recollected and drawn by Abraham Close Lieut. of the Corps of Guides & pioneres." Rough manuscript 14¾ by 9⅝ showing distances from Salem. Clements Library. Brun 324.
2. *Upper Salem and part of the tounds joining it for two or three miles distance. Drawn by Abraham Close of Salem.* Rough manuscript 7⅛ by 10¾. Clements Library. Brun 452.

24. JOHN ABRAHAM COLLET

Born in Switzerland, Collet was trained as an officer. He went to England after serving in the French Army. He emigrated to the Carolinas on the recommendation of Lord Shelburne, and commanded Fort Johnston, at the mouth of the Cape Fear River in North Carolina. Here, he figured in the Stamp Act Crisis of 1767. His reports, and a plan of the fort, indicated its poor condition.

In 1768, Governor Tryon of North Carolina turned over to Collet, the survey and data collected by the recently deceased William Churton of Edenton. Some of the same material had been supplied to Fry and Jefferson, and was employed in their early map. Collet continued to add data, so that his map of North Carolina, printed in London in 1770, accurately depicted the settlements and road network. Collet's abilities were recognized, and he was recommended as Geographer to the Southern District in 1767, to have the same rank as Samuel Holland, the Deputy Surveyor of the Northern District. This may reflect the early friction between local residents and deBrahm.

With the outbreak of the Revolution, Collet was resented by the colonists, and had to flee when Fort Johnston was burned on 18 July 1775. He later served in the Prince of Wales American Volunteers, under Sir Henry Clinton and Lord Rawdon. After the war, Collet was appointed Consul at Genoa in 1782. He petitioned for a pension as late as 1791, citing his services in North Carolina.
1. *A General Map of the Southern British Colonies in America. Comprehending North and South Carolina, Georgia, East and West Florida,...from the modern surveys...deBrahm, Capt. Collet, Mouzon & others; and...B. Romans....* Printed map in *The American Military Pocket Atlas...taken from...deBrahm and Romans; Cook, Jackson, and Collet; Maj. Holland...R. Sayer & J. Bennett, London, 1776.* This is based in part upon Collet's 1770 engraved map. A manuscript preliminary draft is preserved in the Public Record Office in London. A manuscript map of Fort Johnston, dispatched to Lord Shelburne in 1767, is in the Clements Library. Brun 597.

25. COX

Not identified. Source of data for Hills' map 5.

26. ABRAHAM D'AUBANT

D'Aubant was commissioned as Ensign in the Engineers 17 March 1759. His promotions were at the usual rate, making captain, 2 March 1777. During the Revolution, D'Aubant served as

Commanding Engineer at Rhode Island during the British occupation, and later in New York. He reported the services of the Engineers on Rhode Island to John Montresor, Chief Engineer in America, in letters dated March 31 and September 30, 1777. These referred to, or enclosed, various plans. While in New York, D'Aubant proposed (jointly with Alexander Mercer) additional defensive works, in a letter dated 8 December 1781.

D'Aubant's remaining career was successful. He was promoted to major general in 1796 and to lieutenant general in 1802. He had been brigadier on the General Staff at the capture of San Fiorenza, Corsica in 1794. His name is not found in the Army list after 1805.

1. *Goat Island: Am: D'Aubant commg. engr.* [*Rhode Island*] Finished, colored manuscript 7¼ by 8¾. Clements Library. Brun 273.
2. *Plan and section of the excavation and the fort at Bristol Ferry. A: D'Aubant commg. engr & Capt.* [*Rhode Island*] Finished, colored manuscript 10 by 15¼, with inset. Clements Library. Brun 280.
3. *Plan of Fort Brown, for 4 guns en barbette; with a small redout, and a line for 60 men, and a barrack. Am: D'Aubant c engr: March 1st. 1779.* [*Rhode Island*] Finished, colored manuscript 15 by 12⅞, with inset. Clements Library. Brun 297.
4. *Plan of Fort Fanning. For 10 guns, and 300 men. Am: D'Aubant c. engr: March 1st. 1779.* Finished, colored manuscript 16½ by 13. Clements Library. Brun 298.
5. *Plan of the Town and environs of Newport Rhode Island Exhibiting its defences formed before the 8th. of August 1778 when the French fleet engaged and passed the batteries; the course of the French fleet up the Harbor: the Rebel attack: and such defensive works as were erected since that day untill the 28th. of August when the Siege was raised; also the works proposed to be erected in the present year 1779. A D'Aubant commanding engineer.* Finished, colored manuscript 44¾ by 50½. Clements Library. Brun 303.
6. *Plan of the Town of Newport and the adjacent country with a project for its defence.* Finished, colored manuscript 18½ by 20⅛. Clements Library. Brun 304.
7. *Sketch of Dumplin Point with a project for a battery of 4 guns and a redout: for 90 men with a barrack in the battery- Am: D'Aubant. commg. engineer* [*Rhode Island*.] Finished, colored manuscript 21½ by 15. Clements Library. Brun 315.
8. *Sketch of Howland's Point with a project for its defence. Am: D'Aubant comg. engineer* [*Rhode Island*.] Finished, colored manuscript 21½ by 15. Clements Library. Brun 316.

27. HENRY DE BERNIERE

De Berniere was an ensign in the 10th. Regiment of Foot, at Boston on the eve of the Revolution. General Gage, the commander of the British forces in Boston, considered war imminent. On 22 February 1775, he ordered Captain Brown of the 23rd. Regiment and De Berniere to disguise themselves as countrymen and to reconnoiter and sketch the roads, passes, heights etc. New instructions were issued 20 March to proceed to Concord to determine the status of the Provincial magazine. De Berniere and Brown returned, accompanied by a local Loyalist, having been recognized on the road. Both Brown and De Berniere accompanied the expedition against Concord and Lexington.

De Berniere was promoted to lieutenant in the 10th. Regiment, to rank from 30 June 1775. His relationship to John De Berniere, lieutenant in the 18th. or Royal Irish Regiment, ranking from 4 February 1769, is unknown.

1. [*Environs of Boston*] Roads from Boston to Roxbury and Dorchester. Somewhat rough manuscript 10½ by 19½. Formerly in the Force collection. Library of Congress. G 4056 R6 1775 M3.
2. [*Environs of Boston*] Roads about Roxbury toward Cambridge

and Milton. Somewhat rough manuscript 19¼ by 10½. Formerly in the Force collection. Library of Congress. G3764 R8 1775 M3.
3. [*Environs of Boston*] Roads from Roxbury to Needham, Lincoln and Concord. Somewhat rough colored manuscript 21½ by 45. Library of Congress. G4050 1775 M3.
4. *Sketch of the Action on the Heights of Charlestown From 17th. June 1775 between his Majesty's Troops under the Command of Major Gen. Howe, and a larger group of American Rebels. Copied by T.A. Chapman from an original Sketch by Henry De Burriere of the 14th. Regiment of Infantry now in the hands of J. Gist Esq.* Finished manuscript 19½ by 13¼. Library of Congress.
5. *Plan of Battle of Bunker Hill.* Detailed manuscript in color. Signature "H. Clinton, Maj. Gen." in lower right. Sold at a London auction 1 October 1923. *Boston Evening Transcript,* Tuesday October 2, 1923.

28. WILLIAM GERHARD DE BRAHM

De Brahm was born in southern Germany in 1717, where he received an excellent education in languages, mathematics and history. He entered the army of Charles VII, and participated in eleven campaigns in Germany, Turkey and France. He resigned his commission as Captain Engineer in 1748. Renouncing Roman Catholicism, he was befriended by the Bishop of Augsberg, when banished from the Bavarian Palatinate.

De Brahm was placed in charge of a group of German emigrants to South Carolina, arriving to settle Ebenezer in 1751. He found his talents in great demand. He was employed repairing the fortifications at Charleston, Savannah and elsewhere. He also produced the first map of South Carolina and Georgia in 1757, and other surveys.

De Brahm was appointed Surveyor General of the Southern District in 1764. He in turn appointed Bernard Romans as an assistant. De Brahm produced a lengthy manuscript report covering South Carolina, Georgia and East Florida. The magnificently illustrated and comprehensive report covers land forms, plants, trees, commodities, and a Cherokee vocabulary. The maps were employed by Henry Mouzon, for his map, published in 1775. The regional maps of the Revolutionary period were largely based upon his original work.

Frequently in conflict with local political appointees, De Brahm was suspended in 1774, but reappointed. The war, and his advancing age, prevented further mapping. He later moved to Philadelphia where he was considered most peculiar. He authored metaphysical works prior to his death in 1799. A superb account of De Brahm was recently published by Louis DeVorsey, Jr. It includes substantial related historical material. Another valuable compilation is *The Southeast in Early Maps* by W.P. Cumming.

There had been previous surveys of local areas, and printed maps; but the modern mapping of the south east begins with the work of De Brahm, the first trained and disciplined surveyor to work in the region. Although additional detail was added in succeeding surveys, De Brahm's work was not exceeded in accuracy until the advent of the Coast and Geodetic Survey. De Brahm used the previous surveys by William Bull, the lieutenant governor; and Captain Hugh Gascoigne, in his monumental map of South Carolina and Georgia, published by Thomas Jefferys in 1757. De Brahm recognized their contribution in the map title. Bull's surveys had been made as early as 1738, and Gascoigne's in 1729.

De Brahm's Atlantic Pilot, published in London in 1772, and his other works were reproduced in varying form, sometimes without recognition of the source, by the publishers of printed maps during the Revolution. His contribution was recognized in Jeffreys' *The American Atlas* and *A General Topography of North America,* in Sayer and Bennett's *Military Pocket Atlas,* and Faden's *The North American Atlas.*

29. J. DECOSTA

1. *A Plan Of The Town and Harbour of Boston and the Country adjacent with the Road from Boston to Concord shewing the Place of the late Engagement between the King's Troops & the Provincials together with the Several Encampments of Both Armies in & about Boston Taken from an Actual Survey Inscribed to Richd. Whitworth Esqr. Member of Parliament for Stafford By his most Obedient Servant J. De Costa.* Printed map 19 by 14⅜, with quaint depiction of the action at Concord. In lower right, "C. Hall Sc." Data or assistance was furnished by Jonathan Carver.

30. ANTHONY DENNIS

Dennis, a Shrewsbury, New Jersey surveyor, was the son of Jacob, also a land surveyor. They were jointly appointed deputy surveyors by the Board of Proprietors in 1754. Between them, they made numerous property surveys in the present Ocean and Monmouth Counties. Dennis was a source of data for Hills' maps 34 and 37.

31. MATTHEW DIXON

Dixon was present with the engineer contingent at the Battle of Dettingen in Germany in 1743, but was not a member of the corps. In the following year, he was made a sub-engineer. Dixon was employed as an engineer in India in 1747, and was a captain at the reduction of Louisburg in 1758. He also served during the Siege of Havana in 1762. He attained the rank of major, serving in the New York campaign in 1776 and 1777. In 1784 he was the commanding engineer at Plymouth, with the rank of colonel.
1. *A Plan of...Part of Long Island....* See Wheeler map 7.

32. AZARIAH DUNHAM

Dunham, a storekeeper and surveyor of New Brunswick, New Jersey, was active in local and state affairs. He was appointed Deputy Surveyor for Middlesex and Somerset in 1752, and was the author of an excellent survey of the division line between Somerset and Middlesex Counties (1766) and other works. A member of the Committee of Observation, Dunham relayed the news of Lexington, which he had received by express rider five days after the battle. He was commissioned Lieutenant Colonel in the New Jersey Militia in April 1776. Dunham is cited as the source of data in Hills' maps 15, 34 and 36. The original surveys were accessible to Hills, in the Office of the Proprietors of East Jersey in Perth Amboy.

33. SAMUEL DUNN

Dunn, mathematician, geographical editor, teacher and publisher of books on astronomy and related subjects, became established in London about 1751. He published *A Directory of the East Indies, A New Atlas of the Mundane System,* and contributed maps for Sayer and Bennett's *A General Atlas....*of 1768, and their *The American Military Pocket Atlas....*of 1776. Dunn died in London in 1794.
1. See Carver no. 6.

34. ELIAS DURNFORD

Four generations of the Durnfords had served in the Engineers by 1890. Elias entered the corps in 1759, preceded by Augustus who was appointed in 1755.
Elias served with distinction at the sieges of Belleisle and Havanna. At Havanna, he was appointed Aide to Lord Albemarle,

the commander. In North America, he served as Surveyor-General of West Florida, and commanded the garrison at Mobile when compelled to surrender to Galvez 14 March 1780. Moncrief, in a letter dated 30 September 1781, referred to a report by Lt. Durnford reporting improvement in the fortifications in East Florida. Moncrief wrote Durnford on 11 December advising on the defense of Savannah. Elias was promoted to Colonel in 1793, serving as Chief Engineer at sieges in the West Indies. He died in Tobago in 1794.
1. [*Pensacola*] *Captain Elias Durnford Engineer.* Careful, colored manuscript 21¼ by 14½. Enclosed in letter of 1 July 1776. Public Record Office. MPG527.
2. [*Pensacola*] *Surveyed and Drawn by Elias Durnford Cpt of Engineer.* Careful, colored manuscript 20¾ by 14½. Enclosed in letter of 25 November 1778. Public Record Office. MPG358.
3. *Position Of The Detachment under Lieut. Col. Baum & Attacks of the Enemy on the 16th. August at Walmscock near Bennington 1777. Lieut: E. Durnford Engineer.* Careful, colored manuscript 14⅞ by 11¾. Library of Congress. Faden Collection No. 65.
4. *Position of the Detachment Under Lieut. Coll. Baum at Walmscook....* Printed map 13½ by 10⅝. Wm. Faden. 1780. See under Burgoyne, No. 3 in Section, Maps in Books. See also Hutchins No. 3. and No. 4.

35. BENJAMIN EASBURN

Easburn, a Philadelphian, was Surveyor General of Pennsylvania prior to Nicholas Scull. His draft of the Delaware Counties, made in 1732, is referred to in a letter from Thomas Penn to Richard Peters in 1749. A Plan of Philadelphia by Easburn was published by Andrew Dury in London in 1776, and subsequently. See under Andrew Dury, No. 6.

36. WILLIAM EDEN

Eden, a statesman and political figure, was born in 1744. He was educated at Eton and Oxford, receiving an M.A. in 1768. He became Under Secretary of State in 1772 and was seated in Parliament in 1774. He was appointed to the Board of Trade and Plantations in 1776, and he managed Great Britain's secret service on the continent.
A proponent of conciliation, Eden joined Lord Frederick Carlisle and George Johnstone, the Governor of West Florida, in an ineffective Peace Commission in 1778. Eden later became secretary to Carlisle when Viceroy of Ireland, and a distinguished and successful statesman. He was created Lord Auckland in 1793. Eden died in 1814.
1. [*New York and Environs*] A rough manuscript 7 by 7, of 16 July 1776. Enclosed in a letter from Eden, dated at St. James, 23 August 1776. Private collection of Mr. John Reed.

37. LEWIS EVANS

Evans was born in Wales and emigrated to Pennsylvania by 1736. He worked as a surveyor and draughtsman in Philadelphia, where he became associated with prominent and farsighted individuals who were interested in various aspects of natural history, exploration and publishing. He accompanied the botanist John Bartram, on a wilderness trip in 1743. Evans realized the importance of French exploration and settlement of the Ohio River, Great Lakes and other western lands, bringing them to public notice by a series of maps published in 1749 and 1755.
Evans' *A General Map of the Middle British Colonies in America* was initially published in 1755. Authorized editions were published in 1760, and to accompany Pownall's *A Topographical Description of...North America,* printed by J. Almon in London in 1776. Pirated editions were published by Kitchin, Jefferys, Sayer

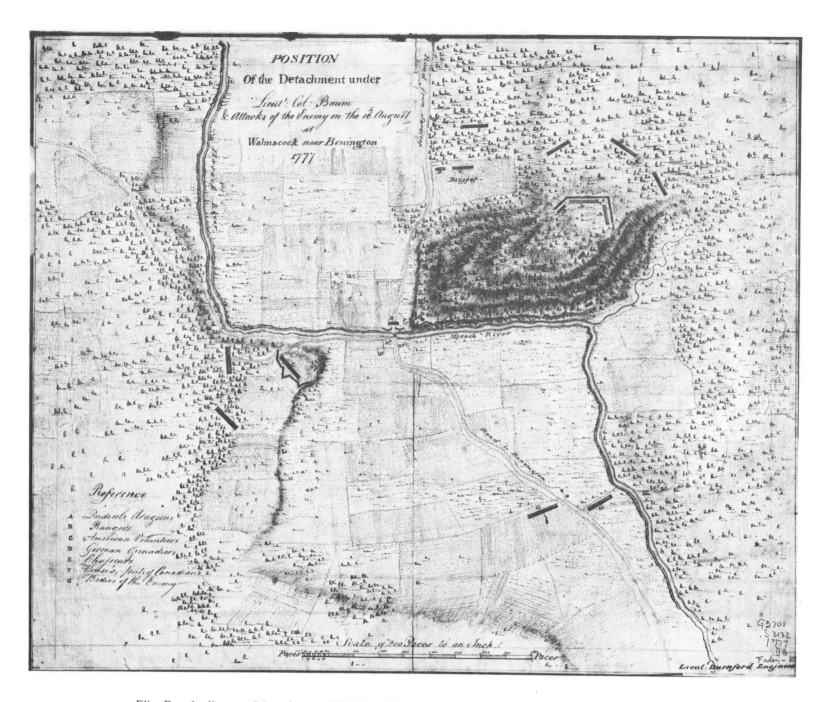

Elias Durnford's map of American and British positions near Bennington, Vermont, August 16, 1777. See 34/4.

and Jefferys, Sayer and Bennett, and later by Laurie and Whittle. Versions of his map appeared possibly as late as 1816, although Evans died in Philadelphia in 1756. Excellent studies of Evans were published by Henry N. Stevens in 1905 and 1920, and by Lawrence H. Gipson in 1939.

1. *A Map of the Middle British Colonies in North America First Published by Mr. Lewis Evans of Philadelphia, in 1755; and since corrected and improved, as also extended. With the Addition of New England, and bordering Parts of Canada. From the Actual Surveys now lying at the Board of Trade.* By T. Pownall M.P. with a Topographical Description of such Parts of North America as are contained in this Map. J. Almon, London. March 25th., 1776. Printed map 31 by 18¼. Inset "...remaining parts of Ohio R., &c."

38. EDWARD FAGE

Fage was the son of Edward Fage of Maidstone, Kent. His relationship to a mathematical instrument maker of the same name,

who flourished 1667 to 1673, is not established. Fage was trained at Woolwich and commissioned in the Royal Artillery. While in Rhode Island, he received a letter of thanks from Major James Pattison dated 8 May 1779, for sending a accurate and neat plan of the area. He was the probable author of a four page table of distances between the defensive works at Newport and the surrounding country.

Fage was promoted captain-lieutenant in September 1779. In August 1780 he was at Flushing, N.Y., recovering from an illness, when ordered to New York. Fage was the author of a letter to Maj. Gen. William Phillips, dated 18 February 1781. The letter concerned data on the French fortifications in Rhode Island from Mr. Brenton, and included maps. Fage's later career was successful. He received steady promotions to the rank of major general in 1808. His will indicates he was resident in Greenwich in 1808, had a son John, and made a bequest to Joseph Barney, Drawing Master at Woolwich.

1. *Plan of the adjacent coast to the northern part of Rhode Island, to express the route of a body of troops under the command of*

Lieutt Colonel Campbell of the 22d: Regiment to destroy the Enemies batteaux vessels, galley &c &c &c which was accomplished May 25th: 1778. Laid down and drawn by Edwd. Fage Lieutt. of Artillery. Careful, colored manuscript 16¾ by 13¼. Clements Library. Brun 300.

2. *Plan of the works, which form the exterior line of defence, for the Town of New-Port in Rhode Island; also of the batteries and approaches made by the Rebels on Honeymans Hill during their attack in August 1778. The line of works command a valley extending from Codington Cove to the head of Eastons Pond, the distance about one mile and a half; on the opposite side of the valley rises Honeymans Hill which overlooks most of our works, but at a distance that renders it of little consequence... This plan surveyed and drawn by Edward Fage Lieut: of artillery November 1778.* Careful, colored manuscript 26¼ by 17½. Clements Library. Brun 307.

3. *[Newport and Environs c. 1778]* Unfinished, colored manuscript 23½ by 18¾. Unsigned. Clements Library. Brun 277.

4. *Plan of the Southern Part of Rhode Island with the Harbour and Such of the Adjacent Coast as is necessary to express the entrance of the Three Rivers into the Narragansett Bay.* Careful, colored manuscript 33 by 25¼. Duke of Northumberland Collection, Alnwick.

5. *Plan of Rhode Island the Harbour, the Adjacent Islands, and Coast. Edwd. Fage Lieut of Artillery.* Careful, colored manuscript 7⅜ by 13½. British Museum. Crown Collection CXX42.

6. *Plan of Rhode-Island surveyed and drawn by Edwd: Fage Captn. Royal Artillery in the years 1777, 78 & 79.* Careful, colored manuscript 26¼ by 37⅛. Clements Library. Brun 299.

7. *[Narragansett Bay and Rhode Island]* Unfinished manuscript 21¼ by 29½. Unsigned. Clements Library. Brun 274.

8. *[Lower Rhode Island Area]* Unfinished, colored manuscript 16¾ by 23. Unsigned. Clements Library. Brun 68.

9. *Original Plan of Brentons Neck; and all the ground to the southward of the Town of New-Port Rhode Island 1779, E. Fage.* Careful, colored manuscript 36⅜ by 26¼. Clements Library. Brun 279.

39. PATRICK FERGUSON

Ferguson, second son of James Ferguson of Pitfour, Aberdeenshire, was born in 1744. He was commissioned in the 2nd. Royal North Dragoons in 1759. He served in Germany, transferred to the 70th. Foot in Tobago. At that time, Ferguson began experimenting with a breech loading rifle, improving on the design of Isaac de la Chaumette, which had been patented in 1721. He presented his work to the authorities in England in 1774. The arm was tested at Woolwich in 1776. A small corps was armed with it, and was employed in the Philadelphia campaign.

Ferguson was an active soldier, serving in the Little Egg Harbour, N.J. operation in October 1778, and at the capture of Stony Point in 1779. He was promoted major in Frazer's 71st. Highlanders, and participated in the southern campaigns in command of a group of 300 Loyalists armed with his rifle. Ferguson was the author of, and recipient of, a number of communications with Clinton, André and others concerning the obstructions to the navigation of the Hudson, descriptions of defense positions, and related subjects. Ferguson was killed at Kings Mountain in October 1780, while commanding his Rifle armed Loyalists against the Rifle armed Southern Militia.

1. *Plan of a two story building converted into a strong point, By Patrick Ferguson.* Pencil sketch 6 by 12¾. Clements Library. Brun 7.

2. *Plan for a fort in North America By Patrick Ferguson.* Ink and pencil sketch 14¾ by 9½. Clements Library. Brun 8.

3. *Long Island Sound Shore from Fairfield to New London by Patrick Ferguson, May 27, 1779.* Careful manuscript 9½ by 7⅞, with descriptive addition. Clements Library. Brun 318.

4. *Hudson River from Peekskill to Slaughters Landing by Patrick Ferguson 1779.* Rough sketch 11 by 7⅞, enclosed in letter to André. Clements Library. Brun 354.

5. *Verplanks Point. By: Patrick Ferguson 1779.* Rough sketch 9 by 7⅜, enclosed in letter to Clinton. Clements Library. Brun 455.

6. *Distances North River. By: Patrick Ferguson.* Detailed sketch manuscript 24 by 14⅝. Clements Library. Brun 339.

7. *[Parts of present Dutchess, Putnam and Westchester Counties, New York]* Rough sketch 28 by 16. Clements Library. Brun 391.

8. *[Parts of present Union and Bergen Counties, New Jersey]* Sketch of British attack on Paramus 16 April 1780. Clements Library. Brun 493.

9. *Proposed fortifications for Savannah. By Patrick Ferguson 1780.* Unfinished manuscript 6½ by 10¼. Clements Library. Brun 638.

40. PATRICK FINNEGAN

Finnegan served as a Lieutenant in the 16th. Regiment. In addition to the map made by him, another interesting one was at least temporarily in his possession. This is a map of the Siege of Savannah. It is considered to be the work of a Swiss or German engineer serving in the Regiment of Trumbach or Wissenbach. It was endorsed by Lt. Finnegan. It was auctioned at the sale of Lord Rawdon's papers in London.

1. *Plan of the Siege of Charles Town in South Carolina under the command of His Excellency Sir Henry Clinton, and under direction of Collenel Mount Crieff as Chief Engineer.* Finished, colored manuscript 17¼ by 25¼. Library of Congress. G3701 S3333 F5.

41. JOSHUA FISHER

A native of Pennsylvania, Fisher made a chart of Delaware River, first engraved in Philadelphia by James Turner in 1755, and printed by John Davis. The valuable chart was included in Sayer and Bennett's *North American Pilot....,* various Faden publications, and as late as 1800 in Laurie and Whittle's *Pilot.* Fisher is cited as a source of data for Hills' maps 5 and 39.

42. LIEUTENANT FORTH

1. *A Plan of...Part of Long Island....* See Wheeler map 8.

43. SIMON FRASER

Fraser, a Loyalist from Albany, appears in the minutes of the Commission for Detecting Conspiracies on 30 July 1778. He eventually went to Shelburne, Nova Scotia in 1783. Fraser's relationship with Col. Simon Fraser, of Frasers Highlanders, active in the same area of New York in 1765, is unknown. Brigadier Gen. Simon Fraser of the Highlanders, was killed at the Battle of Freeman's Farm 19 September 1777.

1. *Plan of the general attack on Fort Mifflin the [10-16] of [November, 1777] The Rebels evacuated it and burn'd the barracks and line of pickets about 11 o'clock at night, taken in possession early next morng:* Finished, colored manuscript 11¼ by 12⅛. Clements Library. Brun 544.

44. JOSHUA FRY

Fry was born in England about 1700, probably attended Oxford, emigrated to Virginia, and taught mathematics at the College of William and Mary at Williamsburg. Fry moved into the undeveloped back country hoping to acquire large properties, and lived on the Hardware River near Carter's Bridge. He acted as a Presiding Magistrate, County Lieutenant, and County Surveyor.

Becoming the leading citizen of Albemarle, he was a member of the House of Burgesses, was appointed Crown Commissioner, and was a member of the commission to settle the disputed Virginia-North Carolina line.

Fry became acquainted with Peter Jefferson while the latter was at Shadwell, and fostered his appointment as one of the surveyors of the Fairfax line, which was completed in 1749. Fry and Jefferson were selected by Acting Governor Lewis Burwell as best qualified to make a map of Virginia in 1750. The map had been proposed 12 years previously. The large amount of previous data and surveys in their hands made it possible to complete a preliminary map by 1751. The first edition was published by Thomas Jefferys in London in 1751. Subsequent issues and new editions were published, the last by Laurie and Whittle in 1794. It was the principal map of the area during the Revolution, widely employed by both sides.

1. *A Map of the Most Inhabited Part of Virginia containing the whole Province of Maryland with Part of Pennsylvania, New Jersey and North Carolina Drawn by Joshua Fry & Peter Jefferson...Printed for Robert Sayer...London, 1775.* Printed map 46¾ by 28¼. See under Peter Jefferson and Robert Sayer and Thomas Jefferys.

45. WILLIAM FYERS

Fyers was appointed an Ensign in the Engineers 11 November 1773 on graduation from Woolwich. He was in Boston during the early revolutionary period, took part in the Battle of Long Island, in the invasion of Charleston, and at Portsmouth Virginia in 1781. Capt. Mercer and Lt. Fyers were reported fortifying Stony Point in a letter from General Pattison dated 9 June 1779. Fyers was the author of a report to Sir Henry Clinton on the state of the Refugee Post on the West side of the Hudson on 11 July 1780.

Fyers' later military career was successful. He served in the low lands in 1807 with the rank of Colonel and was promoted Major General in 1811.

1. *Plan of the post of Portsmouth as it is occupied by His Majesty's Forces under the command of Major General Phillips April 1st. 1781. Shewing, in yellow, the works proposed, in addition to those already constructed by order of Brigadier General Arnold. Wm. Fyers lieut & sub engineer [Virginia.]* Finished, colored manuscript 20¼ by 23½. Clements Library. Brun 577.

46. GEORGE GAULD

Gauld's name appears in the register of the University of Aberdeen as a student between 1750 and 1754, as a teacher of mathematics in 1759, and as "A.M." in 1807. He served as a schoolmaster in the Royal Navy aboard the *PRESTON* in the Mediterranean, and aboard the *CENTAUR* in English waters from 1757 to 1760.

He traveled to the West Indies aboard the *TARTER* in 1764. He was employed in making hydrographic surveys of Florida, the West Indies, and the Carribean area between 1765 and 1775. Many of these activities were in association with Phillip Pittman, Bernard Romans, and David Taitt; some under the supervision of John Stuart, Superintendant of Indian Affairs. In May 1779 he was aboard the schooner *WEST FLORIDA*, presumably making surveys.

Printed charts of the west coast of Florida and Louisiana, of the Tortugas and Florida Keys, and of the island of Grand Cayman were published and sold. An account of observations on the Florida Keys, Reef and Gulf, with sailing instructions for the coast of West Florida, was published about 1796, in book form. His surveys and manuscripts were used as a source of data by Des Barres in *The Atlantic Neptune,* and by others without crediting Gauld.

1. *Plan of the Bays of Pensacola and Mobile with the Sea Coast and country Adjacent By Geo. Gauld, M.A. For the Right Honble. The Board of Admiralty 1765.* Careful manuscript 40¼ by 27½, with soundings. Hydrographic Department, Taunton. D964.

2. *A Survey of the Coast of West Florida From Pensacola to Cape Blaise Including the Bays of Pensacola, South Rosa, St. Andrew and St. Joseph, with the Shoals lying off Cape Blair. By George Gauld, M.A. For the Right Honorable the Board of Admiralty 1766.* Careful manuscript 65½ by 27¾, with soundings. Hydrographic Department, Taunton. A9464.

3. *A Sketch of the entrance from the sea to Apalachy, and Part of the environs taken by George Gauld esqr surveyor of the coast and Lieutenant Philip Pittman assistt engineer [1767.]* Finished, colored manuscript 32 by 17¾, with soundings. See report Haldimand to Gage 5 August 1767. Clements Library. Brun 660.

4. *[Mississippi Sound, Lake Ponchartrain to Biloxi] Survey by George Gauld, M.A. For the Right Honourable the Board of Admiralty 1768.* Careful, detailed manuscript 79 by 40½, with soundings. Hydrographic Department, Taunton. D962.

5. *A Map of West Florida, Part of Et: Florida, Georgia, part of So: Carolina including [Seminole] & Choctaw Chickasaw & Creek nations with the road from Pensacola through ye: Creek Nation to Augusitus & Charles Town Compiled under the direction of ye: so [   ] John Stuart esqr: His Majesty's [   ] superintendant of Indian affairs in the Southern Department of Nth: America & by him humbly to His Excellency ye: Honble: Thomas Gage esqr: general & commander in chief of all His Majesty's Forces in Nth. America &c. &c. &c. By: Bernard Romans, David Taitt, and George Gauld.* Careful, detailed manuscript 66 by 101, with soundings, with inset of W. Florida and Carolinas. Pensacola Harbor from drafts by Duncord [Durnford]. Sent to Gage by Stuart, 22 April 1773. Clements Library. Brun 663.

6. *A plan of Manchac 1774. By Geo. Gauld surveyor of the sea coasts &c. For His Excellency Sir Henry Clinton k.b. commander in chief &c. &c. &c. at the request of Brigr. General Campbell 1779 [Archibald Campbell.]* Finished, colored manuscript 17¾ by 22¾. Clements Library. Brun 676.

7. *A Plan of Part of the Florida Keys, from Bahia Honda to Cayo Largo; Survey by George Gauld For the Right Honourable the Board of Admiralty 1775.* Careful, detailed manuscript 55½ by 33⅞, with soundings. Hydrographic Department, Taunton. D959.

8. *A Plan of the Tortugas and Part of the Florida Kays. Surveyed by George Gauld, M.A. for The Right Honourable The Board of Admiralty. 1773.* Careful, detailed manuscript with soundings. Hydrographic Department, Taunton. D966.

9. *[Untitled and unsigned rough drafts of areas covered by number 7 and 8]* 184 by 47. Hydrographic Department, Taunton. D959a.

10. *A Survey of the Bay of Espiritu Santo in East Florida by Geo. Gauld, M.A. 1765.* Careful, detailed manuscript with soundings. Hydrographic Department, Taunton. X64.

11. *A Draught of Part of the Coast to Westward of the River Mississippi with Part of the Islands of New Orleans &c. By George Gauld M.A. for the Right Honourable the Board of Admiralty. 1777.* Careful, detailed manuscript 166 by 37½, with soundings. Hydrographic Department, Taunton. D965.

12. *A Plan of the Coast of Part of West Florida & Louisiana including the River Mississippi from its entrance as high as the River Yazous surveyed by George Gauld M.A. for the Right Honourable the Board of Admiralty. 1778.* Careful, detailed manuscript 85 by 40, with soundings. Hydrographic Department, Taunton. D958.

13. *Lake Maurepas to B. de Baros etc. G. Gauld 1768.* Uncompleted manuscript. Hydrographic Department, Taunton. E19/13.

14. *Chandeleur I. to Galveston B. Entrance including Mississippi R. 1777.* Rough draft of number 11. Hydrographic Department, Taunton. E19/14.

15. *Rough of Mobile Bay by G. Gauld 1776*. Incomplete preliminary survey, 50 by 44½. Hydrographic Department, Taunton. E19/10.

16. *A Plan of the Mouths of the Mississippi By George Gauld M.A. For the Right Honourable the Earl of Dartmouth*. Preliminary survey 15 by 11¾, with much descriptive data. Enclosed in a letter to Governor Chester 7 June 1774. Public Record Office. PRO 530. See also Romans No. 6.

47. JAMES GRANT

Grant was employed by Samuel Holland in surveying the coast and harbours of New England. Other members of the same group were George Sproule, Charles Blaskowitz, and Thomas Wheeler. His official designation was deputy surveyor of lands, for the northern district of North America, and was most generally teamed with Thomas Wheeler. Many of these surveys were incorporated into, or were the source of data for, *The Atlantic Neptune* of J.F.W. DesBarres. Grant was also the source of the Plan of Perth Amboy, included in the manuscript atlas of New Jersey by John Hills.

1. *Plan of Perth Amboy from an actual survey*. Careful, colored manuscript 7¾ by 8¼. Map 1, in John Hills manuscript atlas of New Jersey. Library of Congress. See also under Charles Blaskowitz, Thomas Wheeler and George Sproule.
2. *A Plan of the Sea Coast from Ogunkett River to Cape Elizabeth, including the Bays of Wells, Saco, and Black Point, also, Wells and Winter Harbours. Surveyed by James Grant, deputy surveyor under direction of Samuel Holland, Surveyor General*. Careful, colored manuscript 36 by 31. Public Record Office. C.O. 700 Maine No. 15.

48. ALEXANDER GRAY

An ensign in the 40th. Regiment of Foot.
1. *Fort Griswold 1781 By Alexr. Gray ensn 40th. regt.* [*Connecticut*.] Outline plan of the British attack September 6, 1781. 12⅝ by 8. Clements Library. Brun 317.

49. JAMES MURRAY HADDEN

Hadden, son of Captain John Hadden of the Royal Marines, entered the Royal Military Academy at Woolwich in 1771. He was commissioned a second lieutenant in the Royal Artillery in 1774. Hadden arrived in Quebec in July 1776, and joined the Army under Burgoyne. He played an active role in the campaign, and was taken prisoner following the Battle of Saratoga. He was exchanged a short time later. His later military career was distinguished. He died at Hovpenden in 1817.

The following maps were in *Hadden's Journal and Orderly Books* in the possession of Horatio Rogers prior to 1884, the date of their publication at Albany, N.Y. The size of the original maps is not known. The journal is an excellent and detailed account of the campaign.
1. *Lake Champlain. Sketch of the Action in Lake Champlain 11 Oct. 1776*. Rough sketch map, opposite page 22.
2. *Magazine at Windmill Point and South Bay*. Rough sketch map, opposite page 33.
3. *Ticonderoga and the Works There*. Rough sketch map opposite page 83.
4. *Lake Champlain to Stillwater*. Rough sketch map opposite page 90.
5. *Toward Swords farm*. Rough sketch map opposite page 152.
6. *Battle of 10th. of Sept.* Rough sketch map, opposite page 164.

50. DANIEL HAMMILL

Hammill served as a Major in the New York Militia under the command of Brig. General James Clinton. Clinton, brother of George, the future governor of New York, escaped from the unsuccessful defense of Fort Montgomery in 1777, with a wound. Hammill was captured by the attacking forces commanded by Sir Henry Clinton. He agreed to defect when promised the colonelcy of a new Irish regiment to be raised from deserters.

Hammill petitioned Sir Henry Clinton for money in a letter dated 6 October 1777. He had sustained imprisonment in Poughkeepsie for 15 months after having been expelled from his house, farm and family in Dutchess County. He also had lost his saddle bags when pursued by Rebel Light Horse on the road from Dutchess County, and had lost a trunk on his Majesty's vessel *PRESTON* when he had to flee New York. A Daniel Hammill is recorded as a "conductor" for the British Army in New York on 1 July and 26 August 1781.
1. *West Point or Fort Defiance. Daniel Hammill*. Finished manuscript 8 by 12½. Clements Library. Brun 461.

51. SAMUEL HAMMONS

He is co-author of a chart as "Master Attendt. Navy Yard."
1. See under Dugald Campbell map 3.

52. ANDREW SNAPE HAMOND

Hamond was born at Blackheath, Kent on 17 December 1738. His father was Robert Hamond, a wealthy and influential London ship owner and merchant. Hamond entered the Navy as a midshipman in 1753, at the age of fourteen. His first command was a cutter in 1763. Successive commands included the *BARFLEUR*, Admiral Lord Howe's flagship, in 1770, during which he cemented his relations with Howe.

Hamond's part in the Revolution revolved about his command of the *ROEBUCK*, a 44 gun frigate. He played a part in the decision to land the Philadelphia-bound expedition under General Howe in the Chesapeake at the head of the Elk, rather than the shores of the Delaware. This was based upon his exploration of the Delaware, which he considered too dangerous to navigate under the prevailing conditions. During the 1777 actions on the Delaware, Hamond distinguished himself as an able and aggressive officer, who incidentally reaped large rewards from the capture of many vessels. He was knighted in the following year. His map was made during this period. Hamond's later naval career was distinguished. He later served as a Member of Parliament. He died on the Isle of Wight in 1802.
1. [*Southeast Pennsylvania*] Careful manuscript tracing showing the Susquehanna, Delaware, major cities and road network, 16½ by 9, part colored. It is fastened inside the cover of volume II of his diary. University of Virginia Library.

53. ALSOP HAMPTON

Source of data for Hills' map 21.

54. DAVID HARTLEY

Hartley, British statesman and diplomat, was born in 1732. He was a leader of the group favoring reconciliation, and actively wrote and campaigned to this end. A pamphlet, published in London in 1776, recounts the status of relations between England and the Colonies. Another pamphlet of letters on the American war was published in 1777, and reprinted several times during the next two years. Hartley represented England as peace commissioner, but his name is overshadowed by the better known Benjamin Franklin, John Adams and John Jay.

1. *A sketch of the United States of America according to the Definitive Treaty of Peace at Paris, September 3, 1783.* Unfinished manuscript 9¼ by 7. It outlines new states along the Ohio and Mississippi Rivers by parallels of latitude and longitude. Clements Library. Brun 5.

55. JOHN HAYMAN

Hayman was commissioned an ensign in the 17th. Regiment of Foot in January 1777 and promoted lieutenant, to date from November 1778.

1. [*Yorktown and Surrounding area, Virginia*] Careful manuscript 18¾ by 20⅛. In lower right, "12th. June 1782." British Museum. Additional manuscripts 15, 535.6.

56. S. HAYS

Source of data for Hills' map 21.

57. JOHN HILLS

Ensign Hills is included as one of three "extra draughtsmen" in a return of the assistant engineers in the engineers department of 19 September 1778 reported by John Montresor, Chief Engineer. Hills' assignment was the 38th. Regiment at New York.

His contempt of discipline was the subject of a letter of complaint, answered by General Pattison, Commandant at New York, on 10 April 1779. He was ordered placed under arrest unless he indicated a sense of contrition for his misbehavior, in writing. Failure to do this would result in court martial.

Hills is the subject of another letter from Pattison to Lord Viscount Townshend on 8 November 1779. Pattison had recommended that Hills be transferred from ensign in the 38th. to second lieutenant in the Artillery. Hills resigned the latter as his interests were in the "professional branch of engineering." As a consequence, he had for some time been permitted to act as an engineer in the Army, and had acquitted himself with credit.

The returns of the engineering department of 14 January 1780 and 25 February 1780 include the name of Lieut. Hills, reported by Alexander Mercer, Commanding Engineer, at New York. The British Army Lists from 1781 to 1784 include Hills in the 23rd. Regiment of Foot, a commission as second lieutenant dating from 5 October 1781.

Another complaint was made of his ill treatment of a distinguished Loyalist, David Ogden of New Jersey, in a letter dated 24 May 1780. In spite of these conflicts, Hills produced a superb collection of maps of the operations of the Army. Some of these were rendered a considerable time after the event, some of which Hills had not observed himself. Several were included in later printed form.

Hills credits his sources of data, particularly in his maps of New Jersey. The sources were principally local surveyors, who were contemporary, or nearly so. A good number were strong and active supporters of the patriot cause. Hills obviously had access to a number of original surveys or copies, many of which had been made for the Proprietors of East Jersey, and possibly for the equivalent West Jersey body. It is probable that these were obtained from the proprietory office at Perth Amboy when it was in British hands, or from the Loyalist Thomas Milliadge who was a Deputy Surveyor of the Proprietors, or from both. A few surveys were credited to other British or Loyalist surveyors.

An outstanding and unique manuscript atlas of New Jersey, was made for, and retained by, Sir Henry Clinton. This was the only state so recognized and honored during the Revolution.

Following the Revolution, Hills established himself as a surveyor and draughtsman in Philadelphia. His name appears in the 1793 directory with James Hardie, A.M., and in later years alone at a different address. He appears for the last time in the 1816 directory. The name of Mary Hills, "academy for young ladies" appears at the same address in 1801 and intermittently to 1816.

Hills produced maps of Philadelphia, of the stage routes between New York and Baltimore, of New Jersey, and surveys of various properties such as Frankford Creek Farm. The New Jersey map was undertaken as early as 1784 when Hills advertised his interest, giving Princeton and New York addresses. This was never completed, although an uncompleted draught was submitted to the Assembly in 1796.

1. *Boston Harbour, with the Surroundings, &c.* Careful, unlabeled manuscript 51 by 29, unsigned. Library of Congress. Faden Collection 35.

2. *Plan of the Peninsula Of Chesopeak Bay Compiled from actual Surveys By John Hills Assistant Engineer 1781.* Careful, colored manuscript 24⅞ by 47. In lower right "Copied from the original by I. Hills, Asst. Engr." British Museum, Crown Collection CXXII34.

3. *Plan of the Peninsula of Chesopeak Bay Compiled from actual Surveys by John Hills Assistant Engineer 1781.* Careful, colored to Turkey Point were taken in 1777. Careful, colored manuscript, dissected, 24¾ by 48½. Newberry Library. Ayer Collection 240.

4. *Plan of the Peninsula of Chesopeak Bay Compiled from actual Surveys by John Hills Assistant Engineer 1781.* Careful colored manuscript 24¾ by 48¾. Series of profiles of a part of the bay. Soundings in the main channel "taken in the passage up to Elk River in 1777 by John Hills...." Clements Library. Brun 561.

5. *A Complete plan of part of the Province of Pennsylvania, East and West Jersey shewing the transactions of the Royal Army under the command of their Excellencies Sir W. Howe and Sr. Hy. Clinton Knts. of the most honorable order of the bath in marching from Elk River 1777 to the embarkation at Navisink 1778. This plan is compiled from the original surveys of Scull, Biddle, Fisher, Cox, Millage, Dennis, Williams, Morgan, Rue, Clinton, Ryartson, & several principal surveyors by I. Hills, vol. with the Brigade of His Majestys Foot Guards. New York August 1778.* Careful, colored manuscript 19½ by 62, with extension 19½ by 21¾ at lower left. Clements Library. Brun 521.

6. *A plan of part of the provinces of Pennsylvania, and East & West New Jersey...By John Hills.* In Faden's, *Atlas of Battles of the American Revolution.*

7. *Sketch of the Surprise of Germantown, by the American Forces...By J. Hills.* In Faden's, *Atlas of Battles of the American Revolution.*

8. *A Sketch of Haddonfield. West New Jersey County. By J. Hills March 1778.* Finished, colored manuscript 8¼ by 10¼. Clements Library. Brun 511.

9. *Sketch of the Road from Penny Hill to Black Horse through Mount Holly 1778.* Careful, colored manuscript 26¼ by 19⅜. Library of Congress. Force Collection G3701 S322 1778 H54.

10. *Sketch of the Road from Black Horse to Crosswick.* Careful, colored manuscript 24¾ by 17⅞. Library of Congress. Force Collection G3701 S222 1778 H53.

11. *Sketch from information of the different roads about Freehold in the Jerseys.* Careful, colored manuscript 27 by 36, unsigned. Clements Library. Brun 510.

12. *Sketch of part of the road from Freehold to Middletown shewing the skirmish between the rear of the British Army under the command of His Excellency Genl: Sir Henry Clinton and the advanced corps of the Rebel Army June 28th. 1778. Copy'd from I. Hills. Sketch by I.H.* Careful, colored manuscript 19¼ by 26¾. Inset of Middletown. Clements Library. Brun 512.

13. *Sketch of Part of the Road from Freehold to Middletown Shewing the Skirmish between the Rear of the British Army under the command of his Excellency Genl. Sir Henry Clinton and the*

advanced Corps of the Rebel Army June 28th. 1778 by I. Hills July 1778. Careful, colored manuscript 20½ by 16½. Library of Congress. Force Collection G3701 S322 1778 H51.

14. *Sketch of Part of the Road from Freehold to Middletown Shewing the Skirmish between the Rear of the British Army under Command of His Excellency Gen'l Sir Henry Clinton and the advanced corps of the Rebel Army June 28th. 1778.* Careful, colored manuscript 20½ by 16½, unsigned. Library of Congress. Force Collection G3701 S322 1778 H52.

15. *Plan of Middlesex County in the Province of East Jersey. Copied from the original by Lieut. I. Hills, asst. engr. N.B. by Az. Dunham in 1776.* Finished, colored manuscript 31¼ by 60¾. Clements Library. Brun 497.

16. *Sketch of the Position of the British Forces at Elizabeth Town Point...on the 8th. June 1780...by John Hills.* In Faden's, *Atlas of Battles of the American Revolution.*

17. *Plan of Somerset County in the Province of New Jersey. Copied from the original by Lieut. I. Hills, asst. engr. N. B. Surveyed by Benjamin Morgan 1766.* Finished, colored manuscript 59¼ by 44½. Clements Library. Brun 501.

18. *Plan of Paulus Hook shewing the works erected for its defence and the country adjacent in the Province of East Jersey. Surveyed by I. Hills, assistant engr. July 1781.* Finished, colored manuscript 36 by 27¼. Clements Library. Brun 499.

19. *Plan of Paulus Hook shewing the works erected for its defence. Surveyed by I. Hills, assistant engr. July 1781.* Finished, colored manuscript 12 by 18. Clements Library. Brun 500.

20. *A Plan of the Roads between Hackinsack and the North or Hudson's River in the Province of East New Jersey. From the original surveys in the posession of I. Hills, Lieut in the 23rd. Regt. Surveyor and draughtsman.* Finished, colored manuscript 61 by 23. Public Record Office. W.O. 78/1855. MP958.

21. *Plan from Paulus Hook Ferry in the Province of East Jersey, to King's Ferry in the Province of New York and parts adjacent from actual Surveys 1781. This plan is compiled and reduced from the original surveys of G. Clinton, S. Matcalse, S. Hays, G. Reyerse, Also Hampton, Ratzer and other surveys in the posession of John Hills, assistant engineer. To His Excellency Sir Henry Clinton, K.B. General and Commander in Chief, of His Majesty's Forces &c. in North America. This plan is most humbly dedicated, by His Excellency's most obedt: humble servant. I. Hills assistant engr.* Finished, colored manuscript 47½ by 15½. Clements Library. Brun 519.

22. *A Map of Part of the Province of East Jersey containing Part of Monmouth, Middlesex, Essex and Bergen Counties compiled from the Original Surveys in the Possession of John Hills, Lieut in the 23rd. Regt. Private Surveyor and Draughtsman to His Excellency the Commander in Chief 1782.* Finished, colored manuscript 22¾ by 30½. In W.O. 78/1845. Public Record Office. MPH569.

The following twenty maps were included in a magnificent and unique manuscript atlas *A Collection of Plans &c. &c. &c. in the Province of New Jersey by John Hills Asst. Engr* made for Sir Henry Clinton, and retained by him following the war. The atlas was among his papers auctioned in 1882. The atlas includes copies of some of the preceding maps, and the work of other surveyors is cited as sources in the table of contents. The names of the men are in brackets. This is the only Revolutionary War state atlas. Library of Congress. Phillips 1339.

23. *Plan of Perth Amboy from an Actual Survey* [James Grant.] Finished, colored manuscript 8 by 9. No. 1 in the Atlas.

24. *Sketch of Bonham Town and Redouts for its Defence in the Winter 1776, 77* [A. Sutherland.] Finished, colored manuscript 12¼ by 7½. No. 2 in the Atlas.

25. *Sketch of Brunswick* [A. Sutherland.] Finished, colored manuscript 10½ by 8½. No. 3 in the Atlas.

27. *Sketch of the Ground near Mr. Lows at Raritan Landing.* Finished, colored manuscript 10½ by 8½. No. 4 in the Atlas.

28. *Sketch of Haddonfield. March 1778.* Finished, colored manuscript 8¼ by 6½. No. 5 in the Atlas.

29. *Sketch of the Roads from Penny Hill to Black Horse through Mount Holly. By I. Hills June 1778.* Finished, colored manuscript 27 by 19¼. No. 6 in the Atlas.

30. *Sketch of the Road from Black Horse to Crosswick By I. Hills June 1778.* Finished, colored manuscript 21½ by 19. No. 7 in the Atlas.

31. *Sketch of Allens Town. June 1778.* Finished, colored manuscript 7 by 7¾. No. 8 in the Atlas.

32. *Sketch of Part of the Road from Freehold to Middletown shewing the Skirmish between the Rear of the British Army under the Command of his Excellency Genl. Sir Henry Clinton and the advanced Corps of the Rebel Army. June 28, 1778. By I. Hills.* Finished, colored manuscript 22½ by 17. No. 9 in the Atlas.

33. *Sketch of Middle Town.* Finished, colored manuscript 7 by 7¾. No. 10 in the Atlas.

34. *A Map of Part of the Province of Jersey* [By Morgan, Williams, Dennis, Rue, Dunham, Taylor, Skinner, &c.] *Compiled from the original surveys. By I. Hills Asst. Engineer 1781. N.B. The Doted Red Line is the Line of March of the Royal Army under the Command of His Excellency Genl. Sir Henry Clinton, K.B. &c. &c. &c. 1778.* Finished, colored manuscript 27 by 20. No. 11 in the Atlas.

35. *A Map of Somerset County* [By B. Morgan] *Reduced from the Original Survey. By I. Hills, asst. Engineer 1781.* Finished, colored manuscript 26½ by 18¾. No. 12 in the Atlas.

36. *A Map of Middlesex County* [By A. Dunham and J. Rue] *Reduced from the Original Survey. By I. Hills Asst. Engineer 1781.* Finished, colored manuscript 26¾ by 23¾. No. 13 in the Atlas.

37. *A Map of Monmouth County* [By I. Williams and A. Dennis] *Reduced from the Original Survey By I. Hills Asst. Engineer 1781.* Finished, colored manuscript 52 by 29. No. 14 in the Atlas.

38. *A Sketch of the Northern Parts of New Jersey* [By T. Milliadge] *Copied from the Original By Lieut I. Hills 23rd. Regt. 1781.* Finished, colored manuscript 32 by 38. No. 15 in the Atlas.

39. *A Chart of Delaware Bay and River, from the Capes to Philadelphia being Part of the Province of New Jersey & Pennsylvania* [By Joshua Fisher] *Copied from the Original By I. Hills 1777.* Finished, colored manuscript 55 by 24¾. No. 16 in the Atlas.

40. *Sketch of the Road from Paulus Hook and Hobocken to New Bridge By I. Hills 1778.* Finished, colored manuscript 23½ by 28. No. 17 in the Atlas.

41. *A Plan of Paulus Hook with the Road to Bergen and Parts adjacent in the Province of New Jersey. Survey'd by I. Hills Asst Engineer 1781.* Inset of defenses 1781-2. Finished, colored manuscript 27¼ by 26¾. Map no. 18 in the Atlas.

42. *Plan of Paulus Hook shewing the Works erected for its Defense 1781-2. Survey'd By I. Hills Lieut in the 23d. Regt.* Finished, colored manuscript 14 by 18½. No. 19 in the Atlas.

43. *Plan of the Road from Elizabeth Town Point to Elizabeth Town Shewing the Rebel Works Raised for its Defence. Survey'd by I. Hills Assistant Engr. 1780.* Finished, colored manuscript 23¾ by 17¾. No. 20 in the Atlas. The last map in the manuscript Atlas.

44. *A Plan of the Surprise of Stoney Point...on the 15th. July, 1779. Also the works erected on Verplanks Point, for the defence of Kings Ferry by the British Forces July, 1779, from the Surveys of Wm. Simpson and D. Campbell by John Hills.* In Faden's, *Atlas of Battles of the American Revolution.*

45. *Plan of the Attack of Forts Clinton and Montgomery, which were stormed by his Majestys Forces under the command of Sir Henry Clinton, K.B., the 6th. of October, 1777. Copied from the Surveys of Verplank, Holland, Metcalve, &c., by John Hill, Lieu-*

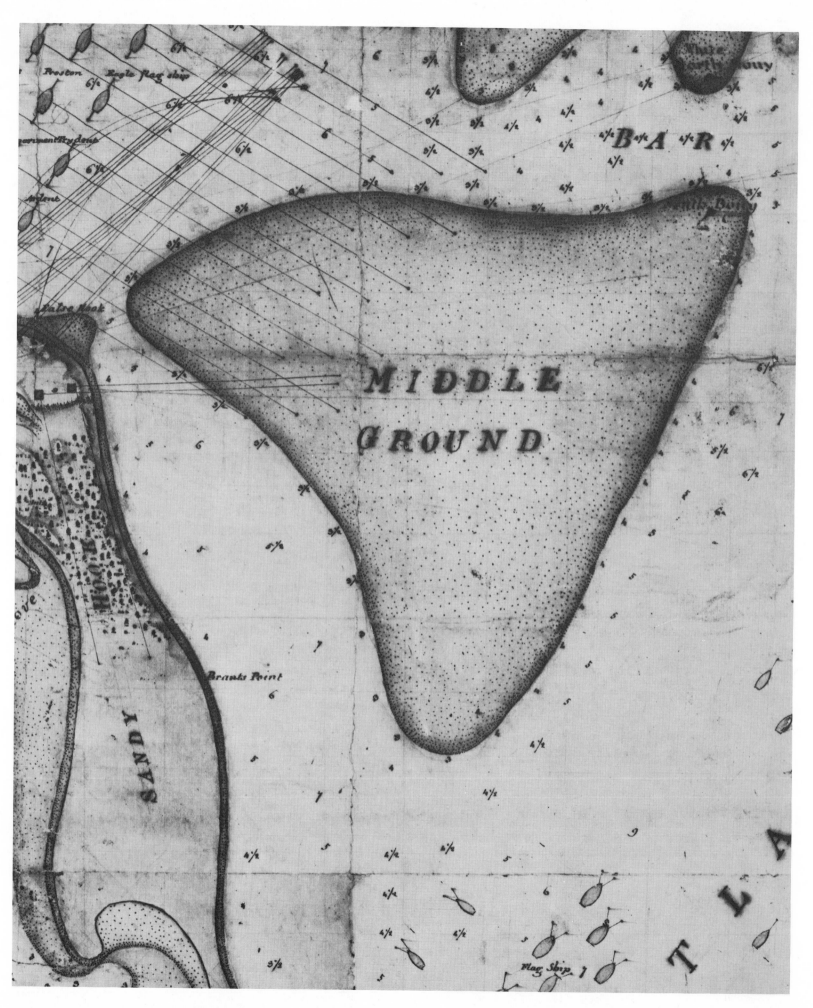

Confrontation of British and French fleets off Sandy Hook, July 12, 1778, section. See 57/51.

tenant in the 23d. Regiment of Foot, or Royal Welch Fusileers, 1782. Finished, colored manuscript 21½ by 35½. Library of Congress. Faden Collection no. 73.

46. *Plan of the Attack of Forts Clinton & Montgomery upon Hudsons River the 6th of Oct., 1777...by John Hills.* In Faden's, *Atlas of Battles of the American Revolution.* Also in Steadman's *American War.*

47. *Sketch of the Roads from King's Bridge to the White Plain's and parts adjacent shewing the encampment of His Majestys Forces under the command of Major General Mathew 1779. By I. Hills.* Finished, colored manuscript 24 by 15¾. Clements Library. Brun 439.

48. *Sketch of the attack of Fort Trumbull, and Griswold near New London in the colony of Connecticut. By a detachment of His Majesty's forces under the command of Brigadier General Arnold. September 6th. 1781. Copied from the original sketch by I. Hills asst: engr:* Finished, colored manuscript 14⅞ by 10¼. Clements Library. Brun 323.

49. *Sketch of the Skirmish At Petersburg between the Royal Army under the Command of Major Genl. Phillips, and the American Army commanded by Major General Stewren: in which the latter were defeated April 25th. 1781. By I. Hills, Lieut. 23d, Regt. & Asst. Engr.* Finished, colored manuscript 9 by 6¾. Colonial Williamsburg. Simcoe Papers 61-211.

50. *A Plan of York Town and Gloucester...1781. From an actual survey in the possession of Jno. Hills.* In Faden's, *Atlas of Battles of the American Revolution.*

51. [*British and French fleets at Sandy Hook July 12, 1778*] from John Hills unlocated original. 24 by 17¼. National Archives.

58. WILLIAM HOGG

Hogg was Master of the armed vessel *CANCEAUX*, employed in the surveys carried out under the direction of Samuel Holland, and others.

1. *A Plan of Piscataqua: River with the Naval remarks &c &c Taken by William Hogg. Master of his Majesty's Armed Ship the CANCEAUX employed upon the Survey of the coast of New England.* Careful, finished manuscript 24⅝ by 34¾, with soundings to the Isles of Shoals. Hydrographic Department, Taunton. A9452.

59. SAMUEL HOLLAND

Holland was born about 1728, probably near Maestricht. He was descended from English refugees who went to Holland about 1660. He entered the Dutch Army at age 17, after a thorough training in mathematics and attained the rank of captain in the artillery before emigrating to England in 1754.

Holland was commissioned lieutenant in the 60th., or Royal American Regiment 29 December 1755, his name being printed as Samuel Jan. Hollandt. He was promoted to captain-lieutenant 21 May 1757, and captain on 24 August 1759. He made a survey of the St. Lawrence in 1761 under Gov. Murray, producing a series of superb maps. His name appears on the record of the regiment through 1772.

Holland started a survey of the Atlantic coast in 1765, after appointment as Surveyor General for the Northern District the preceding year. As one of the few trained surveyors in America, he served in a number of special responsibilities, and in some apparently private capacities, including the authorship of a map, and service on a committee to settle the disputed New Jersey-New York border. The map is *A New Map of the Provinces of N.Y., N.J., part of Pennsylvania, the Government of Trois-Rivieres and Montreal, Drawn by Capt. Holland, engraved by Thomas Jefferys,* 4½ feet by 21 inches. It was offered for sale by G. Duyckinck at Old Slip, New York City, in the *N.Y. Gazette and Weekly Mercury* of 2 May 1768.

The committee to study the New York-New Jersey boundary dispute included Holland, and the equally important and able Surveyor of the Southern District, W.G. De Brahm. The appointment was made 26 June 1769. Any five, of the eleven appointed, were empowered to study and settle the dispute. Of the distinguished committee, only Holland and De Brahm were surveyors. Six members had met, their disagreement being reported in *The New York Gazette* on 9 October 1769, Holland and another dissented. Notably, the Committee had been named on 20 January 1767, but had not previously been convened.

Holland was at Perth Amboy on 20 July 1774 having been engaged in making astronomical observations in conjunction with David Rittenhouse on the Delaware River to settle the New York-New Jersey boundary question, previously surveyed by Montresor. In letters from Perth Amboy on that day, and on 27 May and 27 September 1775, he related an outline of his other surveying activities. The surveys of the Saint Lawrence and the present Atlantic Provinces had been carried out in conjunction with Des Barres, another member of the same 60th. Regiment, and James Cook representing the Admiralty. The latter learned much of surveying by his association with Holland, and was to attain fame by his explorations and discoveries in the Pacific.

The Massachusetts Gazette and the Boston News Letter of 5 May 1774 referred to the surveying activities of Holland and his party. The survey of the sea coast from the Bay of Fundy to Boston had been completed by Holland. Further surveys from Boston to Plymouth were to be done by Mr. Wheeler, and around the cape (Cod) to Rhode Island by Mr. Blaskowitz. Wheeler and Blaskowitz had arrived in Boston the previous week and were immediately to proceed with the survey.

During the summer of 1774, Holland had surveyed the entire New England coast as far south as Newport, R.I., including Boston Harbour Bay, Nantucket, Martha's Vinyard, the Elizabeth Islands. The surveys had been carried out on two scales, 4000 feet to an inch and two miles to an inch. The first delineated all details and variations of the ground and shoreline, and the latter connected all, corrected by astronomical observations and extended bearings. A general map had been prepared of all the surveys, but soundings and naval remarks were omitted because of failure of the Navy to cooperate. The tender *JUPITER* and two seamen had been lost during the summer.

During the summer of 1775, Holland and his party had surveyed in the area of Perth Amboy, as part of the proposed plan of the previous year to survey from Newport to Hudson's River, including Long Island. He noted that unsettled public affairs, and lack of assistance by the Navy had diminished his work. His planned fall survey of the disputed New York-Massachusetts border had not been carried out.

With the advent of hostilities, Holland returned to military life. He appears in the officer list in 1777 as a major with date of rank 4 March 1776. His assignment was to the Guides and Pioneers, to which he was well suited. In the following war years, he carried out the surveys of Forts Clinton and Montgomery, and Long Island. Because of his linguistic abilities, he was probably employed in liaison with the Hessians. He was the author of a letter dated 2 May 1776 from Portsmouth, England to John Pownall regarding ammunition for the Hessian troops.

Following the war, Holland went to Canada, where he took up his interrupted survey of the province. This was completed under General Murray, who had appointed Holland director of the survey. He was appointed Surveyor General of Lower Canada, a position he held until his death.

While in Canada in 1761, Holland was popular because of his fluent command of French. He met, and eloped with, Marie Josephe Rolette, a Canadian beauty whose father objected to her marriage to an officer who had served with Wolfe, the conqueror

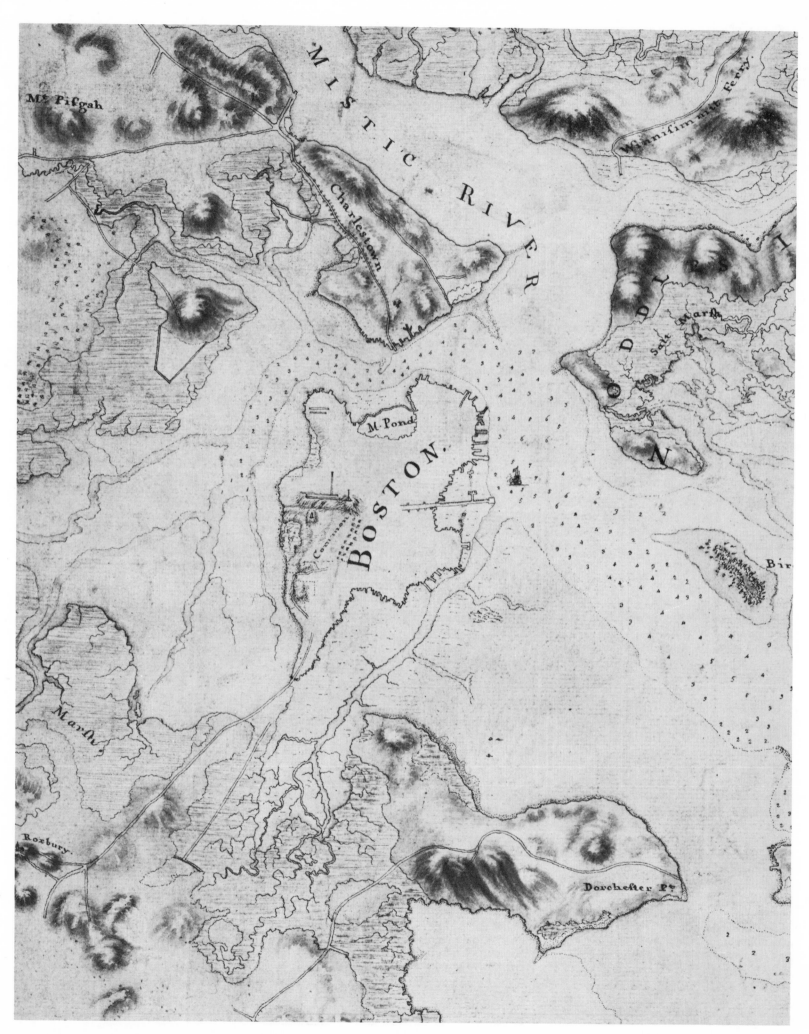

of Quebec in 1755. The couple were subsequently forgiven. Joseph Buchette, descended from Marie's mother, aided Holland in surveying the Eastern Townships of Quebec. He subsequently succeeded Holland as Surveyor General, and was in turn succeeded by his son Joseph, Jr., who held the post until retirement in 1878. Thus one family played a role for over a century.

As a part of his work, Holland spent the summer of 1787 in laying out Baron Riedesel's old headquarters in Sorel into a regular town. This he reported to the Baron by letter, while visiting his old home in Holland during the following summer. Holland had taken his two young sons to visit his birthplace, before returning to England to present his expense accounts. Holland was required to produce his vouchers for the auditing officers for surveying expenses from 1764 to the beginning of the Revolution. The years between Holland's return to Canada, and his death in 1801, were employed in completing the Canadian surveys.

Holland's name was frequently employed to add credibility and stature to maps, some of which he had undoubtedly never seen or composed. For example, the general map of the Northern British Colonies in Sayer and Bennett's *The American Military Pocket Atlas* was "regulated by the astronomical observations of Major Holland." *The American Pilot* of 1798 by Norman, and *The North American Pilot* by Laurie and Whittle of 1800 and 1806 apparently employ the same use of his name in title and map. His printed maps were republished in Le Rouge's *Pilote Américain Septentrional* and in the collected Marine Charts published by the Dépôt des Cartes et Plans de la Marine.

1. *Sketch of the river [Delaware] at about 42 N. Showing the position of boundry markers.* Colored manuscript 9¾ by 14. Attached to the report by Holland and David Rittenhouse, dated Philadelphia 14 December 1774. Public Record Office. C.O. 323/29f.49.
2. *A Plan of the Harbour And Peninsula of Cape Ann In North America drawn from a Survey; the Soundings & Naval observations by Lieut. Henry Mowat, commander of his Majys. armed Ship CANCEAUX.* Careful, finished manuscript 13½ by 18⅞. In lower left "P. D'Auvergne fecit 1776," and below "N.B. this is Surveyed by Samuel Holland Esqr." Library of Congress. G3762 C3 1776 M6.
3. *A Plan of Boston Harbor Surveyed by Samuel Holland Esqr.* Careful, colored manuscript 44¼ by 43½. Hydrographic Department Library, Taunton. 395 press 88.
4. *A Plan of Rhode Island with the Adjacent Islands and Coast of Narragansett Bay.* Careful, colored manuscript 14¼ by 18⅞. Hydrographic Department Library, Taunton. A9455.
5. *A Plan of the Forts Montgomery & Clinton as taken by his Majestys Forces under the Command of Genl. Sir Henry Clinton the 6th. of Octr. 1777 Survey'd by Major Holland Sur. Gen. of the Northern District of North America.* Careful, colored manuscript 20½ by 15. Library of Congress. Faden Collection 70.
6. *A Plan of the Forts Montgomery & Clinton as taken by his Majesty's Forces under the Command of Genl. Sir Henry Clinton the 6th. of October 1777. Surveyed by Major Holland, Surveyor Gen'l of the Northern District of North America.* Careful, colored manuscript 20¾ by 14¾. British Museum. RUSI Collection A 30/49.
7. *A Plan of Fort Montgomery & Fort Clinton, taken by his Majesty's Forces under the command of Maj. Gen. Sir Henry Clinton, K.B. Surveyed by Major Holland, Survr. Gen'l &c. Inset: Part of Hudson's River shewing the Position of Fort Montgomery and Fort Clinton, with the Cheveux de Frieze...By Lt. John Knight of the Royal Navy 1777.* Printed map in Des Barres, *The Atlantic Neptune,* 29½ by 20.
8. *A Plan of Merrituck in the township of Southold on Long Island Surveyed by Major Holland.* Careful, colored manuscript

14¾ by 19. Clements Library. Brun 412.
9. *Plan of Merrituck in the Township of Southold on Long Island. Copy'd from a survey of Major Holland. 1778.* Finished, colored manuscript 19½ by 13⅝. Clements Library. Brun 413.
10. *A plan of Brookhaven or Setalket Harbour with its environs. Surveyed by Major Holland.* Finished, colored manuscript 20½ by 18½. Clements Library. Brun 405.
11. *Plan of Brookhaven, or Setalket on Long Island. Copy'd from a Survey of Major Hollands 1778.* Careful, colored manuscript 18 by 19. Clements Library. Brun 406.

60. NATHANIEL HUBBILL

Hubbill, a captain under the Board of Associated Loyalists of New York, was stationed at Lloyd's Neck on the north shore of Long Island in the spring of 1781. He was in command of the post, or commanded the whale boat crews raiding on Long Island Sound against vessels, shore posts, mills and salt works.

The Board of the Loyalists reported that an expedition of six boats under Hubbill, aided by Captain Glover and Lieutenant Smellage, had captured and destroyed the Fort at New Haven, Connecticut, but failed to capture a schooner, in April 1781. Hubbill signed a certification in favor of Robert Morrell on 21 June 1781, as captain commanding the armed boat company.

1. *A rough draught of New Haven fort taken by Capt. Nathan Hubbill on the night preceding the 19th. of April 1781.* Finished, colored ground plan 11⅞ by 8⅝. Clements Library. Brun 321.

61. JOHN HUMFREY

John Humfrey, a first lieutenant in the Engineers, is listed at Quebec on 21 July 1784.

1. *Sketch of the Action between the British Forces and American Provincials on the Heights of the Peninsula of Charlestown, the 17th. of June, 1775.* Careful, colored manuscript 12 by 10⅜. In left lower corner "John Humfrey 1775." Library of Congress. Faden Collection No. 30.

62. JAMES HUNTER

James Hunter was the author of two views, not maps, of Ticonderoga, made in 1777. These are in the Crown Collection of the British Museum.

1. *Plan of Isle aux Noix at the North End of Lake Champlain 1780.* Careful manuscript 56¾ by 26⅜. In lower left "Hunter As. Eng." Clements Library.

63. JOHN HUNTER

Hunter was born at Leith, near Edinburgh, in 1738, son of a shipmaster in the merchant service. He resided with an uncle at Lyme Regis, where he attended school. Later, he attended school in Edinburgh, followed by attendance at the University of Aberdeen. Hunter elected a naval career, entering in 1754, and serving aboard the *GRAMPUS.* He served aboard the *NEPTUNE* from 1757 to 1759, taking part in the reduction of Quebec. After further shipboard duties, he passed at Trinity House in 1769.

Hunter came to the West Indies, where he was involved in chart making aboard the *CARYSFORT.* Later, he was transferred at Lord Howe's request to the *EAGLE,* Howe's flagship. Hunter was aboard during the campaign prior to the conquest of Philadelphia, at Sandy Hook, and other parts of the east coast. In 1779 Hunter was assigned to the *BERWICK,* leaving America. His later naval career was distinguished, and was on many seas. He eventually was made vice admiral in 1810. He died in London in 1821.

Samuel Holland's pioneer manuscript survey, section showing Boston Harbor with harbor soundings. See 59/2.

1. *A Sketch of the Navigation from Swan pt. to the River Elk at the head of Chesopeak bay. By Mister Hunter, Master of the EAGLE.* Careful, finished manuscript 26 by 19. Inset "Sketch of the river Elk at the head of Chesapeak Bay Eagle Aug. & Sept 1777." Library of Congress. Howe Collection G3701 S3255 1777 H8.

2. *Plan of the River Delaware from Chester to Philadelphia, with the Situation of His Majesty's Ships on the 15th. of Novr. 1777. J. Hunter.* Somewhat rough, colored manuscript 30⅜ by 9¼. Hydrographic Department, Taunton. A9462.

3. *New York, East River, part of Hudson River and adjacent country.* Somewhat rough, colored manuscript. Hydrographic Department, Taunton. A9459.

4. [*East Florida. From Mosquito Inlet to C. Canaveral.*] Somewhat rough, colored manuscript. 35⅞ by 12⅞. Hydrographic Department, Taunton. A9463.

Hunter was the author of the chart of the Delaware River in *The Atlantic Neptune.* The upper part of the survey is dated "15th. Novr. 1777," while the lower part was surveyed in 1779. Hunter was the source, with John Knight, of the chart of New York Harbour in *The Atlantic Neptune.*

64. THOMAS HURD

Hurd was born about 1753. He assisted the surveying operations of Holland and DesBarres in Newfoundland, Nova Scotia and New England. He completed his time as a midshipman on the flagships of Admiral Gambier and Earl Howe, becoming lieutenant of the *UNICORN* commanded by Captain J. Ford. The fast copper-sheathed *UNICORN* captured a large number of American vessels, earning substantial prize money for Hurd.

Hurd returned to surveying as a contributor and participant in constructing the first accurate survey and charting of Bermuda about 1785. He became commander of the *LILY*, sloop-of-war somewhat later. In 1804 Hurd completed surveys off Brest, producing an excellent chart. He was appointed to a committee to study extension of the Hydrographic Department in 1808, and succeeded Alexander Dalrymple as Hydrographer the same year.

Captain Hurd proved an able and practical administrator as he realized the needs of the Navy, and was not connected to any of the current scientific societies. He firmed the connection between the Navy and Hydrographic Department, discontinuing the employment of private surveyors. Numerous surveys were undertaken by naval officers and two surveying vessels were employed. Charts, previously restricted to the use of the Navy, were made available to the merchant marine and the public. Hurd died in 1823.

1. *A Plan of Part of the Sea Coast to the Westward of Penobscot Bay in North America with the soundings and Naval Observations by Thomas Hurd.* Careful, uncompleted manuscript 34 by 36¾. In lower right is "21 Feby. 1775." Hydrographic Department, Taunton. 289.

2. *Coast of North America from Penobscot to St. Johns Original by Captain T. Hurd.* Unfinished and unlabeled on numerous small sheets cemented together, 65 by 35¼. Hydrographic Department, Taunton. E468.

65. THOMAS HUTCHINS

Hutchins was born in Monmouth County, New Jersey, in 1730. He spent his youth on the Pennsylvania frontier, serving in the colonial troops in 1757, during the French and Indian War. He was a lieutenant in the Rangers in October 1759.

Hutchins entered the British service, joining the 60th., or Royal American Regiment as an ensign on 2 March 1762. His first account of the Ohio Country predates this, his journal recording observations from the 7th. to 17th. July 1760, and subsequent trips between 1764 and 1775. His *Topographic Description of Virginia, Pennsylvania, Maryland and North Carolina* was published in London in 1778. It was often accompanied by *A New Map of the Western Parts of Virginia, Pennsylvania, Maryland....and A Plan of the Several Villages in the Illinois Country....* published at the same time. These established his reputation as one of the four early British authors of descriptive accounts of the interior of North America. He was elected a member of the American Philosophical Society in 1771.

Hutchins' career in the 60th. Regiment was not unusual. He was promoted eventually to captain in November 1776, with duty mainly on the frontier. His sympathies were strongly colonial and he resigned his commission. He was considered a spy by Montresor, meriting execution. After coming to America, he was appointed Geographer to the Southern American Army, under General Nathanael Greene in May 1781, and Geographer to the United States on 11 July 1781, but was inactive because of poor health. His great contribution came in perfecting the system for plotting western territory public lands for government sale under the ordinance of 20 May 1785. Quadrilateral land plots had been proposed on the Ohio by Bouquet. Hutchins died in 1789.

Hutchins was one of the four pioneer British authors of accounts of the interior of North America, based upon personal experience. Robert Rogers, of Ranger fame, published his *A Concise Account of North America* in 1765, Jonathan Carver his *Travels Through the Interior of North America* in 1766, and Phillip Pittman his *The Present State of the European Settlements on the Mississippi* in 1770. Hutchins' *A Topographic Description of Virginia....* was published in 1778, although his earliest map was published in 1765. All of his manuscript maps appear to be at least partially perpetuated in the later published maps and accounts.

1. *Section of the level of the country* [*Iberville River to the Mississippi River*] *By Thomas Hutchins.* A careful manuscript profile of a proposed canal, 19½ by 9. Clements Library. Brun 684.

2. [*Canal from the Iberville River to the Mississippi River*] *By: Thomas Hutchins.* A careful manuscript profile of a proposed canal, 19 by 8. This accompanied Hutchins' report of 1 May 1773, from Pensacola. Clements Library. Brun 683.

3. *Copy of a plan of the River Iberville from Lake Maurepas to the Forks, with part of the Comit and Amit-taken from Engineer Durnford's by Tho: Hutchins.* Colored, finished, detailed manuscript 200½ by 50. Clements Library. Brun 672.

4. *Plan of the River Mississippi from the Indian Village of the Tonicas to the River Ibberville, shewing the lands surveyed thereon as also the Rivers Ibberville, Amit and Comit, with the situation of the new town proposed at the Ibberville. A true copy from Enginr. Durnfords by Thomas Hutchins.* Careful, finished, colored manuscript 48¼ by 127. Much was reproduced in Hutchins' 1784 narrative of Louisiana and West Florida. Clements Library. Brun 688.

5. *A Plan of the Lakes Ponchartrain and Maurepas and the River Ibberville and also of the River Mississippi from its Mouth to the River Yazoo, a Distance of 450 miles. By Tho. Hutchins Captain 60th. Regiment.* Irregularly shaped, rather rough manuscript 50 by 36. Public Record Office. MR107.

6. *The rapids of the Ohio, commonly called the Falls, 683 miles below Fort Pitt in 38° :08' No. latitude. By order of ye chief: Engineer. W. Brasier delt.* Careful, finished, colored manuscript 11 by 16 based upon the survey by Hutchins, July 19-23, 1766, while in a party commanded by Capt. Harry Gordon, the Chief Engineer in North America. Clements Library. Brun 692.

7. *A plan of the River Ohio from Fort Pitt to the Mississippi. By order of ye Chief Engineer; Tho: Hutchins assist. draughtsman.* [*William Brasier, del.*] Finished, colored, manuscript strip map 34½ by 72½. Based on data of trip from Fort Pitt, June 18-August 7, 1766, under command of Captain Harry Gordon, the Chief Engineer in North America. A Philadelphia merchant and Indian trader, George Morgan, accompanied the party. Gordon's

own map of the Ohio River is in the Library of Congress. Clements Library. Brun 699.

8. *A scetch of the several Indian roads leading from Fort Pitt to Sioto, Lake Erie &c. Takn. from a draft made on a tour throh. yt. country in 1762 by Mr. Hutchins, then in the indian department. Guy Johnson fect [1764.]* Finished, colored manuscript 7 by 11¼. A copy by Guy Johnson. Clements Library. Brun 717.

9. *Plan of the Indian country through which the troops march'd in 1764 under the command of Col. Henry Bouquet. By Thomas Hutchins. Copy'd from ye original by Lt. Bernard Ratzer.* Finished, detailed, colored strip map 19¼ by 55¼. Copy of the original, used for the following printed map. Clements Library. Brun 698.

10. *A Topographical Plan of that part of the Indian Country through which the Army under the Command of Colonel Bouquet marched in the Year 1764 by Thos. Hutchins Asst. Engineer.* A printed map, with an additional title *A General Map of the Country on the Ohio and Musingham shewing the situation of the Indian-Towns....* In William Smith's *An Historical Account of the Expedition against the Ohio Indians in the year 1764....*, published in Philadelphia in 1765.

11. *A New Map of the Western Parts of Virginia, Pennsylvania, Maryland and North Carolina: Comprehending the River Ohio, and all the rivers, which fall into it; Part of the River Mississippi, the whole of the Illinois River, Lake Erie, part of Lakes Huron, Machigan &c. And all the country bordering on these lakes and rivers. By Thos. Hutchins, Captain in the 60 Regiment. London, 1778. Engraved by T. Cheevers.* Printed map 42¼ by 34¾, to accompany his *Topographical Description of Virginia....*, published in London in 1778, and in subsequent editions.

12. *A Plan of the Several Villages in the Illinois Country, with Part of the River Mississippi &c by Thos. Hutchins.* Printed map 5 by 7¼, to accompany the same.

66. THOMAS JAMES

James, a major in the Artillery, reported to General Gage in letters in October and November 1768 on the increasing ability of the 16th. Regiment in artillery practice, and on the civil disorders in New York. He was in charge of strengthening Fort George at that time.

In 1771 James was a lieutenant colonel, Commandant of Artillery in North America. He petitioned Gage for pay for additional staff officers as the 4th. Batallion of Artillery was to be transferred. Like Gage, he married an American, a member of the DePeyster family of New York. His three sons eventually went into

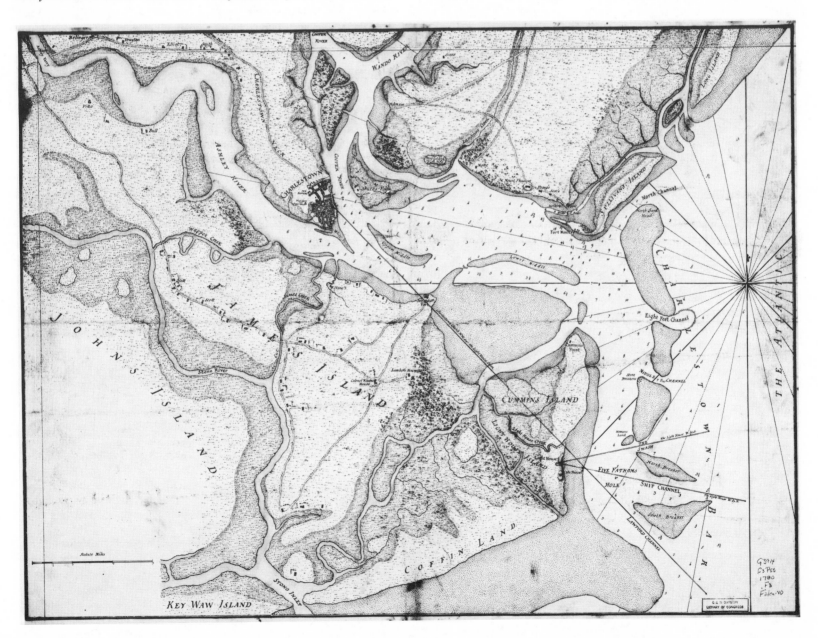

Thomas James' 1780 plan of Charlestown (Charleston, S. C.) and environs, also showing harbor depths. See 66/2.

the British Army. He was an occasional correspondent of Stephen Kemble, Gage's brother-in-law and a major in the 60th. Regt.

1. *A Plan of the attack of Fort Sulivan near Charles Town in South Carolina by a squadron of His Majesty's ships on the 28 June 1776 with the disposition of the Kings Land Forces and the encampments & entrenchments of the Americans from the drawing made on the spot.* Inset "Plan of the platform of Sulivans Fort by Lt. Colonel Thos. James of the Royal Regiment of Artillery." Careful, finished colored manuscript 10¾ by 14½. Clements Library. Brun 623.

2. [*Attack of Fort Sulivan*] Untitled, unfinished manuscript, in color, 27½ by 20. Library of Congress. Faden Collection No. 40.

3. [*Attack of Fort Sulivan*] Unlabeled, unfinished, colored manuscript 14 by 16. Library of Congress. Faden Collection No. 41.

4. *A Plan of the Attack of Fort Sulivan*....Inset "Plan of Platform in Sulivans Fort...Thos. James." Printed map 14½ by 11. London August 10th., 1776.

67. PETER JEFFERSON

Jefferson became acquainted with Joshua Fry while living at Shadwell, where he acted as magistrate. His son Thomas, the future president, was born there. Jefferson soon moved to Tuckahoe, in Goochland County, to take over management of the estate of his deceased friend, William Randolph. He stayed for five or six years, and probably learned the rudiments of surveying from William Mayo. Peter Jefferson, now called "Colonel," was appointed one of the surveyors of the Fairfax Line, through the efforts of Fry. The line was completed in 1749. Acting Governor Lewis Burwell selected Fry and Jefferson as the best qualified to make a map of Virginia, proposed some twelve years previously. Fry was succeeded by Jefferson as surveyor, county lieutenant and burgess, on his death. Jefferson died in August 1757.

1. See under Fry.

68. GUY JOHNSON

Johnson was born in Ireland about 1740, possibly a nephew of Sir William Johnson. He came to New York's Mohawk Valley before 1756, joining Sir William, and later becoming his secretary. Johnson adapted himself well to his surroundings, and life on the New York frontier. During the years 1759 and 1760, he commanded a company of Rangers under Amherst. In succeeding years, he became deputy for Indian affairs under Sir William, married Sir William's daughter Mary, and established an impressive residence, Guy Hall, near Amsterdam.

Johnson served in the New York assembly between 1773 and 1775, strongly supporting the Loyalist cause. During this period, he succeeded Sir William as superintendent of Indian affairs. With the outbreak of war, he marched with a group of 200 Rangers, and Iroquois, to offer his services to Carleton at Montreal. Johnson visited England with Joseph Brant, Mohawk war chief, returning to New York City in July 1776. He stayed here until 1779, when he directed Indian warfare from the Niagara area. He returned to England in 1784, and died in London in 1788.

1. See Hutchins map 8.

69. G.W. DYAIL JONES

Jones was a lieutenant in the 7th. Regiment of Foot, or Royal Fusiliers, in New York in 1779. In the capacity of engineer, he accompanied the expedition under Sir George Collier to reinforce the post at Castine, Maine. His name appears in the army lists through 1792.

1. *A front view of Fort George Majabigwaduce June 1780. By: G.W. Dyail Jones, asst. engineer.* Finished manuscript elevation and ground plan 10¼ by 2¼ and 23 by 4. Clements Library. Brun 153.

2. *A plan, profile and front view of Fort George Majabigwaduce. G.W. Dyail Jones asst. engineer.* Careful, finished manuscript 2¼ by 11 and 4 by 23¾. Clements Library. Brun 158.

3. *Sketch of the neck and Harbour of Majabigwaduce. G.W.D. Jones asst: engr. Augst 22d. 1779.* Finished, colored manuscript 19 by 12⅜. Clements Library. Brun 159.

4. *Sketch of the neck and Harbour of Majabigwaduce 20th. Aug 1779 G.W.D. Jones.* Finished, colored manuscript 19 by 12½. Clements Library. Brun 160.

70. JOHN KNIGHT

The son of Captain John Knight of the Royal Navy, he was born about 1748. He served successively as captain's servant, ordinary seaman and able seaman aboard vessels under his father's command. He probably did not go to sea during the early years, but his name had been entered on the log to insure sufficient time when he came to sit for lieutenant, a common stratagem at the time.

Still under his father's command, he served as midshipman on *TARTER* then *EMERALD*, off the coast of France and in the Channel from 1759 to 1762. Knight passed for lieutenant in January 1763, and served on *ROMNEY* to 1770, engaged in nautical surveys in North America including Nova Scotia. He took command of the schooner *DILIGENT* at Halifax in May 1770. *DILIGENT* had probably been purchased sometime after 1767 for the use of DesBarres and his surveying team.

DILIGENT with six guns and a crew of thirty, was based at Windsor, Nova Scotia, where Knight's family resided. The survey work was carried out in conjunction with *SABLE, TATAMAGOUCHE,* and probably *CANCEAUX,* the vessels marking and charting shoals. On two occasions, *DILIGENT* went ashore, but was refloated. *DILIGENT* was captured by a ruse at Machias, Maine in July 1775. Knight was incarcerated at Cambridge, Massachusetts, then was permitted parole in North Hampton and Hadley.

He was exchanged, serving as lieutenant on *HAERLEM* in 1776. Knight was promoted captain in 1781, rear admiral in 1800 and subsequently vice admiral and admiral. He was knighted for his distinguished service against the French. He died in 1831.

1. *Buzzards Bay and Shoals of Nantucket.* Careful, finished, colored manuscript 39 by 21. On verso "...by Lieutenant Knight 1778." Library of Congress. Howe Collection no. 15.

2. *Part of Long Island, and the Coast Eastward to the Shoals of Nantucket.* Careful, finished, colored manuscript 27 by 9. Library of Congress. Howe Collection no. 16.

71. ELISHA LAWRENCE

Lawrence was born in Monmouth County in 1740, son of John, a noted New Jersey surveyor. Lawrence was sheriff of the county at the start of the Revolution. He immediately declared his support of the Crown and raised a corps of 500 men, the 1st. Batallion of the New Jersey Volunteers, of which he became colonel. He was captured by General Sullivan while on Staten Island in 1777. Following the war, Lawrence was retired as a colonel on half pay and was granted a large property in Nova Scotia. He died at Cardigan, Wales in 1811.

1. [*Northeastern New Jersey*] *Elisha Lawrence lt. Coll: 1 Battn. N. Jersey Volunteers.* Somewhat rough manuscript 25 by 19½. Clements Library. Brun 485.

72. JOSHUA LOCKE

Locke was born at Woburn, Massachusetts, 22 July 1732, son of Joshua and Hannah Reed Locke. He married Abigail Meynard of

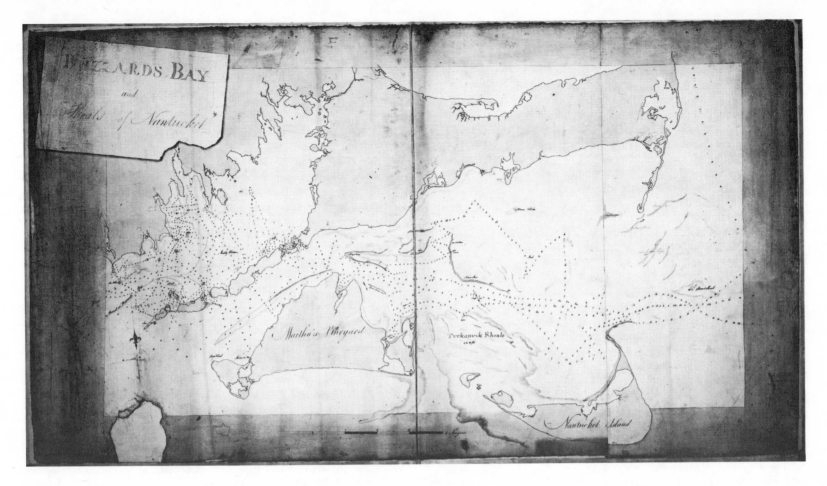

John Knight's 1778 chart of Buzzard's Bay and the shoals of Nantucket, with depths also shown. See 70/1.

Westborough, Massachusetts, in the early 1750's. They, and their six children, moved to Sudbury in 1765. Locke's service in the French and Indian War began as an ensign under General Winslow in Nova Scotia in May 1755. He was possibly the Lieutenant Locke wounded with General Braddock. He served under Major Robert Rogers in his Rangers.

At some time in the prerevolutionary period, Locke served as one of the King's surveyors. Following the outbreak of hostilities, he carried dispatches until June 1779, when he received a warrant to raise a company of men. He was not successful. He left New York for England in December 1779, where he served as a Custom House officer to 1783. He received a military allowance from 1787 to the time of his death in 1810. His family remained in Massachusetts during the entire period.

1. [*Plan of Vermont*] Rough manuscript 12¾ by 15⅞. This was enclosed in an undated letter to Germaine. Clements Library. Brun 170.

73. DANIEL LYMAN

Lyman came from New Haven, Connecticut and graduated from Yale in 1770. He was appointed captain in the Prince of Wales American Volunteers 25 October 1776 and was wounded on 27 April 1777 on the expedition to Danbury under Governor Tryon of New York. The effective defense against the raid was by Generals Arnold and Wooster.

Following convalescence in England, Lyman saw action at Camden, and during the retreat from Charlotte to Charlestown. He also took part in the raid on New London under Arnold on 6 September 1781. He later was promoted major. Following the war, Lyman settled in New Brunswick where he served as a magistrate and member of the assembly. He went to England, dying in London in 1809.

1. *A Sketch of New-London & Groton with the Attacks made on Forts Trumbull & Griswold By the British Troops Under the Command of Brigr. General Arnold Sepr. 6th. 1781 By Captain Lyman of ye Prince of Wales Amr. Volrs.* Careful, colored manuscript 13 by 11. Clements Library. Brun 322.

2. *A Sketch of New London & Groton with the Attacks made on Forts Trumbull & Griswold by the British Troops under the Command of Brigr. Genl. Arnold Sepr. 6th. 1781.* Colored manuscript 19¾ by 16. Library of Congress. Faden Collection no. 98.

74. ALLEN MACDONELL

Macdonell was a resident of Johnstown, Montgomery County, New York, formerly Tryon County. He served as a sergeant in the Rangers during the French and Indian War, later working as a surveyor under the supervision of Lieutenant William Tinling of the Royal Engineers.

During the Revolution, Macdonell apparently served in the Royal American Regiment, and refers to John and Alexander Macdonell, and to Captain Allan Macdonell of the 84th. Regiment, or Royal Highland Emigrants. His wife and daughter requested permission to join him in Canada, after their capture in Albany. Following the war, Macdonell resided in lower Canada. He died in Three Rivers in 1822.

1. *New Settlement-Niagra River Line*. Survey made in March and April 1783. Cited in *The Mark of Honor* by Hazel C. Mathews, University of Toronto Press.

75. FREDERICK MACKENZIE

Mackenzie was born in Dublin about 1725, the son of a prosperous merchant. He was commissioned in the 23rd. Regiment, or Royal Welch Fusileers as a lieutenant in 1745, and was promoted captain in 1775 while in Boston.

Mackenzie's diary is a valuable account, which among others, notes on 7 January 1775 the need for officers capable of taking sketches of the country. On 29 August 1778, he notes that Captain Edward Fage was measuring the distances from his batteries, and he later alludes to the Guides and Pioneers under command of Captain William McAlpine. The diary contains a number of good sketch maps, that of Concord being of particular interest.

In 1780, Mackenzie was promoted to major and was acting adjutant general of New York during part of the occupation. Later he was made lieutenant colonel of the 37th. Foot, living near Exeter on a half pay status. He was active in raising a volunteer defense force during the threat of Napoleonic invasion. Mackenzie was Assistant Barrack Master General, later Secretary of the Royal Military College. He died at Teignmouth, Devon in 1824.

The diary of MacKenzie was published by the Harvard University Press in 1930, and recently republished by the Arno Press.

1. *Positions at Concord 19th. Ap 1775.* Rough sketch 7 by 7¼.
2. *Advanced Posts New York Island 12th. Oct. 1776.* Rough sketch 7½ by 12.
3. *North End of Rhode Island.* Rough sketch 9 by 8¾.
4. *Sketch of the Ground about General Prescotts Quarters Rhode Island 11th. July 1777 F.M.* Rough sketch 12 by 7½.
5. *Disposition of the Night Sentries from the Town Pond to Howlands Bridge 2nd. September 1777* [*Rhode Island.*] Rough sketch 12 by 7¾.
6. *Part of Conanicut Island* [*Rhode Island.*] Rough sketch 8½ by 12.
7. *Sketch of the North End of Rhode Island with the disposition of the advanced posts, Sentries & Patrols 11th. July 1778 F.M.* Rough sketch 11 by 8¾.
8. *View of the Rebels Batteries & Approaches on Honeyman's Hill 26th. Augt. 1778* [*Rhode Island.*] Rough sketch 6½ by 5½.
9. [*Hellgate, New York.*] Rough sketch 7½ by 5½.
10. *Hellgat Fort* [*New York.*] Rough Sketch 5½ by 7¼.
11. *Situation of the French Fleet in the Harbour of Rhode Island November 1780-as per information of a Deserter.* Rough sketch 12 by 7¼.

76. S. MATCALSE

Cited as a source of data for Hills' map 21.

77. THOMAS MILLIDGE

Millidge was born about 1735, probably in Georgia, and came to New Jersey about 1765. He resided in Whippany in Morris County, a center of Loyalist activity at the start of the Revolution. Millidge became a deputy surveyor in Morris, Sussex, and Bergen Counties under Surveyor General William Alexander. Alexander, who called himself Lord Stirling, became a continental general. Millidge was active in property transfers and was a frequent witness to various legal documents. Among others, he witnessed the oath of Ezekiel Beach who stated on 23 December 1775 that he was not a Loyalist.

With the outbreak of hostilities, Millidge joined the New Jersey Volunteers as major, of the 5th., then the 1st. Batallion. He carried all his maps and surveys, for later use. Some were probably employed by John Hills. Following the war, Millidge went to New Brunswick where he made a survey of the St. Croix River, then settled in Nova Scotia. He died at Granville in Annapolis County in 1816.

1. *A scetch of that part of Statten Island from the Old Star to Deckers Ferry and the lands lying to the westd. of the road leading from Deckers Ferry to the Old Star made from a view of the same by Thomas Millidge Major of the 5th. battn of N:JV.* Rough sketch 6⅜ by 12. Clements Library. Brun 428.

2. See Skinner No. 2.

78. CHARLES MIST

A draughtsman employed by Captain William Spry, Commanding Engineer at Halifax, in 1779. Spry's report on the defenses of Nova Scotia are included in *British Headquarters Maps and Sketches* by Randolph G. Adams, Ann Arbor, 1928.

1. *A Chart of the Peninsula of Nova Scotia C.M.* Finished, colored manuscript 23 by 35½. Clements Library. Brun 13.
2. *Plan of Fort Cumberland upon the Isthmus of Nova Scotia 1778. C.M. Halifax 5 March 79: Spry commandg: Engineer.* Finished, colored manuscript ground plan with references, 13⅜ by 19¼. The site of an abortive American attack between 13 and 22 November 1776. Clements Library. Brun 22.
3. *Plan of the Environs of Halifax in Nova Scotia with the temporary works constructed for the protection of the Town, and His Majesty's Naval Yard. C.M. W. Spry, Commandg: engineer.* Finished, colored manuscript 28¾ by 21, overlays of Fort Massey and the Citadel. Clements Library. Brun 29.
4. *Plan and section of the Eastern Battery at Halifax. C.M. 5 March 1779 W. Spry command. engr.* Finished, colored manuscript 16¾ by 10¾. Clements Library. Brun 19.
5. *A Draught of the Harbor & River of Piscataqua with the Island's of Shoals. By Charles Mist.* Unfinished manuscript 31 by 28, with soundings. Clements Library. Brun 165.
6. *A Draught of the Harbor & River of Pisquataqua with the Island's of Shoals. Charles Mist pinxit.* Finished, colored manuscript 32½ by 25¼, with soundings. Clements Library. Brun 166.

79. JOHN MITCHELL

A physician and distinguished botanist, Mitchell emigrated to Urbanna on the Rappahannock River in Virginia about 1700. His correspondents included John Bartram, Cadwalader Colden and Linnaeus. His treatise on Yellow Fever was employed by Dr. Benjamin Rush during the Philadelphia epidemic of 1793.

Mitchell returned to England in 1748 where he was employed by the Ministry to prepare a report on the American Colonies, in the years preceding the French and Indian War. Among others, he noted the evident intrusion of the French into the Great Lakes and Ohio River. He was the author of *An Account of the English Discoveries and Settlements in America,* 1748, *The Contest in America Between Great Britain and France,* 1757, *The Present State of Great Britain and North America,* 1767, and *American Husbandry* in 1775. Although not a surveyor, Mitchell compiled a map of North America in 1750, from the official records and documents to which he had free access. The map was engraved by Thomas Kitchin and published in 1755. The map was an outstanding success, a copy being employed in 1783 as the official map of the Peace Commissioners in Paris in 1783. Mitchell died in London in 1768.

1. *A Map of the British Colonies in North America With The Roads, Distances, Limits, and Extent of the Settlements, Humbly Inscribed to the Right Honourable The Lords Commissioners for Trade & Plantations, By their Lordships Most Obliged and very humble Servant, Jno. Mitchell.* Printed map 72 by 40, inset of Hudson's Bay and Labrador. Fifth edition, in Faden's 1778 catalog it is noted as Mitchell's map of the British Colonies in North America...on 8 sheets, 1775.

80. JOHN MONTRESOR

Montresor was born at Gibraltar in 1736, the son of James, a British military engineer of Norman French descent. He accompanied his father, General Braddock's chief engineer, to America in 1754 and participated in a large number of the operations, especially scouting expeditions and carrying dispatches. Although appointed as an additional engineer, he was not confirmed by the Ordnance Board until 1758, the first of his many disappointing experiences with the establishment. Wounded at Monongahela, Montresor served in northern New York along the Mohawk and at Fort Edward. He accompanied the expedition of Loudoun to Halifax, was present at the capture of Louisbourg and Quebec, and accompanied Murray in the final campaign of 1760. Of particular interest was his overland winter journey from Quebec to New England and the exploration of the Kennebec River route to Canada. The same route was used by the expedition against Quebec under Benedict Arnold in 1775.

Later, Montresor served in Pontiac's War, fortified the portage at Niagara, and accompanied an expedition to Detroit. He was a witness to the Stamp Act Riots in New York in 1765. After a visit to England, to seek preferment, he returned to America in 1766. As captain-lieutenant and barrackmaster, Montresor constructed or improved the fortifications, defenses and barracks about Boston, New York, Philadelphia and in the West Indies. He incidentally surveyed the disputed New York-New Jersey border in 1769. He purchased the present Randall's Island at the confluence of Long Island Sound, the Harlem River and the East River, where he lived with his wife and family.

Montresor was promoted to captain in 1775 and made Chief Engineer in America, but his talents and knowledge were not utilized. He was present at Boston and Long Island during the battles, but played little or no part, being superseded, reappointed, and again superseded. He did act as chief engineer at Brandywine,

and was at least advisor in the reduction of the fortifications on Mud Island, which he had previously designed. When Nathan Hale was captured, he occupied Montresor's tent while awaiting execution in 1776. Montresor incurred Clinton's displeasure, returning to England in 1778, and testified before a House of Commons committee the following year. He retired from the army, residing at Belmont in Kent, and in London, where he died in 1799.

Montresor's Journals give an excellent inside view of the life of a military engineer, particularly in regards to mapping methods, time sequence, and relationship with commanding officers. He is candid in his criticism of army administration, organization; and of many of his contemporaries and seniors. He notes the employment of plane table surveys, and the drafting of a map of North America with particular reference to mountains, portages, passes, sources of rivers at the request of the Marquis of Granby, Master General of Ordnance. He also refers to the employment of a circumferenter to take intersections, and to the use of a theodolite.

Montresor notes a request to make a sketch plan of New York and its harbor on a large scale late in 1765. The survey was started promptly and carried out with so much dispatch that a draught was made in about six weeks, and completed in an additional ten days. Reduction of the large scale to half scale was accomplished in ten more days. Montresor was ordered to survey the islands in New York Harbor, which was carried out with plane table and

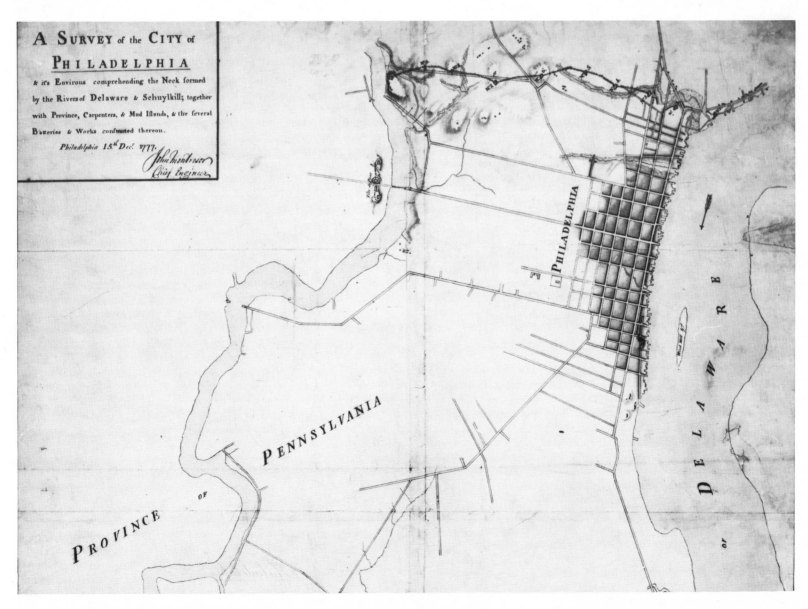

Part of John Montresor's 1777 map showing Philadelphia's defenses from the Delaware to Schuylkill Rivers. See 80/22.

theodolite, and completed in less than a month.

While visiting London, in April 1767, Montresor gave LaRoque the engraver his maps of Canada, Nova Scotia and New York. Two engravers were at work, completing the maps of New York and environs, with the Hook and Channel, which was accomplished in a little more than three weeks. Montresor corrected thirty one errors, apparently authorized publication, and dedicated the map to General Gage. An edition was published the same year.

A large number of maps have been encountered in several collections with Montresor's name stamped on the verso. Many are obviously by others, although the maps were either made under his supervision, or were in his hands in his official capacity, or subsequently. The greater number of Montresor maps in the Library of Congress are in the Force or Faden collections.

Some of the following attributions must be considered tentative, and some of the maps in the anonymous section were possibly the work of Montresor. I particularly want to acknowledge the aid of Mr. Douglas W. Marshall of the Clements Library, with whom I have had many pleasant conversations and much correspondence. His definitive study of the maps of John Montresor will be published in the *Map Collectors Circle*.

1. *A Draught of the Towns of Boston and Charlestown and the Circumjacent Country shewing the Works thrown up by His Majesty's Troops, and also those by the Rebels, during the Campaign:1775. John Montresor, Command. Eng. To Major General Earl Percy.* Careful, colored manuscript 17¼ by 16¾. Duke of Northumberland Collection, Alnwick.

2. *A Draught of the Towns of Boston and Charles Town and the Circumjacent Country shewing the Works thrown up by His Majesty's Troops and also those by the Rebels during the campaign 1775.* Careful, colored manuscript 17½ by 16½. British Museum, RUSI Collection. A30/25.

3. *A Draught of the Towns of Boston & Charles Town & the Circumjacent Country Showing the works thrown up by the King's troops & those by the Rebels showing ye campaign 1775. By John Montresor commanding Engr. at Boston.* Rough, colored manuscript 17⅛ by 16½. Clements Library. M1161.

4. *A Draught of the Towns of Boston and Charlestown and the Circumjacent Country shewing the Works thrown up by His Majesty's Troops, and also those by the Rebels, during the Campaign; 1775.* Careful, colored manuscript 17¼ by 16¾. Dated 5 March 1775. Library of Congress. G3701 S3142 1775 D7.

5. *[Boston and Environs, including Charlestown, Roxbury,Dorchester Neck, Noddle's Island, Hog Island and Castle Wm. 1775.]* Rough, incomplete manuscript 18¾ by 17½. No. 25 in right lower corner. Library of Congress. G3701 S3142 1775 B61.

6. *Boston Neck & Fortifications. Delivd. to H.E. Gl Gage June 30th. 1775-J.M.* Rough, colored manuscript 14¼ by 7½. Library of Congress. G4056 B65 1775 M6.

7. *Plan of the Fortifications on Boston Neck 1775. Delivd. to H.E. Gl Gage June 30th. 1775.* Careful, colored manuscript 14⅛ by 7½. Library of Congress. G3701 S3142 1775 M6.

8. *Plan of the Peninsula of Charles Town shewing the three Posts that His Majesty's Troops have kept and fortified with Buildings therein for Guard Rooms, Boston 3rd. Decr 1775.* Careful, colored manuscript 18 by 11⅞. In cursive "To his Excellency Major General Howe Commander in Chief of his Majesty's Forces &c. John Montresor Commandg. Engr." Library of Congress. G4056 C55 1775 M6.

9. *A Survey of the peninsula of Charles Town shewing the three posts now garrisoned by His Majesty's troops for the winter 10th. Decber 1775. To Major General Clinton John Montresor commandg. engineer.* Finished, colored manuscript 21½ by 14. Inset section. Clements Library. Brun 248.

10. *[Charlestown and Bunker Hill]* Rough manuscript 17⅜ by 11. Library of Congress. G4056 C55 1775 P5.

11. *Major Genl. Howe's Encampment on Bunker's Hill at*

Charles T. June 1775. Rough manuscript 12 by 7⅞. Library of Congress. G4056 C55 1775 M3.

12. *Gov Tryon's Expedition to Danbury 1777.* Careful manuscript 14½ by 18¼. Library of Congress.

13. *Plan de New York Et Des Environs Leve par Montresor Ingenieur en 1775.* Fine, finished, colored manuscript 20⅛ by 29 with inset of the area. Probably the original for the map published in Paris in 1777. Clements Library. Brun 399.

14. *New York et Environs.* Finished, detailed manuscript 48 by 22. Library of Congress. Rochambeau 23.

15. *A plan of New York Island with the circumjacent country as far as Dobb's Ferry to the north, and White-Plains to the east: including the rivers, islands, & roads in that extent. To His Excellency Sir Henry Clinton K.B. general and commander in chief of His Majesty's forces. 1st. Sept. 1778. John Montresor.* Finished, colored manuscript 44½ by 22. Clements Library. Brun 414.

16. *The principal part of the Province of New Jersey Shewing the road and distances to the several towns between the North River and the Delaware. New York 4th. Feb. 1777. Capt. Montresor.* Finished, colored manuscript 34¼ by 25½. Clements Library. Brun 504.

17. *The road from New Bridge and Hackinsack to Burlington. By Captain John Montresor 1776.* Finished, colored manuscript 13¾ by 17⅝. Clements Library. Brun 507.

18. *A Plan of the town spot of Morris Town in Morris County, for about three miles from the Court House, made out from a view of the same. Capt. Montresor. Morris T. N. Jersey.* Finished, colored manuscript 32½ by 19⅛. Clements Library. Brun 503.

19. *[Roads from Windsor to Easton through the Highlands. By: Captain John Montresor.]* Colored sketch map, 12½ by 8½. Clements Library. Brun 470.

20. *[Burlington, N.J. and Bristol, Pa.] Capt. Montresor.* Finished, colored manuscript 7 by 7⅞. Clements Library. Brun 520.

21. *[Philadelphia and Environs] Dedicated to His Excellency Sir Henry Clinton K.B. General and Commander in Chief of His Majesty's Forces, within the Colonies laying on the Atlantic Ocean, from Nova Scotia to West Florida inclusive, &c. &c. &c. John Montresor chief engineer.* Finished, colored manuscript 39¼ by 28. Clements Library. Brun 540.

22. *A Survey of the City of Philadelphia & its Environs comprehending the Neck formed by the Rivers Delaware & Schuylkill; together with Province, Carpenters, & Mud Islands, & the several Batteries & Works constructed thereon. Philadelphia 15 Decr 1777 John Montresor Chief Engineer.* Finished, colored manuscript 32 by 27. British Museum. Crown Collection V 27.

23. *A Survey of the City of Philadelphia and its Environs Shewing the several works constructed by his Majesty's Troops, under the Command of Sir William Howe, since their posession of that city 26th. September 1777, comprehending likewise the Attacks against Fort Mifflin on Mud Island and until its Reduction 16th. Nov. 1777 John Montresor Chief Engineer.* Careful, finished, colored manuscript 33⅞ by 58½. In lower right "P. Nicole Fecit." Library of Congress. G3701 S3237 1777 N5.

24. *Plan of the City of Philadelphia and its Environs Shewing its Defences during the years 1777 & 1778 together with the Siege of Mud Island on the River Delaware. To the Honble. Sir Henry Howe...* Unfinished, careful colored manuscript 33¾ by 42¼. Signed "John Montresor, Chief Engineer in America." Drafting appears to be by the same as the previous map. Library of Congress. G3701 S3237 1778 N51.

25. *A Draught and Calculations of An Entrenchment from Delaware to Schulkill Run in Angles to the Best Advantage the Ground Will Admit.* Careful manuscript 11⅞ by 18¼, of the line of defense north of the city. Atwater Kent Museum.

26. *Project for taking Post at Crown Point May 13th. 1774 by John Montresor.* Manuscript sketch 13 by 20. See Brasier map 1. British Museum. Crown Collection CXXI,54.

27. *Project for taking Post at Crown Point 13th. May 1774 by John Montresor Commdg. Engr. at N. York. Copy W. Brasier Delt. 29th May 1774.* Manuscript plan and section, colored 14½ by 21¼. In C.O. 5/91f.317. Public Record Office. MPC355.

MONTRESOR-PRINTED MAPS
(See also in section on printed maps.)

28. *A Plan of the City of New-York & its Environs to Greenwich, on the North or Hudsons River, and to Crown Point, on the East or Sound River, Shewing the Several Streets, Public Buildings, Docks, Fort & Battery, with the true Form & Course of the Commanding Grounds, with and without the Town.* Engraved, London: 1766, 19¼ by 26½. Inset - Chart of the Entrance to New York.... The map is dedicated to General Gage.
29. Same. London: A. Dury 1776.
30. *A Map of the Province of New York, with part of Pennsylvania, and New England, from an actual survey by. Capt. Montresor.* 1775. London: June 10th 1775 by A. Dury.
31. Same. Same publisher and date. "Tyionderogha or Tienderoga" changed to "Ticonderogs."
32. Same. "Republished with Great Improvements, April 1st 1777."
33. *Boston, its Environs and Harbour, with the Rebels' Works Raised against that Town in 1775, from the Observations of Lieut. Page, of His Majesty's Corps of Engineers, and from the Plans of Capt. Montresor.* William Faden, Oct. 1, 1778. 24½ by 17½.

81. MOORE

Moore was a pseudonym used by Benedict Arnold during the André affair. In the case of this map, Moore was probably the man whose home is shown on the map opposite Fort Constitution.
1. [*Hudson River at Peekskill*] Sketch map in color, 11¾ by 14½. Labeled on verso "Moore's sketch of the navigation of the Highlands." Clements Library. Brun 382.

82. BENJAMIN MORGAN

Morgan, a land surveyor of Somerset County, New Jersey, was appointed deputy surveyor for that county in 1753. In addition, the Board of Proprietors of East Jersey appointed him to act for Roxbury and Mendham Townships in neighboring Morris County. Morgan was a source of data for Hills' maps 5, 17, 34 and 35.

83. HENRY MOUZON, JR.

Mouzon, grandson of a Huguenot immigrant, was born in 1741. He was educated in France and became engaged in surveying as early as 1772, shortly after coming to America. Among his early ventures were maps of parts of Tryon and Mecklenburg Counties, and the Parish of St. Stephan. The latter was the proposed route for a canal to connect the Cooper and Santee Rivers.

Mouzon served as a captain in the American forces, and was severely wounded in the Battle of Black Mingo, South Carolina, on 29 September 1780. Following the war, Mouzon acted as commissioner of roads from 1798. He died in 1807.
1. *An Accurate Map of North and South Carolina, with their Indian Frontiers, showing a distinct manner all the Mountains, Rivers, Swamps, Marshes, Bays, Creeks, Harbours, Sandbanks and Soundings on the Coasts, with the Roads and Indian Paths as well as the Boundry or Provincial Lines, the Several Townships and other Divisions of the Land in Both the Provinces, the whole from Actual Surveys. By Henry Mouzon and others.* Printed map 54 by 38½. Insets of "The Harbor of Port Royal" and "The Bar and Harbour of Charlestown." London: Robt. Sayer and J. Bennett.

May 30, 1775. Portions of the map are based upon the previous surveys of DeBrahm, Cook, Collet, and indirectly, Churton. It proved to be an important Revolutionary War map of the area, being included in Jefferys' and Faden's Atlases, and as a "separate." Copies were used by the leaders of both sides, and it was later printed in France.

84. PIERRE NICOLE

Nicole was a Swiss born captain in the Guides. He was noted by Montresor to be very intelligent, well acquainted with the country and people, from whom he procured intelligence. He obtained the materials needed for the line of defense of Philadelphia, from behind the American lines. Nicole also acted as liaison between the Loyalists and the British Army, and was responsible for the management of substantial sums of money in carrying these out. Nicole was employed as a draughtsman by Montresor, and was very skillful. He died in 1784.
1. *A Survey of the City of Philadelphia....* See Montresor no. 23.
2. *A Plan of the City of Philadelphia....* See Montresor no. 24.
3. [*Paulus Hook*] By: Pierre Nicole. Finished, colored manuscript 11⅝ by 11⅛. Clements Library. Brun 496.
4. [*Paulus Hook and Bergen*] *Surveyed and draughted from the 22d. to 29th. June 1781. By P. Nicole.* Careful, finished, colored manuscript 36¼ by 23. Clements Library. Brun 495.

85. THOMAS HYDE PAGE

Page was born in 1746. As of 1776, his rank as lieutenant in the Engineers dated from 8 June 1774. Page was present at the Battle of Bunker Hill with Montresor, acting as Aide to General Howe. Severely wounded during the battle, he returned to England after only eleven days duty in Boston. His draughts, in conjunction with those of Montresor, form the basis for the contemporary maps of the battle. Montresor notes that Page received a grant of 10 shillings per diem for life, as a result of his wound.

Page, later knighted, had a distinguished career. He was commanding engineer at Dover in 1784 with the rank of captain-lieutenant. Later, he constructed the ferry at Chatham and was chief consultant in large engineering projects in Ireland. These included the improvements in the harbour facilities of the Port of Dublin, and of Wicklow Harbour. His projects also included development of inland navigation in Ireland, culminating in the construction of the Newberry and Royal Shannon canals. Page died in 1821.
1. [*Rough draft of Charlestown*] *Plan of the Action which happened 17th. June 1775 at Charles town, N. America.* Careful, colored manuscript 15 by 9½. Status after the battle but before new works were built. Library of Congress. Faden Collection no. 25.
2. *A Plan of the Action at Bunkers-Hill on the 17th. of June 1775 between his Majesty's Troops under the command of Major General Howe and the Rebel Forces. By Lieut. Page of the Engineers who acted as Aide-de-Camp to Gen. Howe in the action. N.B. The Grand Plan is from an Actual Survey of Capt. Montresor.* Finished, careful, colored manuscript 16¾ by 19½. Library of Congress. Faden Collection no. 26.
3. *A Plan of the Town of Boston and its Environs with the Lines, Batteries and Incampments of the British and American Armies.* Careful manuscript 25 by 17¾. Status before fortification of Dorchester Heights by the Americans. Library of Congress. Faden Collection no. 33.
4. *Boston, its Environs and Harbour with the Rebels Works, by Lieut. Page and other Gentlemen.* Finished, careful, colored manuscript 25 by 17½. Library of Congress. Faden Collection no. 34.
5. *A Plan of the Town of Boston, with the Entrenchments &c. of his Majesty's Forces in 1775: from the observations of Lieut. Page, and from plans of other gentlemen of his Majesty's Corps of Engineers.* Finished, careful, colored manuscript 12⅛ by 17½.

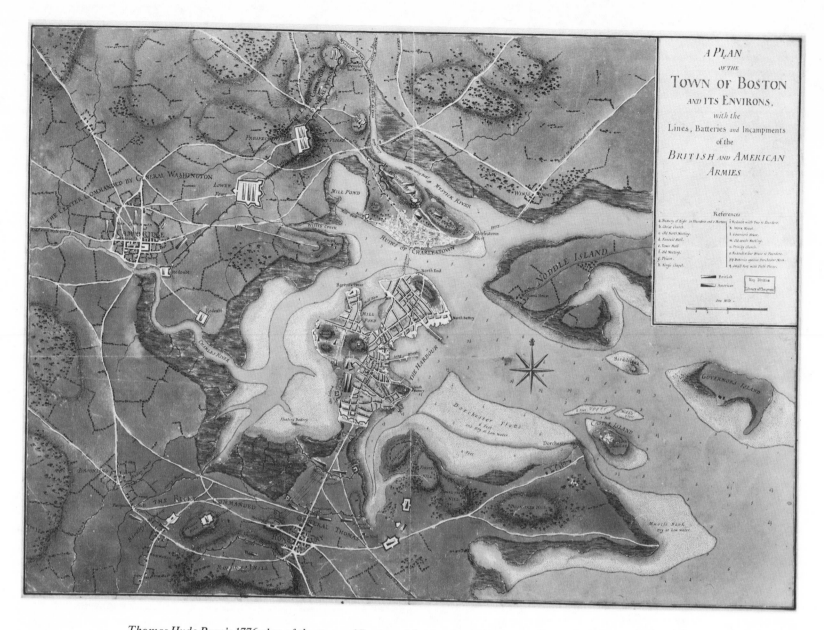

Thomas Hyde Page's 1776 plan of the town of Boston with opposing lines, batteries and encampments. See 85/3.

Library of Congress. Faden Collection no. 32.

6. *A Plan of the Town of Boston, with the intrenchments &c. of his Majesty's Forces in 1775: from the observations of Lieut. Page and from the plans of other gentlemen.* Engraved map, London; William Faden 1st. Oct. 1777. Issued with and without an overlay.

7. *A Plan of the Action at Bunkers Hill, on the 17th of June 1775, between His Majesty's Troops under the command of Major General Howe, and the American Forces.* Engraved map omitting Page's name and referring to "Americans" rather than to "Rebels". Similar map for Stedman's History of the American war in 1793.

86. WILLIAM PARKER

Lieutenant Parker, with the rank of sub-engineer, was assigned to duty at Perth Amboy in June 1777. He was assigned to construction work on Governor's Island, and in October 1779 was mentioned in a letter from General Pattison to Alexander Mercer, as being in need of assistance. A letter from Parker to Mercer, dated 19 November 1780, describes the post and enclosed a sketch map. Parker served as commanding engineer at the Isle of Man in 1784 with the rank of captain-lieutenant.

1. *A Plan of...Part of Long Island....* See Wheeler map 7.
2. *British Refugee Post on Bergen Point, 19th. Novr. 1780* A rough pencil sketch 9½ by 6 inches. Enclosed in a letter from Parker to Alexander Mercer, the Commanding Engineer at New York, dated 19 November 1780. Clements Library. Brun 477.

87. HENRY PELHAM

Pelham, a Loyalist, accompanied the British to Halifax in 1776. He subsequently went to London, where his map was engraved.

1. *A Plan of Boston in New England with its Environs, Including Milton, Dorchester, Roxbury, Brooklin, Cambridge, Medford, Charlestown, Parts of Malden and Chelsea, With the Military Works Constructed in those Places in the Years 1775 and 1776.* Engraved map 26¾ by 39. Published by the author, London, June 2d 1777. Inset of a permit granted Pelham to make the plan, by James Urquhart, Town Major, 28 Aug. 1775. A comprehensive and detailed map, some copies of which were autographed by Pelham.

2. *[Sketch of a Redoubt on Bunker Hill]* Sketch plan and views in manuscript, 9¼ by 5½, on back of letter dated 5 June 1775. This may have been sent to Pelham, but he may be the author of the sketch. Massachusetts Historical Society. Ic 3.6.

88. RENÉ PHILIPEAU

1. [*Savannah and Vicinity*] Careful, untitled manuscript 11 by 6½. Library of Congress. G3701 S334 1778 M6.

89. PHILLIP PITTMAN

Pittman was an ensign in the 15th. Regiment in 1761. Serving as an engineer, he surveyed part of Montresor's route overland from Quebec to New England. Pittman made a series of surveys of the Mississippi, parts of Louisiana, and the Gulf Coast of Florida by 1768. He was promoted to Lieutenant by 1765. He was the author of *The Present State of the European Settlements on the Mississippi, with a Geographical Description of that River*, an important and influential book, published in London in 1770. See biographical sketch of Brasier.
1. See Gauld no. 3.
2. See Brasier no. 5.

90. MATTHEW PITTS

Pitts was referred to as having served as a subaltern for 13 or 14 years while stationed at Brunswick on 11 June 1777. He was also referred to as a witness to Montresor's honesty, in the payment of contractors during the occupation of Philadelphia in 1777 and 1778. He was captain lieutenant of Engineers at Plymouth in 1784.
1. *A Plan of...Part of Long Island....* See Wheeler map 7.

91. JOSEPH PURCELL

Purcell is recorded as a draughtsman, mathematician, and navigator in the employ of the surveyor general, in East Florida between 1763 and 1771. He compiled at least two maps of the Southern Indian District after 1772, under the direction of the superintendent of Indian Affairs, John Stuart. This excellent map of Virginia, North and South Carolina, Georgia and parts of Florida, was used as a source as late as 1794, in Morse's American Geography.
1. *A Plan of Pensacola And its Environs in its Present State From an Actual Survey in 1778 By Joseph Purcell.* Careful manuscript 28⅛ by 19¼. Library of Congress.
2. *A Map of the Road from Pensacola in Wt. Florida to St. Augustine in East Florida. A survey in 1778 by Joseph Purcell.* Careful manuscript 102 by 29. Public Record Office. CO 700Fla 54.
3. *A New Map of the Southern District of North America From Surveys taken by the Compiler and Others. Compiled in 1781 for Lieut. Col. Thomas Brown superintendant of Indian affairs etc. By Thomas Purcell.* Careful, detailed, colored manuscript 74 by 79, with reference table. Public Record Office. PRO 700 No. 15.

92. BERNARD RATZER

Ratzer appears as a lieutenant, rather than an ensign, in the 60th. Regiment in 1756. This indicates that he was considered as having special training. He served with the 1st. Batallion in Jamaica sometime prior to 1774. He was promoted captain-lieutenant, then captain in 1773. He was promoted major in 1783, but appears on the regimental roster for the last time in 1784 as a captain.

Most of Ratzer's mapping was done in upper New York, and in the West prior to the Revolution. Some of his surveys were the basis of maps reproduced during the war years.
1. *Plan of the City of New York survey'd by Bernd Ratzen Lieut in the 60th. Regt.* Colored, poorly preserved manuscript 34½ by 22¾. Part printed, with manuscript corrections. "F. Walden, Fecit." Public Record Office. MPH225.
2. *To His Excellency Sr. Henry Moore...This Plan of the City of New York, Is most Humbly Inscribed By...Bernd. Ratzen...Survey'd in 1767. T. Kitchen Sculpt. London: Jany. 12, 1776; By Jefferys & Faden.* Printed map 32½ by 21¼. Probably second, possibly third issue. This is known as the RATZEN Plan, smaller than the following.
3. *Plan of the City of New York, in North America: Surveyed in the Years 1766 & 1767. London: Published by Jefferys & Faden Jany. 12, 1776. B. Ratzer, Thos. Kitchin Sculpt.* Printed map 45¼ by 32½. Probably second issue. This is known as the RATZER Plan.

The following two maps are presumed to be by Ratzer, and to be precursors of *The Province of New Jersey divided into East and West*. They also resemble the work of Holland and his deputies.

4. [*New York-New Jersey Border, to western Long Island*] Careful, detailed, colored manuscript showing all the division lines between New York and New Jersey, and between East and West Jersey, 35½ by 23¾. Unsigned, date in upper left 1769. Library of Congress. Faden Collection no. 2. Two sections.
5. [*Present Monmouth and Ocean Counties, New Jersey*] Careful, detailed, colored manuscript 23 by 18¾. Library of Congress. Faden Collection no. 2.
6. *The Province of New Jersey, Divided into East and West. Commonly called The Jerseys. Drawn from the surveys of Bernard Ratzer, Lieut. 60th. Regiment, and Gerard Banker.* Engraved map 22 by 30. First issued December 1st. 1777. Later issue 2 December, 1778 with additional data. See Hills map 21, Hutchins map 9.

93. FRANCIS RAWDON

Rawdon was born in 1754, of a noble Irish family. Educated at Harrow and Oxford, he was commissioned ensign in 1771 in the 15th. Regiment of Foot while still at Oxford. Rawdon came to America with the 5th. Foot in July 1774 and was in the Battle of Bunker Hill. He served as aide-de-camp to both Clinton and Cornwallis in Campaigns in New York, New Jersey, the Philadelphia Campaign, on Long Island, at Fort Washington, and at White Plains. He was promoted lieut. col. in 1778 and started the recruiting of a provincial regiment, the "Volunteers of Ireland." He resigned his responsibility as aide, being replaced by Major André on 3 September 1781. He served under Cornwallis in South Carolina, finally returning to England in July 1781.

The remainder of Rawdon's military career was distinguished. He became Baron Rawdon in 1783, Earl of Moira in 1793. He served as major general in the Napoleonic Wars, and was promoted to lieutenant general and general. He served successively as Commander in Chief of Scotland, Governor General and Commander in Chief of India, and finally at Malta, where he died in 1826.
1. *Sketch of the positions of the Army on Long Island upon the morning of the 26th. of August 1776; with the march on the ensuing night; and the action of the 27th.* Finished, colored manuscript 15⅞ by 12¼. Clements Library. Brun 438.
2. *Sketch of Verplanck's Point, taken from Haverstraw Bay. Chart of the coast from Teller's to Verplanck's Point. Slaughter's Landing.* Manuscript sketches 12½ by 7½ in a letter to Clinton, September 1777. Clements Library. Brun 442.
3. *A view of the Great Bridge near Norfolk in Virginia where the action happened between a detachment of the 14th. Regt. & a body of Rebels.* Finished, colored manuscript 8½ by 7⅜. Clements Library. Brun 588.

94. REYERSE

See Ryartson. Source of data for Hills' map 21.

95. ARCHIBALD ROBERTSON

Robertson, a Scots engineer, diarist, and talented amateur artist, has left a valuable, interesting, although incomplete journal of his military years. Born about 1745, he was educated privately before entering the Royal Engineers in March 1759. He came to America after the attack on Havana in 1762 and served at Pensacola where he was commended for his diligence. He was sent to fortify Fort Bute on the Mississippi. While there, the fort was overrun by local Indian tribes bent on insolence and plunder rather than extinction. He returned to England in 1767.

Robertson had been promoted to lieutenant in 1764 and captain-lieutenant in 1765. He had made a tour in 1775 of the fortified French frontier towns in the company of Lieutenant Colonel Campbell. He left England, arriving at Boston Harbor 8 November 1775. After Boston, he served in turn in New York, in the Philadelphia campaign, and in the South. Robertson's later career was distinguished. He was promoted to lieutenant general in 1805 and subsequently retired to his home near Comrie in Perth-Shire where he died in 1813.

Two of Robertson's plans of Pensacola are preserved in the Public Record Office. Other surveys or maps, to which he refers in his journal, have not been found. A 1770 Louisiana map by Elias Durnford, was taken from one by Robertson. Robertson's original journal and maps are in the New York Public Library, with exceptions. An admirable account of Robertson, by Harry M. Lydenberg, was published by the library in 1930, and since republished by the Arno Press. Robertson is sometimes confused with a contemporary artist of the same name.

1. *Plan of the Fort at Pensacola 1763.* Finished, colored manuscript 19 by 14¼. Public Record Office. Z/30/2. Plate 10 in Lydenberg's book.
2. *Plan of the Fort at Pensacola.* Finished, colored manuscript 23⅞ by 17¾. Public Record Office. Z/30/1. Plate 11 in Lydenberg.
3. *A Plan of the Roads between Boston and Albany, surveyed by order.* Unsigned copy of the map by Francis Miller which had been made about 1765, and copied by Brasier is in Clements Library, Brun 270. Finished, colored manuscript 13 by 47. New York Public Library.
4. [*Halifax to Fort Edward, Nova Scotia.*] Sketch map in pencil dated 13 April 1775, 4¼ by 4¾. New York Public Library.
5. [*Chart of the Approaches to Boston Bay.*] Unsigned manuscript 28 by 20¾. New York Public Library, manuscript collection.
6. [*Cambridge to Prospect Hill.*] Unsigned profile 6½ by 13¾. Attribution by Douglas W. Marshall. Clements Library. Brun 181.
7. [*Attack on Fort Washington 16 November 1776.*] Sketch map in pencil, 4¾ by 7. New York Public Library.
8. *Outline of Parapet Deckers Ferry* [*Staten Island.*] Sketch map in pencil, 4¾ by 7. New York Public Library.
9. *Battle of White Plains.* Unsigned manuscript 13½ by 20¾. Dated "Octb 28, 1777." New York Public Library.
10. [*New York City from Kips Bay to McGowans Pass.*] Unsigned, incomplete manuscript 52 by 41½. New York Public Library, manuscript collection.
11. [*Long Island Roads from Moriches to the East.*] Sketch map in pencil, 6⅛ by 4. New York Public Library.
12. [*Long Island Roads between Bakers, Islip, Moriches and Blue Point.*] Sketch map in pencil, 6⅛ by 4. New York Public Library.
13. *British Troops near Charleston, April 1780.* Colored manuscript, unsigned, 14 by 13½. New York Public Library.
14. [*Charlestown Neck, South Carolina, 21st. May, 1780.*] Sketch map in pencil, 6¼ by 3¾. New York Public Library.

Robertson indicates that he made other maps, which have not been found. They are as follows;-
15. *Sketch of the roads between White Plains and Dobbs Ferry, November 2, 1776.*
16. *Sketch of the ground, Battle of Brandywine, September 15, 1777.*
17. *British Troops in September 1777.*
18. *Attack of Monmouth, after the Battle.*
19. *Drawing of Fort Sullivan, June 3, 1780.*

96. BEVERLY ROBINSON

Robinson was born in Virginia in 1722, son of the Honorable John Robinson, the president of the colony. In 1746, he raised a militia company for duty in Canada. While in New York, he met and married Susanna, daughter of the wealthy Frederick Philipse. He so successfully managed his wife's large estate on the Hudson, north of Peekskill, that he was one of the state's wealthiest land-owners.

During the early part of the Revolutionary ferment, Robinson favored the Colonies but opposed independence. He refused to take the oath of allegiance, taking refuge in New York. Appointed a colonel, he formed two units, "The Loyal American Regiment," and the "Corps of Guides and Pioneers." His principal activity was obtaining intelligence and in negotiating defections.

Robinson and his family went to England following the end of the war. He had been appointed to the first council in New Brunswick, but never filled the post. He received a grant of £ 17,000 for his losses. He died in England in 1792. Two of his four sons, one a graduate of Columbia College, were knighted, one becoming a lieutenant general in the British Army. The others were founders of distinguished Canadian families.

1. *Valley of the Hudson River from Fishkill River to Teller's Point. By: Beverly Robinson.* Careful manuscript 14⅞ by 26½. Clements Library. Brun 453.

97. BERNARD ROMANS

Romans was born in the Netherlands about 1720, was probably educated in England as an engineer, and came to America about 1757. He was appointed Deputy Surveyor of Georgia in 1766 and a short time later went to East Florida to survey the property of Lord Egmont, the associate of Oglethorp in founding Georgia. Here, Romans acquired property of his own.

William Gerard De Brahm, Surveyor General for the Southern District, selected Romans to act as deputy surveyor. However, as the result of disagreement, Romans sold his property in Florida in 1773, and moved to New York. Here, he was made a member of the New York Marine Society, and of the American Philosophical Society. The Proceedings of the Society published his description of an improved mariners compass, from a letter dated at Pensacola in 1773.

Romans' *A Concise History of East and West Florida* was published in New York in 1775, which incidentally criticizes *The American Pilot* by De Brahm, published in 1772, the apparent root of the disagreement. During the next few years, Romans was active in various New England cities. A receipt signed by him for payment for a set of charts of the navigation to the southward of Georgia, to Isaac Beers of New Haven, is preserved.

Romans supported the colonial cause, and in April 1775 was appointed as a member of a committee to take Fort Ticonderoga. He accompanied the expedition led by Benedict Arnold, and independently captured nearby Fort George. He aided in the removal of the ordnance, later transported to Boston by Henry Knox. He was appointed to report on the construction of fortifications at Fort Constitution on the Hudson River, at the recommendation of

General Washington. The area was found to be commanded by the higher ground of West Point, across the river. After study, Lord Stirling recommended its occupation.

Romans was commissioned captain in the 1st. Pennsylvania Company of Artillery in February 1776, and accompanied the unsuccessful expedition to capture Quebec. He resigned his commission on 1 June 1778, following an unsatisfactory solution to a disagreement with another officer. In January 1779, Romans married Elizabeth Whitney of Wethersfield, Connecticut. A son, Hubertus, was born of the union. Romans later joined the Southern Army, and was captured in 1780. A prisoner at Montego Bay, Jamaica, he was repatriated late in 1783. He died at sea in January 1784 under mysterious circumstances, possibly murdered.

His maps made in, or employed by, America during the Revolution are described in *American Maps and Map Makers of the Revolution*. The following, all printed, were published and used by the British.

1. *A General Map of the Southern British Colonies...from modern surveys of DeBrahm, Capt. Collet, Mouzon & others; and from the large hydrographical survey of the Coasts of East and West Florida. By B. Romans, 1776.* Insets of Charlestown and St. Augustine. Printed map in *The American Military Pocket Atlas....*"taken principally from the actual surveys...DeBrahm and Romans; Cook, Jackson and Collet; Maj. Holland...." London, R. Sayer & J. Bennett, 1776. The source of this map appears to be Romans' *A Concise History of East and West Florida,* or preliminary draughts which are no longer in existence.

2. *A Plan of Mobile Bar, surveyed by B. Romans, 1771. Plan of the Harbour of Pensacola. By B. Romans, 1771.* Printed maps included in editions of *The West-India Atlas....*some bearing "by the late Thomas Jefferys," and published by R. Sayer, London 1794, and subsequently. The same map is included in a later edition of the same atlas by Sayer's successors, J. Whittle and R.H. Laurie, London, 1818.

3. *Map of East Florida from St. Augustine to Tampa Bay. By Bernard Romans.* Unfinished, but very detailed manuscript 21 by 34, with notes by Romans. Probably the original of his *Part of the Province of East Florida.* Clements Library. Brun 645.

4. *A Map of the Middle Part of East Florida, and the Grand Bahama Bank; drawn for the private use of ___ as taken from the Original Journals and Field-works of B. Romans.* Colored, finished manuscript, 50.7 by 191.5 cm. See above note. T.W. Streeter sale catalog. II, 1185.

5. *A map of part of West Florida done under the direction of the Honourable John Stuart esqe:& by him humbly inscribed to His Excellency Thomas Gage esquire General and Commander in Chief of all His Majesty's forces in North-America. Surveyed and drawn by Bernard Romans. Between the month of June 1772 & January 1773.* Finished, detailed coast chart 21½ by 29¾. Mentioned in a letter from Stuart, dated 22 April 1773 at Charles Town, to Gage. Clements Library. Brun 662.

6. *A map of West Florida, part of Et: Florida, Georgia, part of So: Carolina...Bernard Romans, David Taitt, and George Gauld.* Finished, detailed, careful manuscript 66 by 101. Inset of West Florida and the Carolinas. See Gauld No. 5. Clements Library. Brun 663.

98. JOSEPH RUE

Joseph Rue was appointed deputy surveyor general for Middlesex County in 1752, by the Board of Proprietors of East Jersey. He was also appointed collector for South Amboy in 1759. He is cited as a source of data on Hills' maps 34 and 36.

99. RYARTSON

Samuel Ryartson, correctly Ryerse, was a deputy surveyor for the Proprietors of East Jersey in Bergen County, New Jersey, and agent for the Ramapo Tract. The rugged Ramapo Hills in North Jersey were a source of iron ore. A descendant of Dutch settlers, he and his sons Joseph and Samuel were Loyalists.

Source of data for Hills' map 5.

100. CLAUDE JOSEPH SAUTHIER

Sauthier, son of a saddler, was born in Strasbourg in 1736. Trained as an architect and surveyor, he came to America before 1768, probably directly to the Carolinas. Here, he drafted a series of maps of the communities in North Carolina, based on his own surveys and began his long association with Tryon. The maps were made between 1768 and 1770. Governor William Tryon recommended payment of the sum of £ 50 for these services. A former officer in the Foot Guards, Tryon had little sympathy for the colonials, and tended toward military solutions of problems. He defeated a group of colonial dissidents at Alamance on 16 May 1771. This event was commemorated by handsome maps by Sauthier.

Tryon was transferred to New York as Governor in 1771 and was accompanied by Sauthier. Tryon faced a conflict over the New York-New Hampshire border, and was involved in the purchase of extensive properties in the Mohawk Valley. Both were included in maps by Sauthier. Tryon returned to England in April 1774, accompanied by Sauthier. Sauthier produced a magnificent manuscript copy of Le Clerc's Geometry which he presented to Tryon in London the same year. Tryon returned to New York by the start of the Revolution.

Sauthier made a fine manuscript map of the operations on Manhattan for Lord Percy, and returned to England with Percy as his private secretary. He remained in his employ until 1790, making a survey of his estate. Sauthier eventually returned to Strasbourg, where he died in 1802.

1. *Plan of the Town of NewPort with its Environs Survey'd By order of His Excellency The Right Honorable Earl Percy, Lieutenant General Commanding His Majesty's Forces on Rhode Island &c &c &c in March 1777.* Careful, finished, colored manuscript 28⅜ by 38. Duke of Northumberland Collection. Alnwick.

2. *[New York State showing Counties, Manors, Townships and Estates about 1778.]* Careful, finished manuscript 44½ by 62½. Markedly similar to, and probably a preliminary study for, Faden's 1779 "A Choreographical Map of the Province of New-York...." Clements Library. Brun 371.

3. *A Plan of the Division Line Between the Provinces of New-York and Quebec, in the 45th. Degree of North Latitude Survey'd in the Year 1771 & 1772 By Thomas Valentine & John Collins, Esquirs.* Careful, finished, colored manuscript 53 by 9¾. In lower left "Drawn By C.J. Sauthier." Library of Congress. G3702 B 1772 53.

4. *Map of Staten Island In the Province of New-York Survey'd By Order of His Excellency General Howe Commander in Chief of His Majesty's Forces in North America. August 1776 By C.J. Sauthier Ingineer Geographer.* Careful, colored manuscript 34¾ by 27¾. Duke of Northumberland Collection. Alnwick.

5. *A Map of Part of New-York Island Showing A Plan of Fort Washington now Call'd Ft. Kniphausen with the Rebels Lines on the fourth part, from which they were driven on the 16th. of November 1776 By the Troupes under the Orders of the Earl of Percy. Survey'd the same day by order of His Lordship By C.J. Sauthier.* Careful, colored manuscript 15 by 30. Library of Congress. Faden Collection no. 61.

6. *Plan of the City of New-York as it was when his Majesty's Forces took Possession of it in 1776. Showing all the works the Rebels did in the course of the preceding winter mark'd yellow, and the part of the City which was burnt the same year by a pale red colour & dott'd lines. Surveyed in October 1776 by C.J. Sauthier.* Careful, colored manuscript 31⅜ by 23¼. Duke of

Northumberland Collection. Alnwick.

7. *Plan of Fort George and the Lower Battery in the City of New York. The Addition of Works of the Rebels are with a Yellow edging. By C.J. Sauthier.* Careful, colored manuscript 14 by 27¾. In CO 5/1107/810-11. Public Record Office. MPG 366.

8. *A Plan of Fort George at the City of New-York.* Careful, colored manuscript 14¾ by 25¼. In lower center "Surveyed and drawn by C.J. Sauthier." Library of Congress. Faden Collection no. 95.

9. *A Map of the Inhabited Part of Canada from the French Surveys, with the Frontiers of New York and New England from the large survey by Claude Joseph Sauthier. Inscribed to Major Gen. John Burgoyne.* Printed map 33½ by 22¼. Engraved by Wm. Faden., 1777.

10. *A Map of the Province of New-York Reduced from a large Drawing of that Province compiled from Actual Surveys by order of His Excellency William Tryon Esqr. Captain General & Governor of the same By Claude Joseph Sauthier to which is added New-Jersey, from the Topographic Observations of C.J. Sauthier and B. Ratzer. Engraved by William Faden (Successor to the late Mr. Thos. Jeffreys) 1776.* Printed map 21¾ by 27. August 1st. 1776.

11. *A Topographical Map of Hudsons River with the Channels Depth of Water, Rocks, Shoals, &c...from Sandy-Hook, New York and Bay...as high as Fort Chambly on Sorel River. By Claude Joseph Sauthier....* Engraved by William Faden, Charing Cross. Printed map 20¾ by 31¼. October 1st. 1776.

12. *A Topographical Map of the Northn. part of New York Island, Exhibiting the plan of Fort Washington, Now Fort Knyphausen, with the rebel lines. By C.J. Sauthier. Engraved by William Faden.* Printed map 10¼ by 18¼. March 1, 1777.

13. *A plan of the Operations of the Kings Army under the Command of General Sr William Howe K.B. in New York and East New Jersey against the American Forces...from the 12th. of October, to the 28th. of November 1776, wherein is particularly distinguished the engagement of White Plains the 28th. of October. By C.J. Sauthier.* Printed map 19½ by 28½. Feby. 25th. 1777, William Faden, London.

14. *A Chorographical Map of the Province of New York in North America divided into Counties, Manors, Patents and Townships: compiled from actual Surveys by Claude Joseph Sauthier. London: William Faden, 1779.* Printed map 53½ by 71.

101. NICHOLAS & WILLIAM SCULL

Nicholas Scull, Pennsylvania surveyor during the first half of the 18th. century, was cited as a source of data by Lewis Evans for his 1749 map. Scull also supervised the Heap view and plan of Philadelphia, made in 1753, and republished many times. He produced the first large scale map of Pennsylvania in 1759.

Nicholas' five sons, James, Peter, William, Edward and Jasper were surveyors. Edward made surveys of the Lackawaxan area in 1749, mapped west of the Susquehanna River, and is cited as a source of data for the Lewis Evans map of 1755. William's map of Pennsylvania of 1770 was published in London by Sayer and Bennett in 1775. It was included in their American Atlas, and that of Faden. William was commissioned a captain in the 11th. Pennsylvania Regiment in 1776, retiring in 1778 to join the Geographer's Department of the Continental Army under Robert Erskine. William was a member of the American Philosophical Society from Reading, Pennsylvania.

Scull is cited as a source of data for Hills' map 5.

102. MICHAEL SEIX

A captain in the 22nd. Regiment, Seix commanded a party of 30 men sent to capture the American battery near Bristol, Rhode Island on 25 May 1778, during a British foray.

1. *A Plan of the Adjacent Coasts to the North Part of Rhode Island, To Express the Route of a Body of Troops Detached to Destroy the Rebels Batteaux, Vessels, Stores &c. &c. accomplished May 25th. 1778.* Careful, colored manuscript 16½ by 13¼. Duke of Northumberland Collection, Alnwick.

103. JOHN GRAVES SIMCOE

Simcoe was born in Cotterstock, Northamptonshire in 1752, son of Captain John Simcoe of the Navy. His grandfather was the Rev. William Simcoe, Vicar of Woodhaven, Northumberland. Simcoe received a good education by tutors, at the free school in Exeter, at Eton, and at Merton College, Oxford, before being commissioned an ensign in the 35th. Regiment of Foot in 1770. He received promotions and a transfer, becoming a captain in the 40th. Regiment of Foot in 1775, and commanded the grenadier company.

While in winter quarters at New Brunswick in 1776, Simcoe went to New York to solicit command of the Queen's Rangers, a Loyalist Regiment. He arrived too late. However, on October 15, 1777, Sir William Howe appointed him to succeed Major Wemys as commander, with the provincial rank of major.

Simcoe proved to be a distinguished and aggressive leader of this unit. His exploits have been memorialized in *A Journal of the Operations of the Queen's Rangers*, written by him and first published at Exeter in 1787. The well written account, illustrated with maps by George Spencer and Adam Allen, succeeded in making this unit's exploits a well recorded and well known part of the war. Many of the preliminary map drafts were Simcoe's own work, although all the final renderings were by Spencer.

Following the war, Simcoe's military career was distinguished by further promotions to major general in 1794 and lieutenant general in 1801. He served as Governor of Lower Canada from 1791 to 1796, establishing an essentially military type of government. He later served in other military and diplomatic capacities, prior to his retirement. He died in 1806 at Topham, Devonshire.

During his lieutenant governorship, Simcoe made a map of Upper Canada and the Great Lakes, and of the Campaign of Anthony Wayne against the Indians in 1793 and 1794. Both maps are in the Clements Library.

1. *City of Williamsburg, Virginia.* A careful, detailed, but unfinished manuscript map of the town 9⅜ by 6½. There is an attached signature "John Graves Simcoe Lt. Col. Comdt. Queens Rangers." Colonial Williamsburg, Simcoe Papers (61-57).

2. *Sketch of Roads around New Kent and Diascond Virginia.* A rough manuscript of the road network, labeled but unsigned, 8 by 6½. Colonial Williamsburg, Simcoe Papers (63-29h).

3. [*Roads of Gloucester Neck Va. July 20, 1781.*] Careful manuscript of the road network, road junctions and taverns indicated, 8¼ by 6⅞, unsigned. Colonial Williamsburg, Simcoe Papers (M-49-5).

4. *Sketch of Roads in Gloucester, Va.* A rough manuscript of the road network, indicating the distances between intersections, 8½ by 6¼. Colonial Williamsburg, Simcoe Papers (63-29).

104. ANDREW SKINNER

Skinner, a Scottish land surveyor, was associated with George Taylor in surveys of North Britain in 1776, in North America in 1781 and 1782. He surveyed the Harbour of Nassau and the Island of New Providence in the Bahamas in 1788. See under George Taylor.

1. [*Part of the present Fairfield County, Connecticut*] *copied for the Adjutant General by Andrew Skinner.* Finished, colored manuscript 12½ by 23¼. Clements Library. Brun 319.

2. *A Map Containing part of the Provinces of New York and New Jersey Drawn from Surveys Compiled By Thomas Millidge Major 1st. Batallion New Jersey Volunteers 1780.* Careful, colored manu-

script, dissected on linen, 35⅜ by 66¼. In lower right "This map is Drawn for Oliver Delancy Esquire Adjutant General of N. America & Major of the 17th Light Dragoons By Andrew Skinner 1781." Library of Congress. G3800 1781 M5.

3. *A map of the environs of Brooklyn surveyed by order of His Excellency General Sir Henry Clinton k.b. Commander in Chief of His Majesty's forces &c. &c. by Andw Skinner 1781.* Finished, colored manuscript 28¾ by 20⅝. Clements Library. Brun 375.

4. *A map of the Delaware and Chesapeak Bays with the Peninsula between them. Copied by Andrew Skinner 1780.* Finished, colored manuscript 22¾ by 17½. Clements Library. Brun 563.

105. I. or J. SMITH

1. *A particular description of that part of the Coast of Connecticut extending from Byram River to Stratford Point. These observations were made by a Gentleman belonging to His Majestys Customs in Connecticut. Copied by I. Smith.* Finished manuscript of the coast and harbors 19 by 7½. Clements Library. Brun 320.

106. GEORGE SPENCER

Spencer was born in 1758, and lived in the area of New Haven, Connecticut. He served as a lieutenant in the Queen's Rangers, under the command of John Graves Simcoe. The maps illustrating Simcoe's *A Journal of the Operations of the Queen's Rangers* were made mainly by Spencer, some drafts being the work of Simcoe and Adam Allen.

At the end of the war, Spencer, with his family of four, and two servants, left New York for Shelburne, Nova Scotia, where he was granted 50 acres of land, one town lot, and one water lot. His losses as a Loyalist were estimated at £1500. He died in 1834.

1. [*Approaches to Philadelphia.*] A careful manuscript in color, 7¼ by 6. It shows the Delaware River from Philadelphia to Derby Creek, the ship channel, islands, and fortifications. Huntington Library.

2. *Affair at Quintin's Bridge: 18th. March 1778.* Careful, finished manuscript 8¾ by 8½. The title and references A through I are below. Huntington Library.

3. *Surprize of the Rebels at Hancock's House* [*New Jersey.*] Careful manuscript in color, 6⅝ by 6½, unsigned. Title below and references A through G. Huntington Library.

4. *The Skirmish at Crosswicks* [*New Jersey.*] Careful manuscript in color, 8 by 6½. References A through G. Huntington Library.

5. *Battle of Monmouth 28th. June 1778* [*New Jersey.*] Careful colored manuscript 10⅝ by 6¼. Inset map of roads between Freehold and Middletown. In lower left is "Copy G S." Monmouth County Historical Association, Freehold, N.J.

6. *Battle of Monmouth 28th. June 1778* [*New Jersey.*] Careful colored manuscript 15 by 6. Inset of the "Skirmish of the Queens Rangers with the Jersey Militia." Monmouth County Historical Association, Freehold, N.J.

7. *Singular Position Occupied by Lieutenant Colo. Simcoe with the Queens Rangers and Legion at North Castle* [*Virginia.*] Careful colored manuscript 16 by 8. A notation "This Plan is delineated to elucidate the principal on which Lt. Colo. Simcoe chose his position as described in the 150th. Page." In lower left, "from a sketch by Lt. Colo. Simcoe taken on the Spot copy G. Spencer Lt. Qs. Rs." Huntington Library.

8. *Plan of the Post at Great Bridge on the South River of Elizabeth River, Virginia.* Careful colored manuscript, 6⅜ by 8¼. References A through H. In lower left "from a survey by J. Stratton, Lt. Royal Engineers," and in lower right "Copy G. Spencer Lt. Qs Rs." Huntington Library.

9. *Plan of the Post of Great Bridge on the South Branch of Elizabeth River in Virginia, Established the 5th. of February*

1781. Careful colored manuscript 5¾ by 7¼. Colonial Williamsburg. Simcoe Papers (61-206).

10. (*Action at HoopersTown 15th. Apl. (17)80 Cornet George Spencer*) (*New Jersey*) Rough sketch, 6¼ by 7. Included in a report from Capt. Benjamin Wickham to Simcoe. Title is on verso. Clements Library. Brun 473.

11. *The Landing at Burrell's April 17th. 1781.* Careful colored manuscript, 12⅛ by 11¾. Square cartouche in lower right with references A through E. In lower left "taken on the Spot by G. Spencer Lt. Q. Rs." Huntington Library.

12. *Rebels dislodged from Williamsburg landing, April 17, 1781.* Unlabeled and unfinished colored manuscript 7¾ by 6. Colonial Williamsburg. Simcoe Papers (61-207).

13. *Rebels dislodged from Williamsburg landing, April 17, 1781.* Careful colored manuscript 8 by 6⅛. Cartouche in lower right with references A through G. Colonial Williamsburg. Simcoe Papers (61-210).

14. *Sketch of Action at Petersburgh April 25th. 1781* [*Virginia.*] Careful colored manuscript, 7¾ by 5⅞. Cartouche in upper left with references A through H. Huntington Library.

15. (*Affair at Osburns*) (*Virginia*) Careful, unlabeled and unfinished manuscript 7⅞ by 8⅛. Square cartouche on right. Colonial Williamsburg. Simcoe Papers (61-208).

16. [*Affair at Osburns.*] Careful, unlabeled and unfinished manuscript 9 by 6⅞. Colonial Williamsburg. Simcoe Papers (61-209).

17. *Affair at Osburns, Virginia.* Careful, unlabeled and unfinished manuscript 8 by 5¾. Title at center below. Colonial Williamsburg. Simcoe Papers (61-212).

18. *Sketch of the Action at Osburns April 27th. 1781.* Careful colored manuscript 12¾ by 11¾. Rectangular cartouche on right with references A through H. In lower left "taken on the spot by G. Spencer Lt: Q.R." Huntington Library.

19. *Sketch of the Action at Osburns 27 April 1781.* Careful colored manuscript, 8¾ by 9⅝, labeled in cursive. Rectangular cartouche in upper left. Huntington Library.

20. *Point of Fork 4th. June 1781* [*Virginia*] Careful colored manuscript, 11¾ by 11¼, of the forks of the James River. Rectangular cartouche in upper left corner with references A through H. In lower left "taken on the Spot by G. Spencer Lt. Q.Rs." Huntington Library.

21. *Attack on the Rebels under Genl. _____ at the Point of Fork.* Careful, unfinished and unlabeled manuscript 9 by 7¼. Rectangular cartouche in upper left, with letters A through H, but without references. Colonial Williamsburg. Simcoe Papers (66-13).

22. [*Point of Fork*] Careful, incomplete and unlabeled manuscript 8⅞ by 7. Colonial Williamsburg, Simcoe Papers (66-12).

23. *The Great Bridge, on Elizabeth River Virginia.* Careful manuscript labeled in cursive, 4½ by 8⅜. Descriptive data on right. Colonial Williamsburg. Simcoe Papers (61-205).

24. *Action at Spencers plantation seven miles from Williamsburg....* Careful, finished manuscript 8⅜ by 6⅜. Descriptive references on right. A through H relating to the infantry of the Queen's Rangers, and O through S relating to the cavalry. Colonial Williamsburg. Simcoe Papers (61-218).

25. *Action at Spencers plantation seven miles from Williamsburg....* Careful, unfinished manuscript 8⅜ by 6¼. Similar to the preceding, the same references on the right. Colonial Williamsburg. Simcoe Papers (61-219).

26. *Action at Spencer's Ordinary June 26, 1781.* Careful colored manuscript 8⅜ by 7¾. References to right, A through N, within a curved border. In lower left "taken on the spot G. Spencer Lt. Queen's Rangers." Huntington Library.

27. [*Action at Spencer's Ordinary*] Unfinished and unlabeled manuscript 7⅛ by 6½. Rectangular cartouche in upper right. Colonial Williamsburg. Simcoe Papers (61-215).

28. [*Action at Spencer's Ordinary.*] Careful, unlabeled and incomplete manuscript 6⅞ by 7. Very similar to preceding, but provision for labeling below. Colonial Williamsburg. Simcoe

Papers (61-214).

29. [*Action at Spencer's Ordinary.*] Careful, unlabeled and incomplete manuscript nearly identical in size and description to preceding. Colonial Williamsburg. Simcoe Papers (61-213).

30. *Ambuscade of the Indians at Kingsbridge August 31st. 1781.* Careful, colored manuscript 7¾ by 6. References A through I in a rectangular cartouche in upper left. In lower left "from a sketch by Lieut. Colo. Simcoe, taken on the spot, copy G. Spencer Lt. Qs Rs." Huntington Library.

31. [*Simcoe's Position at Oyster Bay*] *Long Island, New York.* Careful colored manuscript showing location of the redoubt, 7½ by 5¾. References A through H below. Huntington Library.

32. *Retreat from Generals Clinton and Morgan.* Careful manuscript 7⅞ by 5¾. References A through F in a rectangular cartouche in upper left. In lower left "by Lt. C. Simcoe" and below "From a Sketch by Lieut. Colo. Simcoe, taken on the Spot. Copy G. Spencer Lt. Qs Rs." Huntington Library.

33. *March of the Queen's Rangers, Emmerick's Corps, the Cavelry of the Legion under Lt. Col. Tarleton, and a Detachment of the Yagers; The whole commanded by Lt. Coll. Simcoe; to surprise a Corps of Rebel (Light) Troops under Col. Gist.* Careful, colored manuscript 8 by 6. References A through H below. Huntington Library.

34. [*Nine small scale maps, action at Osburns, landing at Burrells, Skirmish at Richmond, Skirmish at Crosswicks, Action at Spencers, Route of the Queens Rangers, Ambuscade of the Indians at Kingsbridge, Point York, and the Affair at Quintons Bridge.*] All on one sheet of careful manuscript 9½ by 7. Colonial Williamsburg. Simcoe Papers (61-221).

107. GEORGE SPROULE

Sproule was born on Long Island about 1741. He was an ensign in the 59th. Regiment, serving under Samuel Holland in 1767 in eastern Canada. There, he made surveys of Cape Breton Island and Louisbourg (Clements Library, Brun 28, 34, 35). He acted as Holland's assistant after the death of Haldimand, and became a lieutenant in the 16th Foot by 1778.

Sproule supervised engineering projects about New York, including the works at "Morris House" 6 October 1779. His report on the works on Staten Island was forwarded in a letter from Alexander Mercer to DeLancey, dated 9 December 1780. Sproule subsequently settled in Fredericton, New Brunswick, served on the council, and became surveyor general of the province. He died there in 1817.

1. *A Plan of the Sea Coast from Pemaquid River to Bens River in Edgemoggia Reach including St. Georges and Penobscot Rivers Deer Island Isle Haute the Fox and Long Islands with all the other Rivers and Islands also Bays Harbours &c in that extent Surveyed agreeably to the Order and Instructions of the Right Honorable the Lords Commissioners for Trade and Plantations to Samuel Holland Esqr. His Majestys Surveyor General of Lands for the Northern District of North America by Ensign George Sproule of his Majestys 59th. Regt. of Foot and Mr. James Grant Deputy Surveyors of Said District.* A magnificent survey on the scale of ¾ mile to an inch, 62 by 91. Title and scale in upper left corner. Shows soundings close to the shore, and in some of the bays. Hydrographic Department, Taunton.

2. *A Plan of . Rhode Island with the Adjacent Islands and Shores Surveyed in the Year 1774 Under the Direction of Samuel Holland Esqr. Surveyor General &c.* A careful, colored manuscript 47¾ by 38½. Soundings are shown. Descriptive title in upper left. In lower right is "George Sproule Lieut 16 Foot." Duke of Northumberland Collection, Alnwick.

3. *A Survey of the defile and that part of York Island adjacent to Fort Knyphausen surveyed and drawn by Lieut. George Sproule of the 16th. Regt. of Foot assist engineer. Surveyed in November

1778. Alexr. Mercer, commg. engineer.* A careful, colored manuscript 29¾ by 18. Descriptive title in upper left. Clements Library, Brun 447.

4. *British Fortifications on Staten Island December 9, 1780 By George Sproule.* Careful manuscript sections of redoubts, with a report on the works, 5 by 9½, addressed to Capt. Mercer. Clements Library, Brun 330.

5. *A Plan of the environs of Brooklyn showing the position of the Rebel Lines and defences on the 27th. of August 1776. Drawn by Lieut: Geo Sproule of the 16th. Regimt. of Foot assist. engineer. From a survey made by him in September 1776. Drawn in March 1781.* A careful, finished, colored manuscript of the American lines, and of later British lines, 18⅜ by 23. Clements Library, Brun 420.

6. *A Plan of...Part of Long Island....* See Wheeler map no. 7.

7. *A Plan of the Sea Coast of the Province of Massachusetts Bay....* See Wheeler map no. 5. Also in *The Atlantic Neptune.*

8. *A Sketch of the Environs of Charlestown in South Carolina.* Incomplete engraved proof, in colors, 21½ by 15½. In lower right "by Captain Geo. Sproule Assist. Engineer on the Spot, Published 1st. June 1780." Library of Congress. Faden Collection no. 48. Also in *The Atlantic Neptune.*

108. JAMES STRATON

Straton, sometimes spelled Stratton, was commissioned as ensign in the Engineers in February 1775. He was in Rhode Island, with the rank of lieutenant, then served in the New York area from 1777 to 1780. A letter to Sir Henry Clinton dated 6 September 1777 reports the work being carried out on Fort Independence and at Kingsbridge. Straton's name is included in returns, or mentioned in correspondence, in the New York area as late as February 1780. He served in Virginia as early as January 1781, to 1783. Straton returned to England, serving as commanding engineer at Chester, still with the rank of lieutenant. He was promoted eventually to major in 1797. His name disappears from the Army List after 1801.

1. *Plan of an intrenched guard house at the north end of Howlands Neck June 1777. J. Straton lt. of engineers.* Finished, colored manuscript 8¾ by 15½, with inset. Clements Library. Brun 293.

2. *Plan of Portsmouth on Elizabeth River from an exact survey made ye. 21st. January 1781. By James Straton, 2nd. lt. of engineers.* Finished, colored manuscript 19¼ by 24. Enclosed in the letter from Benedict Arnold to Sir Henry Clinton, 23 January 1781. Clements Library. Brun 575.

3. *Plan of the Post at Great Bridge, on the South Branch of the Elizabeth River, Virginia, Established the 5th. February 1781.* Finished, colored manuscript 11⅜ by 16⅜. In lower left "James Straton, Royal Engineer, October 1788." Library of Congress. G3701 S3314 1788 S8.

4. *A Plan of Portsmouth Harbour in the Province of Virginia shewing the Works erected by the British Forces for its Defence 1783.* Finished, colored manuscript 24¾ by 36. In lower right corner "Copied from the Original of Lieut. Stratton Engineer 1782." Library of Congress. Faden Collection no. 92.

5. *Plan of Yorktown and Gloucester in Virginia Shewing the Works constructed for the Defence of those Posts by the Rt. Honbl. Lieut. General Earl Cornwallis with the Attacks of the Combined Army of French and Rebels under the Command of the Generals Count de Rochambaud and Washington which Capitulated October 1781.* Careful, colored manuscript 23 by 35½. Library of Congress. Faden Collection no. 91.

109. JOHN STUART

Stuart, son of a merchant, was born in Scotland in 1718. He established himself as a Charleston merchant about 1748, having re-

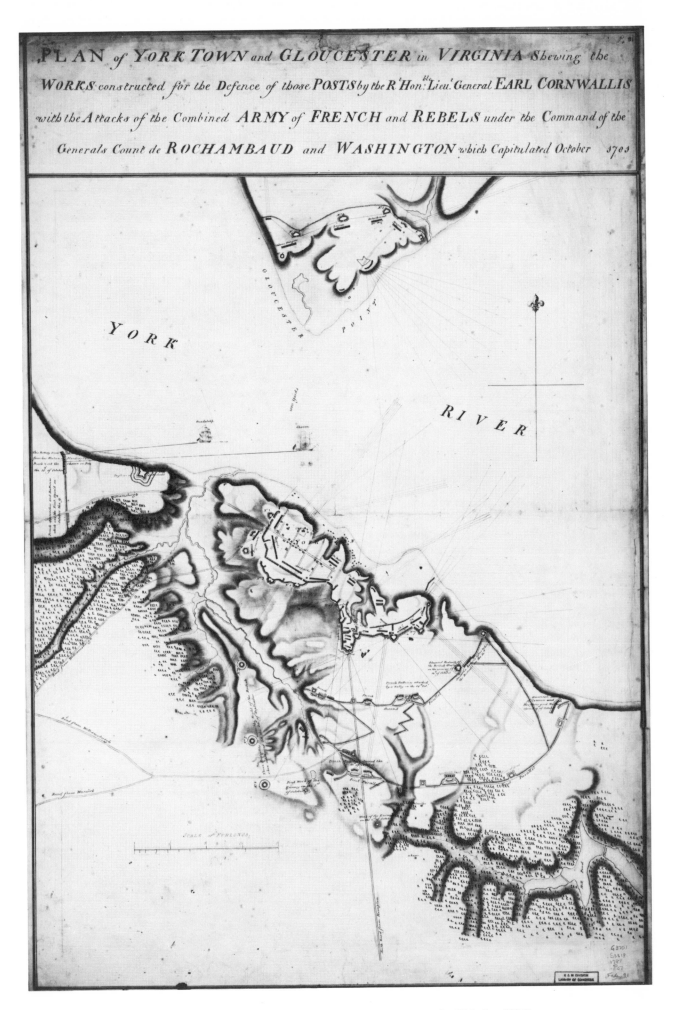

James Straton's plan of Yorktown at surrender October 19, 1781. See 108/5.

45

tired from the sea following the lucrative circumnavigation with George Anson. He may also have been associated with General Oglethorp's Georgia venture.

Mercantile activities being unsuccessful, Stuart turned to arms as a captain in the South Carolina Militia in the war against the Cherokees. He proved a success as soldier and Indian negotiator. Captured at Fort Loudun in 1760, he was saved by the intercession of Chief Little Carpenter, giving Stuart access to the principal Indian leader.

Edward Atkin, superintendent of Indian affairs, died in 1761. Stuart was appointed his successor, although Crown confirmation was delayed. He remained the dominant figure in Indian affairs in the south east until the Revolution. A great deal of mapping activity was carried out in his office, under his supervision. The accurate coast surveys of Romans, de Brahm, and Gauld were employed, the prominent features of the interior being added from the surveys of David Taitt and Savery. Stuart fled to St. Augustine at the start of the Revolution, maintaining control of Indian warfare against the Georgia settlers from there and from Pensacola. He died in 1779.

1. *A Map of South Carolina and a part of Georgia, containing the Whole Sea-Coast...compiled from surveys taken by the Hon. William Bull, Captain Gascoign, Hugh Bryan, and especially William DeBrahm. Republished with considerable additions from the surveys made & collected by John Stuart. London: Wm. Faden 1780.* Printed map 51 by 46½, dated London, June 1, 1780. A republication of Thomas Jefferys' map of 1757.

110. ALEXANDER SUTHERLAND

Sutherland was commissioned ensign in the Engineers in 1770, and was promoted to lieutenant in October 1775. On 1 April 1777, Sutherland completed the defenses at Billingsport on the Delaware River. On 11 June 1777, he was stationed at New Brunswick, N.J. In a letter to General Cornwallis dated 25 July 1781, Sutherland outlined his recommendations for the defense and fortification of the Hampton Roads area of Virginia. He was the author or recipient of several letters in December 1781 in reference to entrenching tools for use in eastern Virginia. He was the chief engineering officer at Gloucester, and was captured in the capitulation of Yorktown.

Sutherland was promoted to captain in 1784 and served in Quebec. He served with distinction in the expedition to Holland in 1793. He led the British column at Valenciennes, and was killed in the Battle of Lannoy in the same year. A namesake, Capt. Alexander Sutherland, commanded the sloop of war *VULTURE* in New York waters in 1779 and 1780.

1. *The British works at Yorktown and Gloucester. By Alexander Sutherland.* Unfinished manuscript 10½ by 15¾. Clements Library. Brun 567.

2. *Sketch of the posts of Yorktown and Gloucester Point Shewing the French and Rebel attacks upon the former in October 1781. Lieut. Sutherland engineer.* Finished, colored manuscript 18 by 25½. Clements Library. Brun 585.

111. BANASTRE TARLETON

Tarleton was born in Liverpool in 1754, son of a wealthy merchant. Educated at Oxford, he entered the Dragoon Guards as cornet in 1775. Tarleton took part in Clinton's expedition against Charleston, then served in the New York-New Jersey area. Here he aided in the capture of General Charles Lee. His aggressive leadership earned him the command of the British Legion, a corps of partisan raiders, with the rank of lieutenant colonel. His later operations were principally in the South, where he distinguished himself as an alert, dashing, vindictive, and occasionally unsuccessful, cavalry leader. He was captured at Yorktown and paroled

to England. After the war, Tarleton's attempt to enter politics was temporarily successful, but he returned to the Army in 1790 as a colonel, serving in Portugal, then Ireland. He died in 1833.

1. *From the Croton River to the Long Island Sound Shore. By: Sir Banastre Tarleton.* Manuscript sketch map 20¾ by 11⅝. Clements Library. Brun 348.

112. GEORGE TAYLOR

Taylor, a Scottish land surveyor, had strong associations with Aberdeen. He may have been the son or grandson of William Taylor who had surveyed in the north-east of Scotland between 1755 and 1766. Taylor made surveys for the Gordon estates in the north-east, a plan of Aberdeen in 1773, maps of the roads of North Britain in 1776, a map of Perth in 1777, and road maps of Ireland. He was either recruited, or volunteered, to serve in North America, where he was commissioned as a captain of Guides. Here, he was the dominant member of a team with Andrew Skinner, another Scots land surveyor, and a previous and subsequent partner. Their service in America lasted less than one year. Taylor's later work was in Ireland, where he surveyed the County of Leath in 1778, and made a chart of Holyhead in 1807.

1. *A Map of the pass, at Jamaica Long Island surveyed by order of His Excellency General Sir Henry Clinton k.b. Commander in Chief of His Majesty's forces &ca. &ca. &ca. March-1782. By George Taylor Capt: of Guides.* Finished, colored manuscript 59¾ by 26⅝. Clements Library. Brun 377.

2. *A Map of the country adjacent to Kings-bridge surveyed by order of His Excellency General Sir Henry Clinton k.b. Commander in chief of His Majestys forces &ca, &ca, &ca. 1781. Surveyed & drawn by Andw Skinner and George Taylor.* Finished, colored manuscript 44⅝ by 32¼. Clements Library. Brun 374.

3. *A Map of New York & Staten Islds And Part of Long Island Surveyed by Order of His Excellency General Sir Henry Clinton K.B. Commander in Chief of His Majesty's Forces &c &c.* Careful, colored manuscript 38½ by 26¼. In lower left "Surveyed and Drawn by George Taylor & Andw. Skinner, surveyors to his Excellency The Commander in Chief." British Museum. Crown Collection CXXI34.

4. *A Map of New York & Staten Islds And Part of Long Island Surveyed by George Taylor & Andw. Skinner.* Careful, colored manuscript 54½ by 26⅜. Somewhat less finished than the preceding. Public Record Office. MR954.

5. *Plan of New York and Staten Islands with part of Long Island Survey'd in the Years 1781 & 82. By George Taylor & Andrew Skinner.* Partially completed manuscript 54 by 31¾. Library of Congress. G3804 N4A1 1782 P5.

113. RICHARD TAYLOR

1. *Delaware River from Capt. Hamond.* Careful, colored manuscript 44 by 20¾. In lower right "Drawn by Richard Taylor For Capt. Jann. Philadelphia." Library of Congress. Howe Collection no. 13.

114. WILLIAM TINLING

Tinling, whose name appears in the Army Lists sometimes as Tingling or Finling, served in expeditions during Burgoyne's campaign up Lake Champlain, as an ensign in the 29th. Regiment of Foot. His date of rank, however, was 31 August 1780. The expeditions were commanded by Christopher Carleton, a major in the 29th, nephew of Sir Guy Carleton, and a daring, colorful leader in forest and border warfare.

Tinling was promoted lieutenant in October 1782, put on half-pay in 1783, but rejoined the regiment in 1784. Tinling, or a man of the same name, served in the 68th. Regiment of Foot, rejoined the 29th. Regiment, and retired in December 1790. He may also be the same man who served as paymaster of the 17th. Regiment of Foot, retired on Irish half-pay in 1802, and who was removed in 1808 for a reason other than death.

1. *Rough Sketch of the Country from Lake Champlain and the River Sorell extending to the Eastward as far as the River St. Francois and the Cohos on the Connecticut; Showing the march of 21 officers & canadians in October and November 1780 under the command of Lieutenant Colonel Carleton, in order to discover the road cut by the Rebels under the direction of Colonel Hazen in the year 1778 & 1779. W. Tinling. ensn. 29th. Regt. For Major Carleton.* Colored manuscript 18¼ by 22¼. Library of Congress. G3701 S31 1780 T5.

115. CHARLES VALLANCY

Vallancy was a Loyalist serving in the King's American Regiment and the Volunteers of Ireland.

1. *Sketch of the Battle of Camden Augt. 16, 1780 by C. Vallancy Lt. Vol. of Irel.* Rough sketch map 11⅜ by 9¾. Library of Congress. G3701 S3322 1780 V3.

2. *Sketch of the Battle of Hobkirks Hill, near Camden, on the 25th. of April, 1781. Drawn by C. Vallancy, Capt. of the Vols. of Ireland.* Printed map 11¾ by 17⅛. Wm. Faden. London. Aug. 1, 1783. The same map, with a few changes, was used in Steadman's American War.

116. THOMAS WHEELER

Ensign Wheeler is noted as employed as a draughtsman, in a return of Montresor dated 11 June 1777. He is again noted in the same capacity as "Thomas Wheeler, draughtsman," at a per diem of 5 shillings and again referred to as an ensign, serving in the capacity of extra draughtsman, attached to, or from, the 40th. Regiment, in a return of the Engineers dated 19 September 1778, made by Montresor. He was transferred from the Engineers to the staff of Sir William Howe on June 11, 1777.

1. *A Plan of Pisquataqua Harbour with its Branches, the town of Portsmouth, with its Environs, also, the Sea Coast, the Isles of Shoals, &c Surveyed by Mr. Thomas Grant, a Deputy Surveyor of Lands, for the Northern District of North America, under the Directions of Samuel Holland, Esqr. Surveyor General of the Same.* Careful, colored manuscript 37½ by 24¾. Descriptive title in upper left beneath "No. 2." The latitude of William Pepperell's house is indicated in the lower right as 43 3'0". Soundings are indicated. In lower right "Drawn by T. Wheeler." Hydrographic Department Library, Taunton A9451.

2. *A Plan of the Sea Coast from Falmouth in Casco Bay to the Light House near New Port in Rhode Island Including the Province of New Hampshire With its Several Townships &c also Nantucket Marthas Vinyard and the Elizabeth Islands surveyed agreeably to the Orders and Instructions Of The Right Honourable the Lords Commissioners for Trade and Plantations to Samuel Holland Esqr. Surveyor General of Lands For The Northern District of North America with the Assistance of the Gentlemen his Deputys.* Careful, colored manuscript, 71 by 142. Descriptive title in upper right. Hydrographic Department Library, Taunton A7353.

3. [*Gouldsborough Bay to Cape Elizabeth Maine.*] Careful, colored manuscript on numerous small sheets which have been joined or superimposed to form a somewhat irregular sheet 59 by 32. Hydrographic Department Library, Taunton A9450.

4. *A Plan of the Bay and Harbor of Boston Surveyed Agreeably to the Orders and Instructions of the Right Honorable the Lords Commissioners For Trade and Plantations Samuel Holland Esqr. His Majestys Surveyor General of Lands for the Northern District of North America By Messrs. Wheeler and Grant.* Careful colored manuscript with soundings, 47½ by 43½. Hydrographic Department Library, Taunton A9453.

5. *A Plan of the Bay and Harbor of Boston, surveyed agreeably to the orders and instructions of the Right Honorable the Lords Commissioners for Trade and Plantations. By Messrs Wheeler and Grant.* Careful colored manuscript with soundings, 21⅜ by 23. Library of Congress, G3764 B6 P55 1775 W5.

6. *A Plan of the Sea Coast of the Province of Massachusetts Bay including part of Merrimack River with Nantucket, Martha's Vinyard and the Elizabeth Island & also the Colony of Rhode Island to the Narragansett Shore opposite the Light House near New Port, surveyed agreeably to the Orders and Instructions of the Right Honorable the Lords Commissioners for Trade and Plantations to Samuel Holland Esqr., His Majestys Surveyor General of Lands for the Northern District of North America by Messrs. Geo. Sproule, Chas. Blaskowitz, Ja. Grant and Thos. Wheeler, his deputies.* Careful, colored manuscript 105 by 216. Hydrographic Department Library, Taunton 9.

7. *Narragansett Bay and the Surrounding Shores, By. T. Wheeler.* Careful, colored manuscript 40 by 29¼, with many soundings. Clements Library, Brun 275.

8. *A Plan of That Part of Long Island Which Lyes between Flatbush and Brookland Ferry Including the Rebel Works from Red Hook to Remsens Mills Surveyed by the Following Gentlemen Lieuts. Pitts, Parker, Bendyshe, Forth, Sproule, Messrs. Dixon and Wheeler under the Direction of Major Dixon Chief Engineer in America.* Careful, colored manuscript 18¼ by 27¼. In right lower corner "Drawn by Thos. Wheeler." Auction Catalog, October 20, 1970.

9. *Part of the City of New York 27th; Augt:1778 Part of Long Island. Drawn by Thos: Wheeler.* Careful, colored manuscript, 22¼ by 28¼. Clements Library, Brun 390.

10. *A Plan of the Attacks Against Fort Mifflin on Mud Island Which Surrendered 16th. November 1777 to the King's Troops Under The Command of the Honorable Sir William Howe, K.B. General and Commander in Chief &c. &c. &c.* Careful, detailed, colored manuscript. Library of Congress. See also under Blaskowitz and under Grant.

117. GEORGE WIGHTMAN

Wightman, or Whiteman, was a lieutenant colonel of the Loyal New Englanders. Three others of the same name were Loyalists. Wightman was the author of three letters in 1779 to 1781 relating to the embarkation of his Loyalist unit, an accurate description of western Rhode Island, and an intelligence report of the French troops in Rhode Island.

1. *A draft of Nererganset Shore from the entrance to the mouth of Potewomet River northward and from the Nererganset Bay to the post rode westward in length about 17 milds in the widest place three milds from the end of Boston Neck to the South Ferey 4 milds from South Ferey to north 2 milds to Updikes Harbor 4 milds across 1 mild from Quaneet to Quitneset Harbor 3 mildes from Calf Paster Pint to Pore Jack Pint 3 milds George Wightman.* Sketch map 12⅝ by 7½. Clements Library. Brun 271.

118. WILLIAM CUMBERLAND WILKINSON

Wilkinson was appointed a lieutenant in the 62nd. Regiment of Foot 1 May 1775. Acting as assistant engineer, he accompanied his regiment in the Burgoyne expedition. He was promoted to captain on 30 October 1782. His name was removed from the Army List about May 1786.

1. *The Encampment & Position of the Army Under His Excy. Lt. Gl. Burgoyne At Swords and Freemans Farms On Hudsons River near Stillwater 1777.* Finished, colored manuscript 43 by 26¾. In

lower left "Wm. Cumb. Wilkinson Lt. 62nd. Regt. Asst. Engineer." Overlay of the first and second position of 19 September, of the third and fourth position, and of the status of 8th. October. Library of Congress. Faden Collection no. 69a.

2. *Plan of the Encampment and Position of the Army under His Excelly. Lt. General Burgoyne at Swords House on Hudson's River near Stillwater on Septr. 17th. with the Positions of that part of the Army engaged on the 19th. Septr. 1777 Drawn by W. C. Wilkinson Lt. 62nd. Regt. Asst. Engr. Engraved by Wm. Faden. Feb. 1st. 1780.* Printed map 13¼ by 12½. Engraved proof. Library of Congress. Faden Collection no. 68.

3. Same as the previous with title omitted. Printed proof, earlier state than no. 68. Library of Congress. Faden Collection no. 68a.

4. Same as the previous with title omitted. Printed proof, same as 2, without title. Library of Congress. Faden Collection no. 69.

5. *Plan of the Encampment and Position of the Army under His Excelly. Lt. General Burgoyne at Swords House on Hudson's River near Stillwater on Septr. 17th with the Positions of that part of the Army engaged on the 19th Septr. 1777 Drawn by W. C. Wilkinson Lt. 62d. Regt. Asst. Engr.* Engraved by Wm. Faden. Printed map 13¼ by 12½. Overlay in upper right. Feb. 1st. 1780.

6. *Plan of the Encampment and Position of the Army under his Excelly. General Burgoyne at Braemus Heights on Hudson's River near Stillwater, on the 20th. September with the position of the Detachment & c. in the Action on the 7th of Octr. & the Position of the Army on the 8th Octr. 1777. Drawn by W. C. Wilkinson Lt. 62 Regt. Asst. Engr.* Engraved by William Faden. Printed map 13¼ by 12¼. Feb. 1st. 1780. Both printed maps were included in various editions of *A State of the Expedition From Canada As Laid Before The House of Commons By Lieutenant-General Burgoyne....;* and in Faden's *Atlas of the Battles of the American Revolution.*

119. JOHN WILLIAMS

Williams was a New Jersey land surveyor who flourished between 1757 and 1764. He was the author, or co-author, of surveys of timberlands in present Monmouth and Ocean Counties, and in Morris County. He is cited as a source of data for Hills' map 34.

120. RICHARD WILLIAMS

Williams was appointed second lieutenant in the 23rd. Regiment of Foot, or Royal Welsh Fusiliers 17 August 1768, and promoted first lieutenant 13 May 1773. The Regimental Muster Book shows that he was absent with the "King's Leave" on 24 January 1775. On 11 April 1775, he was transferred from Lt. Col. Bernard's Company to that of Captain Horsfall. When the Regiment mustered at Boston 29 January 1776, he was on the sick list. An accomplished amateur artist, he made a fine panoramic rendering of the area surrounding Boston, which is in the Crown Collection in the Map Room of the British Museum. He retired 20 May 1776, and died later that year.

1. *Plan of the Heights of Charlestown & c. R.W., Lieut RWF.* Careful manuscript 14⅛ by 8¾, after the British had established an encampment. Library of Congress. Faden Collection no. 29.

121. JOHN WILSON

In May 1778, Wilson, a volunteer in the 71st. Regiment was ordered to duty as an assistant engineer. In a series of letters in 1781, he indicated his interest in obtaining a company in the 71st., or Fraser's Highlanders; rejected a plan to go into the Engineers because of the poor prospects for promotion; and finally decided to accept. Wilson's name appears in the Army List of 1781 as a practitioner engineer and second lieutenant to date from 24

January 1781. Other records appear to relate to different men of the same name.

1. *Plan of the Town of Savannah Shewing the Works Constructed for its Defence also, the Approaches and Batteries of the Enemy Together with the Joint Attack of the French & Rebels on the 9th. October 1779 from a Survey by John Wilson 71st. Regt Asst. Engineer.* Finished, careful, colored manuscript 37¾ by 28¼. James Moncrief's name is noted in references as the commanding engineer. British Museum. Royal United Services Institution Collection A30/67.

2. *Plan of the town of Savannah, with the Works constructed for its Defence; together with the Approaches & Batteries of the Enemy, and the joint attack of the French and Rebels on the 9th. of October 1779. From a survey by John Wilson 71st: Regt. asst. Engineer.* Finished, careful, colored manuscript 28⅞ by 38. Signature of James Moncrief in right lower corner. Clements Library. Brun 637.

3. *Plan of the decent and action of the 29th. Decr. 1778, near the town of Savannah: by His Majestys Forces under the command of Lt. Colol. Campbell of the 71st. Regt. foot. John Wilson assist. engineer.* Finished, colored manuscript 27¾ by 18¼. Clements Library. Brun 636.

4. *Plan of the Siege of Savannah And the Defeat of the French and Rebels on the 9th. Oct. 1779 By His Majesty's Forces under the Command of Major General Augustin Prevost Surveyed by John Wilson As Engineer.* Photograph 10¼ by 6½, in the map room of the New York Public Library. Location of the original is unknown.

5. See Andre map 46.

The chart of the Coast of South Carolina and Georgia in some copies of J. F. W. Des Barres' *The Atlantic Neptune* has an inset Plan of the Siege of Savannah as surveyed by John Wilson.

122. THOMAS WRIGHT

Deputy surveyor under Samuel Holland. See Wm. Faden nos. 3,4.

Three-pointed dividers, 18th century, used in spherical or plane plotting. The Adler Planetarium and Astronomical Museum.

ANONYMOUS MANUSCRIPT MAPS

Arranged Geographically

The anonymous maps listed here are identified as of the Revolutionary War period, with varying degrees of reliability. A number of them are dated, and are of obvious British or Loyalist origin. Others have been identified on tenuous grounds, and may precede the Revolution.

123. NORTH AMERICA

1. *A Map of North America from Blair 1775.* Careful, colored manuscript 22⅛ by 16, extending from Newfoundland to East Texas and Central Florida. Probably based upon John Blair, F.R.S. Duke of Northumberland Collection, Alnwick.

124. QUEBEC

1. *Plan of the City and Environs of Quebec with its Siege and Blockade by the Americans from the 8th. December 1775 to the 13th. of May 1776.* Careful, elaborate, colored manuscript 27½ by 17¾. Faden collection no. 20. Library of Congress.
2. *Sketch of the Review of the 5th., 26th., 29th., 37th., & 34th. Regts and part of the 1st. Batt. of Royal Artill. on the Plains of Abraham, Aug. 29, 1781 in presence of Prince William Henry.* Careful, colored manuscript 27¾ by 20¾. Faden collection no. 23. Library of Congress.

125. MAINE

1. *Sketch of Different Passes into Canada from our lower Provinces.* Manuscript 11 by 6½. A note at bottom "Arnold's pass is marked." Clements Library. Brun 142.
2. [*Mouth of the Penobscot River*] *Battle of Castine Bay.* Careful manuscript 12¾ by 15¼. Massachusetts Historical Society. IVa 2.2.
3. *Penobscot River and Bay with the operations of the English Fleet, under Sir George Collyer, against the Division of Massachusetts troops operating against Fort Castine August 1779 with full soundings up to the present site of Bangor.* Manuscript 57 by 18. Location of the fort may be in error. Faden collection no. 101. Library of Congress.
4. *The Coastline from Passamaquoddy Bay to the Mouth of the Kennebec River.* Careful manuscript 32¼ by 16. Looks much like the work of Holland and his deputies. Public Record Office. (C.O. 217/54) MPG 216.

126. NEW HAMPSHIRE

1. *The River Mouth showing New Castle, Portsmouth, adjoining creeks and islands.* Careful, colored manuscript 23 by 18½. Looks much like the work of Holland and his deputies. Public Record Office. C.O. 700 N.H. 6.
2. *Plan of a Road from New Hampshire to Canada.* [*Carrying place between the Connecticut and St. Francis Rivers.*] Careful, finished manuscript 12 by 36. Enclosed, Governor J. Wentworth No. 57, 22 April 1774. Public Record Office. (CO5/93op587) MPG1012.

127. MASSACHUSETTS

1. *A Plan of the Sea Coast from Boston Bay to the Light House near Rhode Island Reduced from the Large Surveys to a Scale of Four Statute Miles to one inch.* Careful, colored, finished manuscript 23⅜ by 25½. Looks like the work of Holland's deputies. Library of Congress. G3762 C6 1775 P5.
2. *The Town, Harbour, and Environs of Boston beleagued by the Americans in 1775.* Careful, colored manuscript 12½ by 15¾. Positions "after the 17th. of June." John Carter Brown Library.
3. [*Boston Area.*] Careful, colored manuscript 40¼ by 27½. Prior to fortification of Dorchester by the Americans. Removed from 78/1850. Public Record Office. MPHH 268.
4. [*Boston Area.*] Rough sketch 7¾ by 8¼. The King's Army put at 8000 and the Continental Army at 20,000. Massachusetts Historical Society. Ic4.
5. [*Boston and Surrounding Areas.*] Careful manuscript 16¾ by 13½, lines and fortifications, table of distances, and references. "taken Novr. 28, 1775." Massachusetts Historical Society. Ic3.2.
6. *Plan of the Town of Boston and the Circumjacent Country Shewing the present situation of the Kings Troops & the Rebels Intrenchments 25th. July 1775. The Yellow shews the Rebels Intrenchments.* Careful, detailed colored manuscript 17 by 16¾. New York Public Library, Manuscript Collection.
7. *A Plan of Boston and it's Environs shewing the true Situation of His Majesty's Troops, and also those of the Rebels, likewise, all the Forts, Redouts and Entrenchments erected by both Armies. Drawn by an Engineer at Boston.* Careful, detailed, colored manuscript 25½ by 18. British Museum. Add.Ms. 15,535.5.
8. [*Boston and Enviorns.*] Good, somewhat rough manuscript 18¾ by 17¼. In lower right "No. 25." Library of Congress. G4056 B65 1775 B6.
9. [*Boston Area Roads.*] Careful, finished, colored manuscript of roads Roxbury, Concord, Brookline, Menotomy, 20⅜ by 44⅝. Library of Congress. G3761 P2 1775 R6.
10. [*Boston Area Roads.*] Unfinished, part colored manuscript of roads, Charleston, Cambridge, Brookline, Jamaica Plain, 62¼ by 27⅝, irregular. Duke of Northumberland Collection, Alnwick.
11. [*Boston Area Roads.*] Rough manuscript of roads, Cambridge, Medford, Menotomy, 23¾ by 15. Duke of Northumberland Collection, Alnwick.
12. *A Plan of the Town and Harbour of Boston And the Country Adjacent with the Road from Boston to Concord showing the Place of the late Engagement between the King's Troops & the Provincials, together with the Several Encampments of both Armies in and about Boston 19th. April 1775.* Finished, somewhat schematic manuscript 12 by 7⅝. Duke of Northumberland Collection, Alnwick.
13. [*Boston Harbor.*] Rough, unlabeled manuscript 21¼ by 18½. Library of Congress. Faden Collection no. 36.
14. [*Boston Harbor.*] Finished, colored manuscript 12½ by 15. Position of the French fleet shown. Clements Library. Brun 177.
15. [*Boston Harbor.*] Finished manuscript 12½ by 15⅛, nearly identical with 14. Clements Library. Brun 178.
16. [*Boston Harbor.*] Careful manuscript 20½ by 28¼, western half is missing. New York Public Library, Manuscript Collection.
17. [*Boston Harbor.*] Careful but unfinished manuscript 10½ by 13. Library of Congress. G4056 B65 1775 B61.
18. *A Plan of the Town of Boston 1775.* Fine street map, garrison area is noted. Duke of Northumberland Collection, Alnwick.
19. *Fort on Fort Hill in Boston.* Careful colored manuscript 18¾ by 13½. Maps 36, 38, 39, 41 and 42. by the same hand. Library of Congress. G 4056 B65F6 1776 F6.
20. [*Fort on Beacon Hill.*] Careful colored manuscript of stone redout for Beacon Hill 8½ by 9. Clements Library. Brun 232.
21. *A Plan of Boston Advanced Lines 1775.* Careful, colored manuscript 13⅛ and 13⅝, similar to 18. Duke of Northum-

berland Collection, Alnwick.

22. *A Temporary Project for a Star Redout to contain 150 men on Boston Neck.* Rough manuscript 13¼ by 8. Library of Congress. G4056 B65 1778 T4.

23. *Boston S west part.* Somewhat rough manuscript of the neck and fortifications 12⅝ by 15¼. Library of Congress. G4056 B65 1775 B62.

24. *A Plan of the British Lines on Boston Neck in August 1775.* Careful manuscript 9 by 11½. Library of Congress. Faden Collection no. 37.

25. *South west part of Boston and the Neck.* Rough manuscript 15¾ by 12½. Library of Congress. G3701 S3142 1775 B6.

26. [*Boston Neck.*] Unfinished manuscript 13⅜ by 9½, showing fortifications. Clements Library. Brun 176.

27. [*Boston Neck.*] Careful, colored manuscript 10⅜ by 16⅝, carefully calculated distances. Library of Congress. G4056 B65 1775 P5.

28. [*Boston Neck.*] Careful colored manuscript 16⅝ by 10½, carefully calculated distances. Library of Congress. G3701 S3142 1775 P5.

29. *Plan of Battle of Bunker Hill. Operations on the 17th. June 1775 against Intrenchments & Redoubts on Charlestown Hill By The Rebel forces To Which is Added the Position of the New Fort on Bunkers Hill (400 ft by 75 ft). Completed in September. Details of Land Forces Engaged.* Facsimile 7¼ by 5¾, from auction catalog-lot 392, B.F. Stevens, September 11, 1923. Signed in lower right by H. Clinton, Maj. Gen.

30. *Major Gen. Howe's Encampment on Bunker's Hill at Charles T. June 1775.* Rough sketch map 11¾ by 8. Photostat. Library of Congress.

31. [*Battle of Bunker Hill.*] Rough, accurate, unfinished manuscript 21⅞ by 17¼. British fortifications not complete. Library of Congress. G4056 C55 1775 P51.

32. *Plan of Charles-Town with the Entrenchments and Encampments of his Majesty's Troops after the Action of the 17th. of June 1775.* Careful manuscript 19¾ by 13¼, labeled in cursive. Reminiscent of Montresor. Library of Congress. Faden Collection no. 28.

33. *A Sketch of the Peninsula of Charles-Town with Gen: Howes Intrenchments and the Rebels Redoubt.* Careful, colored manuscript 10¼ by 8¾. Duke of Northumberland Collection, Alnwick.

34. [*Charlestown.*] Rough, untitled manuscript 17¼ by 14½, in color. Reminiscent of Montresor. Library of Congress. Faden Collection no. 27.

35. *Sketch of the Ground about Charles Town.* Careful, colored manuscript 17¼ by 11¼. Library of Congress. G4056 C55 1775 S55.

36. *Fort of Charlestown Point.* Finished, colored manuscript 16⅜ by 12⅜. In same hand as maps 19, 39, 40, 42 and 43. Library of Congress.

37. *A Sketch of Charlestown Neck & c. & c.* Finished, colored manuscript 19¾ by 13½. Initialed "A.F." or "A.S." Duke of Northumberland Collection, Alnwick.

38. [*Dorchester Heights.*] Careful isometric manuscript 19¼ by 6. Library of Congress. G4056 D6 1776 V5.

39. *Fort on the First Hill in Dorchester. Fort on the Second Hill in Dorchester.* Finished, colored manuscript 20⅝ by 14. Same hand as maps 19, 36, 40, 42 and 43. Library of Congress. G4056 D6 1776 F61.

40. *Fort on Dorchester Point.* Finished, colored manuscript 15¾ by 12¼. Same hand as maps 19, 36, 38, 41 and 42. Library of Congress. G4056 D6 1776 F6.

41. *Dorchester Point copied from a actual survey.* Careful manuscript 7¼ by 8¾. Duke of Northumberland Collection, Alnwick.

42. *Plan of the Rebels Works on Prospect-Hill. Plan of the Rebels Works on Winter-Hill.* Careful, colored manuscript 20½ by 14. In same hand as maps 19, 36, 39, 40 and 43. Library of Congress. G4056 S6 1775 P5.

43. *Fort on Noddles Island.* Finished, colored manuscript 20¼ by 13⅞. In same hand as 19, 36, 39, 40 and 42. Library of Congress.

128. RHODE ISLAND

1. *Harbor of Rhode Island & Narragansett Bay.* Fine, finished, colored manuscript with much detailed data. Irregular shape, overall 26½ by 36. British Museum. Royal United Services Institution Collection A 29/19.

2. *A draught of Rhode Island 1777.* Finished, colored manuscript 19½ by 38⅝. Clements Library. Brun 272.

3. *Attacks upon Rhode Island Augt 1778.* Careful, colored manuscript 21 by 14⅜. Library of Congress. Faden Collection no. 88.

4. *Plan of the position of His Majesty's troops at Rhode Island, after the defeat of the Rebels the 29th: of August 1778.* Finished, colored manuscript 11 by 18½. Clements Library. Brun 302.

5. *Plan of the Northern Part of Rhode Island.* Finished, careful, colored manuscript 25½ by 32¾. Detailed disposition of troops, defenses. Huntington Library. HM 15473.

6. *A Plan of the Adjacent Coast to the North Part of Rhode Island, to Express the Route of a Body of Troops, detached to Destroy the Rebel's Batteaux, Vessels; Store &c &c Accomplished May 25th 1778 Under the orders of Lt. Coll. J. Campbell, 22d Regt.* Careful, colored manuscript 13¼ by 16¾. Duke of Northumberland Collection, Alnwick.

7. *Seconnet Passage.* Sketch of the batteries, manuscript 16 by 12¾. Clements Library. Brun 314.

8. *Newport.* Unfinished manuscript 17 by 15¼, of town and fortifications. Clements Library. Brun 276.

9. *Plan of the Town of Newport, and the adjacent country: with a project for its defence (Nr 7).* Finished, colored manuscript 20½ by 21⅛. Clements Library. Brun 305.

10. *Providence and Newport.* Sketch map of defenses about the two, 12½ by 7⅞. Clements Library. Brun 310.

11. *Plan of an Intrenchment with Redouts, ordered by Major General Pigot, to be thrown up, for the defence of the town of Newport.* Finished, colored manuscript 18⅞ by 21¼. Clements Library. Brun 294.

12. *Plan of the North Battery, near Newport.* Finished, colored manuscript 17½ by 10. Clements Library. Brun 301.

13. *Redout No. 2 of the intrenchments for 68 men and 3 guns with a guard house and barrier. No. 12.* Finished, colored manuscript 20 by 20. Clements Library. Brun 313.

14. *Redout No. 3 of the intrenchments for 68 men and 3 guns with a guard house & barrier. No: 13.* Finished, colored manuscript 21½ by 12. Clements Library. Brun 312.

15. *Redout No. 5 of the intrenchments for 68 men and 3 guns with a guard house & barrier (Nr 14).* Finished, colored manuscript 21 by 12. Clements Library. Brun 311.

16. *Plan of a battery for six guns and a redout for one hundred men and two royals: erected upon Windmill Hill eight miles and a half N.N.E. of Newport. (Nr 3).* Finished, colored manuscript 21½ by 17⅜. Clements Library. Brun 284.

17. *Plan of a Barrack for 300 men, and officers, erected at Windmill Hill with an abbatis. December 1777. Plan Nr. 18.* Finished, colored manuscript 28 by 17¾. Clements Library. Brun 282.

18. *Plan of the works on Windmill Hill. December 31st. 1777. Plan nr 19.* Finished, colored manuscript 29½ by 22. Clements Library. Brun 306.

19. *Plan of a redout for 50 men & 4 guns, for the defence of Easton's Bar & the support of the right of the town lines (nr 8).* Finished, colored manuscript 15 by 21½. Clements Library. Brun 286.

20. *Plan of a redout for 57 men and 4 guns, inclosing Hubbards House (Nr 9).* Finished, colored manuscript 21 by 15. Clements Library. Brun 287.

21. *Plan of a redout for 28 men & 2 guns, for the defence of the pass at Howlands Bridge (Nr. 10).* Finished, colored manuscript 15

by 21¾. Clements Library. Brun 290.

22. *Plan of a redout for three guns en barbette inclosing a barrack for 96 men and officers erected at Burrington Hill, 8⅓ miles NE of Newport. (Nr: 15).* Finished, colored manuscript 15 by 21½. Clements Library. Brun 289.

23. *Plan of a redout for 3 guns and 30 men, erected October 1777 in Lopez's Bay, for the defence of the Seakonnet Passage, and of the coast from Little Sandy Point to Black Point. Plan Nr. 17.* Finished, colored manuscript 21¾ by 15. Clements Library. Brun 288.

24. *Plan of a battery for four guns, erected at Fogland for the defence of the Seakonnet Passage. Four miles to an (   ) half N. E. of Newport. (Nr. 4).* Finished, colored manuscript 15 by 19. Clements Library. Brun 283.

25. *Plan of a redout with barracks for 136 men and officers erected at Fogland for the support of the enclosed battery and pass.* Finished, colored manuscript 21 by 15. Clements Library. Brun 291.

26. *Plan of a redout with barracks for 136 men and officers erected at Fogland, for the support of the enclosed battery, and of the pass. (Nr 11).* Finished colored manuscript 21¾ by 15. Clements Library. Brun 292.

27. *Plan of Tomony-Hill Fort.* Finished, colored manuscript 18¼ by 11. Clements Library. Brun 308.

28. *Plan of ye South Battery.* Finished, colored manuscript 18 by 11¼. Clements Library. Brun 309.

29. *Plan of Bristol Ferry Fort.* Finished, colored manuscript 6¼ by 11. Clements Library. Brun 295.

30. *Plan of Bristol Ferry Fort, as it was December 8, 1776, and exhibiting the additions and alterations made to it since.* Finished, colored manuscript 15¼ by 21½. Clements Library. Brun 296.

31. *Plan of a redout erected at Connanicut 700 yards from East Ferry. 750 from west, defending the Isthmus of Beaver Tail, the North Causway, and the East Ferry for sixty eight men. (Nr. 6).* Finished colored manuscript, 15 by 21¾. Clements Library. Brun 285.

129. CONNECTICUT

1. [*British Raid on New London.*] Finished, colored manuscript 11½ by 15. Much detail, labeled in French. Dartmouth University Library. Scavenius Collection.

2. [*Fort Griswold.*] Manuscript sketch 7¾ by 9½. Library of Congress. Faden Collection no. 99.

3. *Gov. Tryon's expedition to Danbury, 1777.* Careful, colored manuscript 14½ by 18¼. Reminiscent of Montresor. Library of Congress. G3701 S3162 1777 G6.

130. NEW YORK

SHORE AND BAY

1. [*Approaches to New York Harbor.*] Outline manuscript 22 by 28, the shore from central New Jersey to Jamaica Bay, across central New Jersey. In W.O. 78/1848. Public Record Office. MPH571.

2. [*Disposition of British Fleet defending New York at Sandy Hook.*] Finished manuscript 9¾ by 17½, naming some vessels. Clements Library. Brun 436.

3. *A Chart of Sandy Hook Bar, the Entrance of Hudson's River; Shewing the Position of the British Fleet, under the Command of Admiral Lord How, and the Works Erected at Sandy Hook, for the Defence of the Light House; under the Command of General Charles O'Hara July 13th 1778.* Careful, detailed, colored manuscript 32¼ by 38½. In lower left "...d from the Original in the possession of John Hills Feb. 1813." National Archives.

4. *Disposition of the Force at New York to oppose the Entrance*

of a Superior Enemy. Careful manuscript 16½ by 9. Enclosed in Vice Admiral Arbuthnot 8 October 1779. (Adm. 1/486). Public Record Office. MPI100.

5. *Lord Howe's Position of Defence at Sandy Hook.* Careful manuscript 15⅝ by 9¼, all vessels identified. New York Public Library. Manuscript Division.

6. *Plan of the Narrows shewing, the channel, shoal, depth of water, and the several battery's proposed on each side to prevent an enemy's sailing up to New York.* Finished, colored manuscript 20½ by 29. Clements Library. Brun 423.

7. *Plan of The Narrows Shewing; The Channel, Shoal, depth of water, and several Battery's proposed on each side to prevent an Enemy's sailing up to New York.* Finished, colored manuscript 28⅝ by 19⅝. Library of Congress. G3701 S32161 1776 P5.

STATEN ISLAND

8. *Draft of the Watering Place, & Redouts Constructed to Defend It. 15th. July 1776.* Finished, colored manuscript 15 by 14¼. Clements Library. Brun 340.

9. [*Town of Richmond.*] Finished manuscript 8½ by 6½. Clements Library. Brun 427.

10. *Sketch, shewing the disposition of the batteries, on the right and left, of the Flagstaff Redout - Staten Island, 12th. July 1779.* Clements Library. Brun 443.

11. *Plan of the Redouts at Richmond on Staten Island 30th. October 1779.* Somewhat rough manuscript 12¾ by 15, labeled in cursive. Library of Congress. Faden Collection no. 97.

LONG ISLAND

12. *Plan Of the Attack the Rebels on Long Island by an Officer of the Army.* Careful, colored manuscript 13⅛ by 14¾. Library of Congress. Faden Collection no. 56.

13. *A Sketch of the Action on Long Island between the British & American Armies on th 26th & 27th. of Augst 1776 drawn on Montresors Plan.* Careful manuscript 10¼ by 13½. Huntington Library. HM15464.

14. [*Western Long Island.*] Manuscript 3¾ by 7¹¹/₁₆ of roads, with notes. Clements Library. Brun 364.

15. [*Southwestern Shore of Long Island.*] Unfinished manuscript 13 by 20⅛, shows site Fort George. Clements Library. Brun 396.

16. [*Eastern Long Island.*] Finished manuscript 12¾ by 17¾, including Gardiner's Bay. Clements Library. Brun 349.

17. [*Northeastern Long Island.*] Rough sketch 8 by 12½. Clements Library. Brun 385.

18. *A Sketch of Lloyd's Neck Particularly Shewing the Situation of the Redout, Encampment of the Troops, with the Ground Adjacent and position of the Advanced Picket's.* Finished, colored, detailed manuscript 17 by 20¾, of the Loyalist troops and dispositions. Clements Library. Brun 434.

THE NEW YORK CITY AREA AND ENVIRONS

19. [*New York and Environs.*] Northeast New Jersey and Southeast New York in careful but unfinished manuscript 23¾ by 65½. Extends from above present site of Kingston, N.Y. to Perth Amboy. Shows roads, mills and furnaces. Library of Congress. G3701 S321 1780 06.

20. *The Seat of Action Between the British and American Forces or an Authentic Plan of Staten Island with the Neighboring Counties including Amboy, New York, and the Western Part of Long Island &c. Also the course of Hudson's River from Courtland, the Great Magazine of the American Army to Sandy Hook, from the surveys of Major Holland.* Finished, colored manuscript 17¾ by 15½. Inset of the road between Amboy and Philadelphia. Similar to the engraved map by Sayer and Bennett

George Taylor and Andrew Skinner's 1781 manuscript map section of New York and environs. See 112/3.

dated 22 October 1776, for which this may be the model. Clements Library. Brun 429.

21. [*New York and Environs.*] Parts of the present Kings, Queens, Lower Westchester Counties, and Manhattan, in careful manuscript 20¾ by 28½, showing troops. British Museum. Additional Manuscripts 16, 367.

22. [*New York and Environs.*] Careful, colored, unfinished manuscript 23½ by 49. Hydrographic Department, Taunton. A9459.

23. [*New York and Environs.*] Careful, detailed manuscript 49 by 69, showing troops. Hydrographic Department, Taunton. L690.

24. [*New York and Environs.*] The present Bergen County, N.J., and Westchester County, N.Y., with Manhattan, in manuscript 12½ by 15½. Disposition of British troops, notation "Place where Col. Baylor was surprised" Sept. 28, 1778. Library of Congress. G3701 S322 1776 P6.

25. *Plan of New York and its environs, shewing the Lines projected and partly executed for its defence.* Careful, colored manuscript 52½ by 59, table of works in progress. Public Record Office. MR1140.

26. *New York and its environs, with a note attached locating the landing of troops.* Careful manuscript 9½ by 12. Public Record Office. PRO 30/29/5.

27. *A Topographical Sketch of New York & Adjacent Country 1776.* Somewhat rough, schematic, colored manuscript 22½ by 43. Reminiscent of Sauthier. Duke of Northumberland Collection.

28. *A Topographical Sketch of the Island of New York, with part of the Circumjacent Country.* November 1775. Careful, detailed, colored manuscript 34½ by 23. Clements Library. Brun 449.

29. [*British Troop Dispositions about New York.*] Manuscript 19 by 25¼, with troop strength indicated of July and August 1781. Clements Library. Brun 332.

30. [*British Troop Dispositions about New York.*] Manuscript 18¾ by 25½, almost identical with preceding, September 2nd. 1781. Clements Library. Brun 333.

31. *Plan of New York, Staten and Long Island.* Rough schematic manuscript 23½ by 28, locating troops and fortifications. Removed from W.O. 78/1849. Public Record Office. MPH572.

32. [*British Troop Dispositions about New York.*] Outline manuscript 15¾ by 12⅝, about 1781. Clements Library. Brun 331.

MANHATTAN ISLAND, AND IMMEDIATE AREA

33. [*Lower Manhattan.*] Uncompleted map 20 by 25¼ of almost same area as the Ratzen plan, (not the Ratzer plan). Original 31 references increased to 44 in manuscript. Library of Congress. Faden Collection no. 54.

34. *Ye commencement for draft of New York Island.* Unfinished manuscript 22½ by 20, of the Kip's Bay area. Clements Library. Brun 463.

35. *Land Holdings on Kip's Bay.* Finished, colored manuscript 16 by 18 of area of preceding map. Clements Library. Brun 363.

36. [*Manhattan Island and Adjacent Areas.*] Unfinished, unlabeled, careful manuscript 28 by 20½. British Museum. Additional Manuscripts 16, 3671.

37. *Plan No. 1, New York, Hudsons River &c &c.* Careful, detailed, colored manuscript 34½ by 121, of all fortifications. It is a topographical and historical encyclopedia of the area during the Revolution. A facsimile was produced by B.F. Stevens in 1900. In W.O./1105. Public Record Office. MR463.

38. [*Manhattan Island and Adjacent Area.*] Fragmentary, irregular manuscript 48 by 120 of approximately the same area as the preceding. In W.O. 78/1394. Public Record Office. MR590.

39. [*Part of Manhattan.*] Fragment of careful, detailed manuscript 40½ by 50¼, between Kip's Bay and McGowans Pass. New York Public Library, Manuscript Division.

40. *Sketch of the Hessian Attack on Fort Washington under General Knypheusen on the 16th.* November 1776. Rough but detailed manuscript 9½ by 13¾. Library of Congress. G3701 S2213 1776 S5.

41. *A Plan Of The Attack of Fort Washington now Fort Knyphausen and of the American Lines on New-York Island By The King's Troops on the 16th of November 1776.* Careful, detailed map 10¼ by 18⅛, reminiscent of Sauthier. Library of Congress, Faden Collection no. 60.

42. [*Fort Washington and Vicinity.*] Sketch of the ground between the Hessian Camp and Fort Washington at the time of the attack, 16 November 1776, in manuscript 7⅞ by 12½. Library of Congress. G3701 S3213 1776 F6.

43. [*North Manhattan and Kingsbridge Area.*] Somewhat rough manuscript 12 by 15⅞ of details of disposition of Hessian and British Troops. Library of Congress. G3701 S3216 1778 D5.

44. [*North Manhattan.*] Careful, incomplete manuscript 30¾ by 17¾, showing Fort Kniphausen and Fort Lee. Library of Congress, Faden Collection no. 59.

45. [*Northern Manhattan and Kingsbridge.*] Unlabeled, careful, colored manuscript 23⅝ by 41⅝, showing fortifications. See following, no. 46. Does not show Fort Lee. Library of Congress. G3701 S3216 1776 N4.

46. [*Northern Manhattan and Kingsbridge.*] Unlabeled, careful, colored manuscript 22¾ by 39¾, showing fortifications. Identical in scale and area to preceding, no. 45. Shows Fort Lee. Area is north of about the present 80th. Street. Library of Congress. G3701 S3216 1778 N5.

47. [*Northern Manhattan and Kingsbridge.*] Unlabeled, careful manuscript 12⅜ by 19⅜, showing fortifications. Library of Congress. G3701 S3216 1776 N41.

47. [*Northern Manhattan and Kingsbridge.*] Unlabeled, careful manuscript 13½ by 19¾, elevations indicated by hachures. Library of Congress. G3701 S3216 1777 M33.

48. [*Northern Manhattan and Kingsbridge.*] Finished, colored manuscript, 25 by 29, showing British and American Redouts and encampments. Clements Library. Brun 360.

49. *Sketch of the Heights of Kingsbridge 1777 with the proposed Redoubts colored Orange, Old Rebel Works coloured black.* Careful, finished, colored manuscript 25⅜ by 18. In same hand as no. 50. Library of Congress. G3701 S32146 1777 S5.

50. *Sketch of the Heights of Kingsbridge with the Proposed Redouts Colored Yellow.* Careful, colored finished manuscript 25¼ by 18⅜, by same hand as no. 49. Stamped Montresor on verso. Library of Congress. G3701 S32146 1777 S51.

51. *Sketch of the Environs of Kingsbridge.* Colored, finished manuscript 12¾ by 8½. Clements Library. Brun 437.

52. *A Plan of the Works on Spiken devil Hill with the Ground in front Protracted from a Scale of 200 Feet to an Inch.* Careful, colored manuscript. Library of Congress. G3701 S3216 1778 P5.

53. *Plan of the Narrows of Hell Gate, on the East River near which batteries of cannon, and morters were erected on Long Island, with a view to take of the defences and make a breach in the Rebel Fort, on the opposit shore, to facilitate a landing of troops on New York Island.* Finished, colored manuscript 17 by 13½. Clements Library. Brun 422.

54. *Plan of the Works opposite Hell-Gate.* Outline manuscript 4⅜ by 4½. Library of Congress. G3701 S32142 1776 P5.

WESTCHESTER COUNTY AND THE BRONX

55. [*Westchester County and the Bronx.*] Unfinished, partly colored manuscript 64 by 32¾, of troop dispositions and fortifications. Clements Library. Brun 393.

56. [*Westchester Creek to the Bronx River.*] Unfinished manuscript 6⅛ by 7⅜. Clements Library. Brun 426.

57. [*Westchester County and parts of Manhattan and Queens.*] Finished, colored manuscript 24 by 19½, locating some residents. Clements Library. Brun 392.

58. *Positions of the British Troops between The Hudson River and the Bronx River at Valentine's Hill.* Sketch 9¾ by 15½, locating regiments. Clements Library. Brun 425.

59. *Sketch of the roads on the East side of the North River.* Finished, colored manuscript 20¼ by 14⅛. Clements Library. Brun 440.

WHITE PLAINS, AND SURROUNDINGS

60. *Sketch of Westchester County east of the Bronx River with defense works at White Plains.* Unfinished, unlabeled manuscript 17 by 13¾. Library of Congress. G3803 W5 1776 S5.

61. *Discription of the roads about White Plains.* Rough sketch manuscript 12½ by 14⅜. Clements Library. Brun 337.

62. *Sketch of the Road From Kingsbridge to White Plains.* Careful, colored manuscript. Library of Congress. G3701 S32187 1778 S5.

63. *Battle of White Plains fought October 28th. 1777.* Careful, colored manuscript 20¾ by 13⅜. Acquired with the manuscripts from the family of Archibald Robertson. See under Robertson. New York Public Library, Manuscript Collection.

64. [*Battle of White Plains.*] Careful, colored manuscript 13 by 16¼, of troop dispositions. British Museum. Additional Manuscripts 16, 367e.

65. *White Plains.* Rough manuscript 14 by 12⅝, of part of the battle. Clements Library. Brun 462.

66. [*Battle of White Plains.*] Careful, colored, but incomplete

manuscript 12¾ by 15¾. British Museum. Additional Manuscripts 16, 367.

67. *A Military Sketch of the disposition of the English and American troops and of Howe's Headquarters, after the Battle of White Plains 25 Oct. 1776.* Unfinished and incomplete manuscript 13 by 16. British Museum. Crown Collection II 33.

HUDSON RIVER AND THE HUDSON HIGHLANDS

68. [*Haverstraw Bay.*] Manuscript sketch map 16⅛ by 12⅝, of the west bank. Clements Library. Brun 351.

69. *From Spikendevil to Dobs Ferry along the Hudson.* Finished, colored manuscript 18½ by 11, of the east shore of the Hudson and Long Island Sound with names of landowners. Clements Library. Brun 347.

70. *From Fishkill Creek to the Croton River.* Finished manuscript 28½ by 18¼ of the east shore of the Hudson, Forts Independence and Constitution. Clements Library. Brun 346.

71. *Hudson River from New Windsor to Tappan.* Unfinished manuscript 9½ by 15 with much military intelligence. Clements Library. Brun 353.

72. *Map of North River from Stoney Point to Peeks Kill.* Manu-

script road map 12⅝ by 7¾, labeled in hand of John André. Clements Library. Brun 373.

73. *Lent's Creek and Baillie's Creek.* Manuscript road map 12⅞ by 15⅛, labeled in hand of John André. Clements Library. On verso of Brun 373.

74. *Hudson River from Anthony's Nose to Stony Point.* Sketch 9 by 8 of roads on both shores of the Hudson. Clements Library. Brun 352.

75. *Hudson River from Anthony's Nose to Stony Point.* Sketch 10 by 6 of the roads on the west shore of the Hudson. Clements Library. On verso of Brun 352.

76. *Hudson River from West Point to Dobbs Ferry.* Rough manuscript of the settlements 15⅞ by 12¾, inset of West Point. Clements Library. Brun 356.

77. [*Forts of the Hudson Highlands.*] Rough manuscript 12½ by 8¼. Clements Library. Brun 345.

78. [*Forts at Stony and Verplank's Points.*] Unfinished manuscript 19¼ by 12. Library of Congress. G3701 S32174 1779 M3.

79. [*Stony Point.*] Finished manuscript plan 9¾ by 12, with note urging secrecy. Clements Library. Brun 444.

80. *Verplanks.* Perspective view 9½ by 12½ with note in hand of Sir Henry Clinton. Clements Library. Brun 454.

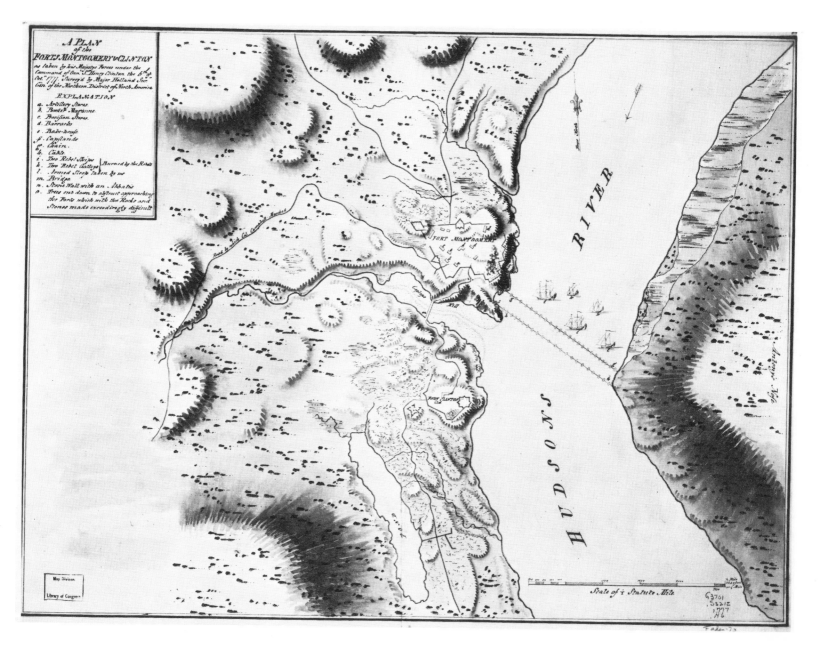

Samuel Holland's plan of Forts Montgomery and Clinton, October 6, 1777. See 59/5.

81. *Sketch of Stoney & Verplank's Points upon the North River, as taken Possession of, and Fortified by His Excellency Sir H. Clinton in June 1779.* Careful, finished manuscript 23¾ by 19. Library of Congress. G3701 S32174 1779 S5.

82. *Hudson's River from Stony Point to Fort Montgomery.* Colored sketch 8½ by 7⅜ of Forts Montgomery and Independence. Clements Library. Brun 358.

83. [*Hudson River from Stony Point to West Point.*] Finished, colored manuscript 26¾ by 88½, details of the military installations, chains across the river, and attacks on the forts. Clements Library. Brun 355.

84. *Sketch of Forts Clinton & Montgomery Stormed the 6th. October 1777 by the Troops under the Command of Sir Henry Clinton K.B. Lt. General of his Majs. Forces and Commander in Chief of New York and its dependancies.* Careful, detailed manuscript 40½ by 21¾, with troop movements. See no. 85. Library of Congress. G3701 S3212 1777 S5.

85. *Sketch of Forts Clinton and Montgomery Stormed the 6th October 1777 by the Troops under the Command of Sr. Henry Clinton K:B: Lt. General of His Majesty's forces and Commander in Chief of New York and its Dependancies.* Careful, colored manuscript 20¼ by 44½, with troop movements. See no. 84. Clements Library. Brun 432.

86. [*Hudson Highlands.*] Unfinished, untitled, careful manuscript 21½ by 30, showing the forts. Library of Congress. G3701 S3212 1777 P3.

87. [*Hudson Highlands at Martelaers Rock.*] A wash profile 11¼ by 6. Clements Library. Brun 357 on same sheet as nos. 88 and 93.

88. *Topographick plan by the eye* [*of the Hudson Highlands.*] Unfinished manuscript 6 by 10. Clements Library. Brun 450 on same sheet as nos. 87 and 93.

89. [*West Point Area.*] Rough manuscript sketch 10½ by 18. Labeled by John André. Clements Library. Brun 457.

90. [*West Point Area.*] Rough manuscript sketch 15½ by 19. Clements Library. Brun 456.

91. *West Point or Fort Clinton.* Outline manuscript 13 by 16¾. Clements Library. Brun 459.

92. [*West Point gun emplacements.*] Rough manuscript sketch 12½ by 15¼. Clements Library. Brun 460.

93. *Geogrephick scetch 1754.* Unfinished manuscript 8½ by 5¾ from New Windsor to West Point, date appears in error. Clements Library. Brun 350.

94. [*Fort Independence to Slaughter's Landing.*] Manuscript sketch 11¼ by 16 of the west shore. Clements Library. Brun 343.

LAKE CHAMPLAIN AND SARATOGA

95. *Plan Lake Champlain from Fort St. John's to Ticonderoga with the Soundings Rocks Shoals and Sands Surveyed in the Years 1778, 1779.* Careful, detailed, colored manuscript 100 by 31⅝, with description of battles. Library of Congress. Faden Collection no. 64.

96. *The Order of Battle in Crossing Lake Champlane.* Unfinished manuscript 14½ by 9¾ of formation prior to the battle of October 11 and 13, 1776. Clements Library. Brun 386.

97. *The Attack and Defeat of the American Fleet under Benedict Arnold by the King's Fleet, commanded by Sir Guy Carleton upon Lake Champlain 11th. October, 1776 From a Scetch taken by an Officer on the Spot.* Careful, detailed manuscript, 6½ by 10¼. Library of Congress. Faden Collection no. 21.

98. [*Crown Point to Fort Edward.*] Portion of a finished, colored manuscript 11 by 9. Clements Library. Brun 334.

99. *Plan of the Position wch. the Army under Lt. Genl. Burgoyne took at Saratoga on the 10th. Septr. 1777 and in which it remained till the Convention was signed.* Careful, detailed manuscript 28 by 20. By the same hand as no. 101. British Museum. Royal United Services Institution Collection A 30/14.

100. *Plan of the Position which the Army under Lt. Genl. Burgoyne took at Saratoga on the 10th. of September 1777, and in which it remained till the Convention was signed.* Carefully drawn for engraving, 18⅞ by 8½. Library of Congress. Faden Collection no. 66.

101. *Plan of the Position of the Army under the Command of Lieut. Gen'l Burgoyne near Still Water in which it encamped on ye 20th. Septr. 1777.* Careful, completed, colored manuscript 28⅛ by 20⅝. By same hand as no. 99. British Museum. Royal United Services Institution Collection A 30/15.

102. *Position of the Army on the 8th. Octbr 1777.* Rough, colored manuscript 10⅞ by 9⅞ of the area at Swords house. Library of Congress. Faden Collection no. 67a.

103. [*Upper New York, Vermont and Massachusetts.*] Finished, colored manuscript 29¼ by 21⅞ of roads, forts, towns and streams. May be prior to Revolution. Clements Library. Brun 466.

104. [*Upper New York, Vermont and New Hampshire.*] Careful manuscript which looks like engraving, 10⅞ by 22⅞. From Lake Champlain to Albany, and eastward to the upper Connecticut River. Library of Congress. Faden Collection no. 62, 63.

131. NEW JERSEY

1. [*North East New Jersey, Staten Island, Long Island.*] Unlabeled, careful manuscript 27 by 13¾ of operations in Long Island, Staten Island, Elizabethtown, Monmouth. To join maps 2 and 3. Duke of Northumberland Collection, Alnwick.

2. [*Delaware, Pennsylvania and Central New Jersey.*] Unlabeled, colored, careful manuscript 41½ by 22½, from Wilmington, Delaware to Imlaystown New Jersey. Joins maps 1 and 3. Duke of Northumberland Collection, Alnwick.

3. [*Pennsylvania, Delaware, Maryland and New Jersey*]. Unlabeled, careful, colored manuscript 19¾ by 15, of south west New Jersey, and the area between the lower Delaware Bay to upper Chesapeake Bay. Joins map 2 and 3, and is accompanied by several descriptive sheets of the operations of the British Army from 12 August 1776 to the end of 1779. Duke of Northumberland Collection, Alnwick.

4. *A Plan of The Operations of the King's Army under the command of General Sir William Howe, K.B., in New York and East New Jersey against the American Forces Commanded by General Washington from the 12th. of October to the 28th. of November 1776 wherein is particularly distinguished The Engagement on the White Plains the 28th. of October by _____.* Incomplete manuscript 19¾ by 29 resembling an engraving. The precursor of *Sauthier's map*, published by Faden. See Sauthier map 13. Library of Congress. Faden Collection no. 58.

5. [*New Jersey and adjacent New York and Pennsylvania.*] Careful, finished manuscript 14 by 17½, particularly roads, towns. Clements Library. Brun 471.

6. [*New Jersey from Burlington to Fort Lee.*] Careful, colored manuscript 19½ by 11¾ showing the disposition of the British troops in December 1776, and the connecting roads. Library of Congress. G3701 S322 1776 M3.

7. [*Paulus Hook.*] Careful, colored manuscript 15½ by 14. In the same hand as no. 8, and very similar to no. 9. Library of Congress. G3701 S3227 1778 P3.

8. [*Paulus Hook.*] Careful, colored manuscript 17¼ by 14¼. In the same hand as no. 7, and very similar to no. 9. Library of Congress. G3701 S3227 1778 P31.

9. *Plan of the Post at Paulus's Hook. 24 July 1778.* Finished, careful, colored manuscript 14½ by 16½. Very similar to nos. 7 and 8. Clements Library. Brun 502.

10. *British Refugee Post on Bergen Point, 19th. Novr. 1780.* Rough pencil sketch of Paulus Hook, 6 by 9½. In report of Sub. Engr. & Lieut. William Parker to Capt. Alexander Mercer, with description. Parker may be the author of the map. Clements Library. Brun 477.

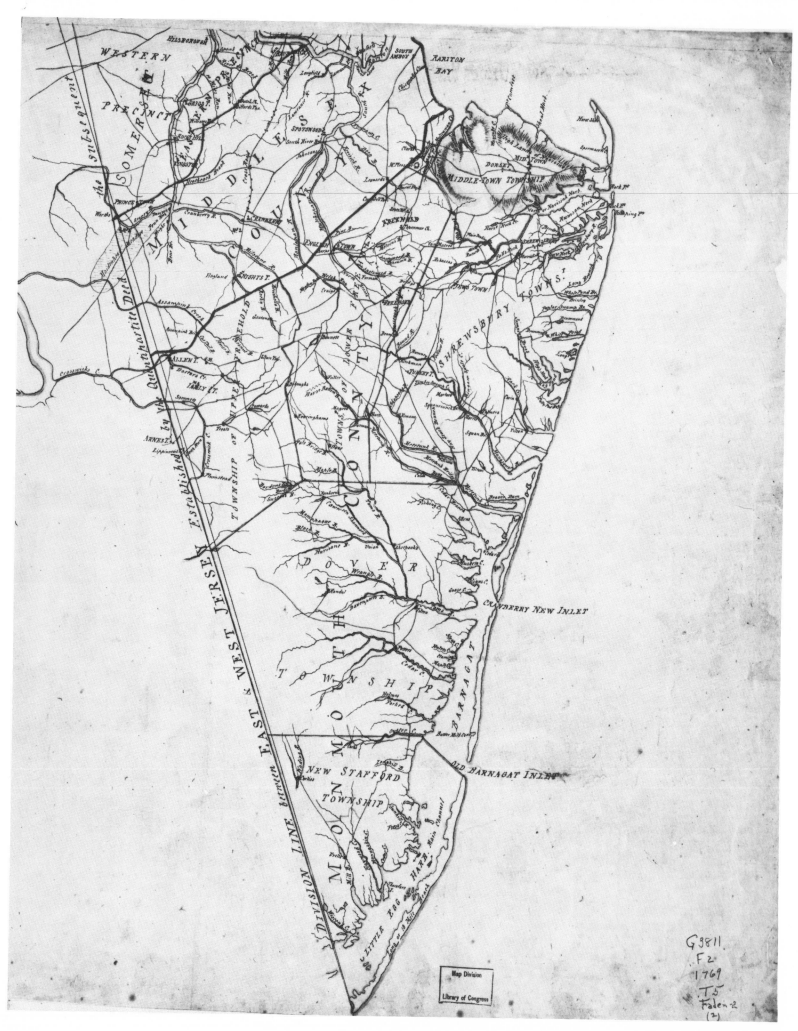

11. [*Fort Lee area.*] Rough manuscript 7¼ by 9, reminiscent of hand of John André. Clements Library. Brun 481.

12. [*Union and Essex Counties.*] Roads between present Newark and Newark Bay, manuscript sketch 23¾ by 19¼. Clements Library. Brun 492.

13. [*Passaic and Hackensack Rivers.*] Road map in manuscript 12½ by 15⅝ of the area between and about the rivers, and Newark Bay. Clements Library. Brun 483.

14. [*Newark.*] Rough manuscript 12¾ by 8 with table of distances. Clements Library. Brun 484.

15. [*Roads between Bergen County and Trenton.*] Manuscript 20 by 30 of the towns and connecting roads. Clements Library. Brun 486.

16. [*Roads in present Union and Middlesex Counties.*] Unfinished manuscript 21 by 17¼ of roads and towns. Clements Library. Brun 494.

17. *Rahway River to Perth Amboy.* Unfinished manuscript 21 by 17¼ of roads and towns. Clements Library. Brun 505.

18. [*Rahway River Area.*] Careful, colored manuscript 15½ by 20, of the River, roads and residents. Clements Library. Brun 506.

19. *Sketch of the position of the Army 17 of June 1780.* Disposition of British units between Elizabethtown and Arthur Kill. Clements Library. Brun 513.

20. *Draught of an Intrenched Camp proposed to be erected near Elizabeth Town.* Careful, manuscript 10⅞ by 8¼. Library of Congress. G3701 S3223 177- D7.

21. *Bridge from Staten Island to the Jersies, by Cn. Laird's description.* Careful manuscript of pontoon bridge over Arthur Kill. Clements Library. Brun 467.

22. [*Roads between Perth Amboy and Elizabethtown Point.*] Rough, manuscript road survey 23¾ by 16. Library of Congress. G3701 S322 1777 A5.

23. *Plan of Gen'l Washingtons Winter Cantonment & Environs - in March 1780.* Careful, colored manuscript 15¼ by 12¾. In Governor Tryon's of 26 February 1780, No. 89. Removed from CO 5/1110. Public Record Office. MPG 1015.

24. [*Sandy Hook.*] Careful manuscript 8⅛ by 8¾, showing garrison. Clements Library. Brun 508.

25. *Camp at Middlebush. 14th. June 1777.* Careful manuscript 6½ by 6. British units identified. Clements Library. Brun 478.

26. *Camp at Middlebush, 16th. June 1777.* Manuscript 7¾ by 6¼, more detailed than no. 25. Clements Library. Brun 479.

27. *Encampment near Brunswick-21st. June 1777.* Careful manuscript 7½ by 12¾. British units identified.

28. *Sketch from Information of the Different Roads about Freehold in the Jerseys.* Finished, colored manuscript road map 27 by 36. Clements Library. Brun 510.

29. [*Roads, North East Monmouth County.*] Careful, manuscript road map 12 by 14¾, with distances. Clements Library. Brun 488.

30. [*Roads, North East Monmouth County.*] Careful, manuscript road map 21½ by 15. Clements Library. Brun 489.

31. *Battle of Monmouth 28th. June 1778.* Finished, colored manuscript 15⅛ by 17, inset of the skirmish of the Queens Rangers. See Spencer no. 6. Clements Library. Brun 475.

32. *Battle of Monmouth. 28th. June 1778.* Finished, colored manuscript 6⅝ by 15½, inset of the skirmish of the Queens Rangers. See Spencer no. 6. Clements Library. Brun 476.

33. [*Roads between Freehold and Trenton.*] Manuscript sketch road map 8 by 12¾. Clements Library. Brun 482.

34. [*Roads between Bordentown and Haddonfield.*] Colored, manuscript road map 12½ by 8⅛. Clements Library. Brun 491.

35. [*Roads between Bordentown, Burlington and Mount Holly.*] Rough, manuscript 6 by 8 inches. Clements Library. Brun 487.

36. [*Roads between New York and Philadelphia.*] Finished, colored manuscript 16¾ by 24¼. Clements Library. Brun 522.

Bernard Ratzer's 1769 East New Jersey survey, embodied into later British war maps. See 92/5; 145/19.

37. *Situation of ye. Rebels just before the attack upon Trenton.* Unfinished manuscript 13 by 8¼, with descriptive data on disposition of the British and American forces. Clements Library. Brun 509.

38. *Plan of the Operations of General Washington against The King's Troops in New Jersey from the 26th. of December 1776 to the 3d. of January 1777.* Careful, finished, colored manuscript 15¼ by 11½, simulating an engraved map. Library of Congress. Faden Collection no. 61a.

39. [*Present Camden.*] Rough, colored manuscript 10¼ by 7⅞, labeled "No. 45." Library of Congress. G3701 S32217 1778 06.

40. *Red Bank.* Careful, finished manuscript plan 13⅝ by 9½ of the fort. Library of Congress. G3701 S32282 1777 R4.

41. [*Roads between Red Bank and Present Camden.*] Manuscript, labeled in cursive, 17 by 11. Shows march of the Hessians against Red Bank. Library of Congress.

132. PENNSYLVANIA

1. *Progress of the Army from their Landing till taking possession of Philadelphia.* Somewhat rough, colored manuscript 10⅜ by 9½. Howes and Kniphausen route shown separately. Library of Congress. Faden Collection no. 82.

2. [*Route of British March upon Philadelphia.*] Careful, detailed, colored manuscript 17¾ by 21. Dates all operations from landing at Elk 25 August, to 26 September 1777. In right upper "No. 20" stamped "Montresor," on verso. Library of Congress. G3701 S32 1777 M3.

3. [*Route of British March upon Philadelphia.*] Careful, manuscript 7¼ by 8⅞, of "progress of the army from the landing at Elk to the taking of possession of Philadelphia." Library of Congress. G3701 S32 1777 T5.

4. [*Philadelphia.*] Careful, colored manuscript 27½ by 35¼ of roads and streets. Clements Library. Brun 539.

5. [*Philadelphia.*] Careful, colored manuscript 17½ by 19, showing line of defense. Library of Congress. Faden Collection no. 85.

6. [*Philadelphia and immediate environs.*] Somewhat rough, colored manuscript 15¾ by 12½. "No. 44" in left upper. Library of Congress. G3701 S3237 1778 P5.

7. [*Southeastern Pennsylvania.*] Unfinished manuscript 38 by 52½, of roads between the Delaware and Susquehanna Valley. Clements Library. Brun 538.

8. [*Southeastern Pennsylvania.*] Finished, part colored manuscript 34¼ by 57½, of roads, towns, mills, etc. Clements Library. Brun 556.

THE DELAWARE RIVER AND FORTS

9. *The Course of Delaware River from Philadelphia to Chester.* Careful manuscript closely resembling engraving, inset "Mud Island." 24¼ by 15. Many additions in red ink, date April 30, 1778 is struck out. Precursor of Faden's map of the same name published April 30, 1778, and republished with changes, 1 January 1785. Library of Congress. Faden Collection no. 84.

10. [*Delaware River from Chester to Philadelphia.*] Untitled, incomplete, part colored manuscript 27¼ by 17¼, resembling engraving. A less finished, and slightly different version of no. 9. Library of Congress. Faden Collection no. 83.

11. [*Delaware River Forts.*] Fine, finished, colored manuscript 6½ by 14¼ of the forts at Red Bank, Billingsport, down to Chester. Column of references, and note referring to October and November, 1777. Duke of Northumberland Collection, Alnwick.

12. *Plan of Fort Mifflin on Mud Island with the Batteries on Province Island.* Careful, colored manuscript, 4 by 7. Library of Congress. Faden Collection no. 86.

13. *Plan and Sections of the Redoubt at Billingfort and Plan of the Rebel Fort marked yellow.* Careful, colored manuscript 14⅝ by 10⅛. Library of Congress. G3701 S32207 1777 P5.

BATTLE OF GERMANTOWN

14. *A Sketch of the Battle of German Tn. 4th. October 1777 where the Rebels were repulsed.* Careful, colored manuscript 10¼ by 13⅜, rubber stamp "Montresor" on verso. Houghton Library, Harvard University.
15. *A Sketch of the Battle of German Tn. 4th. October 1777 where the Rebels were repulsed.* Careful, colored manuscript 10¾ by 13½. Library of Congress. G3701 S3236 1777 S5.
16. *A Sketch of the Battle of German Tn. 4th. October 1777 where the Rebels were repulsed.* Careful, colored manuscript 10⅝ by 13¼. "Montresor" stamped, on verso. Library of Congress. G3701 S3236 1777 S51.
17. [*Philadelphia Area and Paoli.*] Careful, unfinished manuscript 29¾ by 36, on multiple sheets, of military operations. Military units identified. New York Public Library. Manuscript Collection.
18. *British Camp at Trudruffin from _____ with The Attack made by Major General Grey against The Rebels near White Horse Tavern.* Careful, colored manuscript resembling engraving, 16⅛ by 10, with corrections. Precursor to Faden's map of July 1, 1778 with similar title. Library of Congress. Faden Collection no. 81.
19. *Plan of Washingtons Position.* Rough manuscript of Valley Forge 8 by 12⅝. Notation "Mr. Parker late a Mercht in Virginia now at Philadelphia." Clements Library. Brun 546.

BATTLE OF BRANDYWINE

20. *Battle of Brandywine 11th. Sept. 1777 in which the Rebels were defeated by the Army under the Command of General Sir William Howe.* Careful, colored manuscript 18¼ by 22½. Library of Congress. Faden Collection no. 79.
21. *Battle of Brandywine in which the Americans were defeated September the 11th. 1777 By General Sr. William Howe.* Engraved, corrected proof 17 by 19¼, numerous corrections in manuscript. Date changed from April 13, 1778 to April 13th. 1784. Name of Wm. Faden altered to "Geographer to the King." Library of Congress. Faden Collection no. 78.
22. [*Battle of Brandywine.*] Careful manuscript 17¼ by 23½, descriptive text in careful manuscript, corrected in rough cursive. Marked similarity to no. 23. Library of Congress. G3701 S3233 1777 B32.
23. *Battle of Brandywine.* Careful manuscript 30½ by 24½, labeled in cursive. Library of Congress. G3701 S3233 1777 B31.
24. [*Battle of Brandywine.*] Careful, colored manuscript 28¾ by 18⅞. "Montresor" stamped, on verso. Same scale, but different hand from no. 23. Library of Congress. G3701 S3233 1777 B29.

MISCELLANEOUS: PENNSYLVANIA

25. *Encampment near Cecil Church, 1st. Septr. 1777.* Careful manuscript 7½ by 6¼. Clements Library. Brun 559.
26. [*Road between Newcastle and Chester Town.*] Sketch map 12½ by 8, of area between Chesapeake and Delaware Bays. Clements Library. Brun 562.
27. *Disposition of the Camp near Elk, 28th. Augt. 1777.* Careful sketch manuscript 7¾ by 6¼. Clements Library. Brun 558.
28. *Camp at head of Elk, 27th. Augt. 1777.* Careful sketch manuscript 7¾ by 6¼. By same hand as no. 27. Clements Library. Brun 557.
29. [*Delaware and Chesapeak Bays.*] Finished, colored manuscript 13⅜ by 6⅞, Philadelphia to Cape Henry. Clements Library. Brun 554.

30. [*Delaware and Chesapeak Bays.*] Finished, colored manuscript 13¼ by 7⅛, almost identical to no. 29. Clements Library. Brun 555.
31. *Plan of part of Western Front.* Rough manuscript 32 by 24⅜, of headwaters of the branches of the Susquehanna River and Lakes Ontario and Erie. Shows major forts. Library of Congress. G3822 S9 1778 P5.

133. VIRGINIA

1. *A Plan of the Entrance of Chesapeak Bay with James and York Rivers wherein are shown the Respective Positions (in the beginning of October) 1° Of The British Army Commanded By Lord Cornwallis At Gloucester and York in Virginia, 2° of the American and French Forces under General Washington, 3° and of the French Fleet under Count de Grasse By an officer.* Engraved proof 20½ by 16, with manuscript additions "London, Published by Wm. Faden, Charing Cross, Novr 26th. 1781." Library of Congress. Faden Collection no. 90.
2. *Four Positions of the English and French Fleet, as the latter was coming out of Chesapeak Bay.* A series of four manuscript sheets 11 by 17½, with relative positions of the vessels identified. British Museum. Royal United Services Institution Collection 30/79.
3. [*Siege of Yorktown.*] Finished, colored manuscript 16 by 12¾, positions of the French and American units. Clements Library. Brun 583.
4. [*Siege of Yorktown.*] Careful, detailed, unlabeled manuscript 18 by 15. Dartmouth College Library. Scavenius Collection.
5. *Plan of the Siege of Yorktown Virginia.* Somewhat rough, finished colored manuscript 45¾ by 44, much detailed data from 29 August to 19 October 1781. Dartmouth College Library. Scavenius Collection.
6. *Position of the Troops, under Earl Cornwallis, on the 28 and 29 September 1781; when the Enemy first appeared.* Careful, finished, colored manuscript 30 by 21¼, of part of Yorktown. Clements Library. Brun 581.
7. *Position of the Army under the Command of Earl Cornwallis between the Ravines on the 28th. and 29th. of Sept 1781.* Careful, colored manuscript 12½ by 11⅝. Norfolk Museum, Norfolk Virginia.
8. [*Yorktown Area.*] Finished manuscript 6 by 7¼ of the towns about Yorktown. Clements Library. Brun 590.
9. *Williamsburgh & the slip of land between York & James Rivers from thence to Hampton.* Rough manuscript 16 by 12¾ of roads. Clements Library. Brun 589.
10. *March of the Army under Lieut. General Earl Cornwallis in Virginia from the Junction at Petersburg on the 20th. of May, till their arrival at Portsmouth on the 12th. of July.* Somewhat rough, colored manuscript 21½ by 15⅛ of daily progress, in great detail. British Museum. Royal United Services Institution Collection A29/35.
11. *Action Near Spencers Ordinary.* Rough sketch 6 by 6¾, describing movements. Dartmouth College Library. Scavenius Collection.
12. [*Confluence of the James and York Rivers, and Chesapeak Bay.*] Rough sketch of roads 14⅜ by 8⅞. Clements Library. Brun 570.
13. [*Confluence of the Matapony, Pamunkey Rivers with the York River.*] Careful manuscript 20 by 13½, identifying plantations. Clements Library. Brun 571.
14. [*Elizabeth River Area, Cape Henry to Nansmond River.*] Finished, colored manuscript 19¼ by 11¾. Clements Library. Brun 572.
15. [*Norfolk Area.*] Finished manuscript 20 by 31, of roads, town and plantations. Clements Library. Brun 576.
16. [*Portsmouth and Norfolk.*] Finished, colored manuscript 11¾ by 7¾. Clements Library. Brun 578.

Odometer, second quarter of the 18th century, calibrated in miles, poles and links. Colonial Williamsburg.

17. [*Portsmouth and Norfolk.*] Finished, colored manuscript 12⅞ by 15½. Inset of "Rebel Fort." Clements Library. Brun 579.
18. *A Sketch of the east end of the Peninsula where on is Hampton* [*by*] *W.P.M.* Finished, detailed manuscript 20 by 28¼, of roads, plantations. Endorsed by Lt. Colonel DeLancey. Clements Library. Brun 584.
19. *Plan of part of the Province of Virginia.* Finished manuscript 7½ by 14⅛, of the northern end of the Shenandoah Valley and cantonment of Burgoyne's Convention troops. Clements Library. Brun 574.

134. NORTH CAROLINA

1. *A plan of part of the principal roads in the Province of No. Carolina.* Finished manuscript 29¾ by 21, of towns, plantations, roads, bridges. Clements Library. Brun 598.
2. *Battle of Guildford fought on the 15 of March 1781.* Rough manuscript 12⅝ by 15¾. Library of Congress. Faden Collection no. 53.
3. *Battle of Guildford Fought on the 15th. of March 1781.* Manuscript, part engraved, 7⅜ by 8½. Library of Congress. Faden

Collection no. 52.
4. *Battle of Guildford fought on the 15 of March 1781.* Finished, colored manuscript 8¼ by 7¼. Identical with the map in Steadman's *A History of the Origin, Progress, and Termination of the American War*, London 1794. Clements Library. Brun 592.
5. [*Wilmington Area.*] Sketch map 12 by 12, of the roads and ferries. Clements Library. Brun 596.
6. *Plan of Wilmington in the Province of Nth. Carolina.* Finished manuscript 17¼ by 19½.
7. [*Part of Brunswick County.*] Rough manuscript 10¾ by 14¾. Clements Library. Brun 593.
8. [*Part of Brunswick County.*] Rough manuscript 7½ by 12. Clements Library. Brun 594.
9. [*North East North Carolina.*] Finished manuscript 17 by 14½, of roads and towns. Clements Library. Brun 595.

135. SOUTH CAROLINA

1. *South Carolina and Parts Adjacent Shewing The Movements of the American and British Armies.* Careful, finished manuscript 21¾ by 18, resembling engraving. Public Record Office. MPI 327.
2. [*Western South Carolina.*] Manuscript 19½ by 19, of Fort Rutledge and old Cherokee boundary. Clements Library. Brun 617.
3. *Plan of the Battle Fought near Camden August 16th. 1780.* Finished manuscript 8¼ by 7¼, identifying units. Clements Library. Brun 624.
4. *A Sketch of the Battle near Camden in South Carolina 16 Augst. 1780.* Finished, colored manuscript 11½ by 13, identifying units and officers. Clements Library. Brun 631.
5. *Plan of the Battle fought near Camden August 16th. 1780.* Detailed, somewhat rough manuscript 10⅞ by 14, units identified. Library of Congress. Faden Collection no. 51.

CHARLESTON CAMPAIGNS

6. [*Sullivans and Long Islands.*] Rough sketch 15¾ by 12⅞, about 1776. Clements Library. Brun 632.
7. *View of the Attack upon the Fortress of Sulivan's.* Careful, detailed manuscript 13 by 8. In Sir P.A. Parker's letter of 9 July 1776 (Adm. 1/486). Public Record Office. MPH 199.
8. *Eye Sketch of the Harbour of Charlestown in South Carolina.* Manuscript 14½ by 8¾, accompanying "Observations on the Attack on Charleston, S.C.," published in *Journal of Southern History* XI, Feb. 1945. Clements Library. Brun 612.
9. *A Sketch of Charles Town from Memory as it was in the Year 1777, N.B. all the Marshes are impassable.* Careful, detailed manuscript 14⅝ by 22¼. Public Record Office. MPH 136.
10. *Draught of Part of the Province of South Carolina; Shewing the march & encampments of the British Troops under the command of Major Genl. Prevost. Upon an expedition into that Province.* Careful, detailed manuscript 28½ by 20¼. Insets of post at Stono, attacked by Rebels 20th. June 1779," and post at Wapoocut, 24th. & 25th. of May. Clements Library. Brun 611.
11. *Sketch of the Coast from South Edisto to Charles Town 1 st. March 1780. Sketch of the Rebel Redoubt on Stono River destroyed by Genl. Prevost.* Careful, detailed manuscript 13¾ by 11½. Library of Congress. Faden Collection no. 46.
12. [*Siege of Charlestown.*] Sketch of the fortifications, 12⅛ by 15, 1780. Clements Library. Brun 629.
13. [*Siege of Charlestown.*] Rough sketch 9 by 7⅜, units identified, 1780. Clements Library. Brun 630.
14. [*Charlestown Area.*] Finished manuscript 8 by 10¾, of the area south of the city. Clements Library. Brun 616.
15. [*Charlestown and its approaches from the sea.*] Finished manuscript 10⅝ by 10½. Clements Library. Brun 606.
16. *Sketch of the Harbour of Charles Town as described by Captain Durfee Latitude of Ship Barr 32° 38' 1st March 1780.* Rough

manuscript 7⅜ by 11½. Library of Congress. Faden Collection no. 50.

17. [*Defenses at Charlestown.*] Unfinished sketch 9 by 7⅜, 1780. Clements Library. Brun 608.

18. [*Disposition of the British Forces before Charleston.*] Sketch of troops 7¼ by 6⅛, inset detail. Clements Library. Brun 609.

19. *Distribution & Strength of Corps, 1780.* Careful sketch 8 by 8½. Clements Library. Brun 610.

20. *Plan of Charleston and its Defences, 1780.* Plan of the town 11¾ by 8½, numbers of guns. Clements Library. Brun 620.

21. [*Sullivans Island.*] Sketch 8 by 12¾, inset profile, and additional data. Clements Library. Brun 633.

22. *Sketch of the Harbour of North Edisto 2d March 1780.* Careful sketch 7½ by 11½. Library of Congress. Faden Collection no. 47.

23. *A Plan of the Military Operations against Charlestown, the Army being Commanded by L.G. Henry Clinton K.B. and the Fleet by Vice-Admiral Arbuthnot, from an original drawing sent by an officer in the army.* Finished, detailed manuscript 17¾ by 22. Almost identical with one of the same title, published by Sayer and Bennett 27 May 1780. Clements Library. Brun 626.

24. *Charles Town Harbour & Adjacent Islands, Country, Rivers & c.* Careful, colored manuscript 30 by 21¾. British Museum. Royal United Services Institution Collection A30/34B.

25. *Charles Town Neck Exhibiting the Plan of the Town and all the Fortifications in December 1781.* Careful, detailed, colored manuscript 30 by 21¾. British Museum. Royal United Services Institution Collection A30/34A.

26. [*Positions of British on John's Island.*] Careful, uncompleted manuscript 30 by 21¾, status of April and May 1780. New York Public Library. Manuscript Collection.

27. *Plan of the Seige of Charlestown in South Carolina.* Finished, colored manuscript 10⅜ by 11⅝. Clements Library. Brun 628.

28. [*Charlestown Fortifications.*] Rough pencil sketch 7½ by 12½, status of 1780. Clements Library. Brun 613.

29. *Hornwork at Charleston's outer defences at neck of peninsula.* Unfinished manuscript 8 by 9. Clements Library. Brun 614.

30. [*Charlestown Fortifications.*] Manuscript 8 by 12¾ of the outer defense line. Clements Library. Brun 615.

31. [*Charlestown and Defenses.*] Finished, colored manuscript 18 by 14¾, status prior to evacuation in December 1782. Dartmouth College Library. Scavenius Collection.

136. GEORGIA

1. *A Chart of Tibee Inlet in Georgia A:B: July 30th. 1776.* Finished, colored manuscript 14¾ by 18½. Sailing directions on verso signed "Willm. Lyford, Branch Pilot for the Barr and River of Savannah in Georgia." Clements Library. Brun 634.

2. [*Savannah River and Sound.*] Finished, colored manuscript 24¼ by 41¼, in great detail. Clements Library. Brun 640.

3. [*Savannah River from Augusta to Ebenezer.*] Detailed manuscript 8 by 32, showing Colonel Archibald Campbell's route. Two page memorandum and distance table. Library of Congress. G3701 S334 1779 R6.

4. *Plan of the Siege* [*of Savannah*] *by French and American forces 1779.* Careful manuscript 30 by 9, with the attack of 9 October 1779. Public Record Office. CO5/657/229.

5. *Plan of the French and Rebels Sieg of Savannah in Georgia in South America Deffend: trough the Br. Gen. August Prevost 1774.* Careful, colored manuscript 24¾ by 16½, European in spelling and appearance. Isometric view of the town. Library of Congress. Faden collection no. 42.

6. [*Siege of Savannah.*] Rough, colored manuscript 22 by 20½. Library of Congress. G3956 .537 1778 M31.

7. [*Siege of Savannah.*] Finished, colored manuscript 7 by 11. Clements Library. Brun 641.

8. [*Siege of Savannah.*] Careful, unfinished manuscript 17 by 10. Library of Congress. G3956 S37 1778 M3.

9. [*Siege of Savannah.*] Somewhat rough, part colored manuscript 22 by 20½. Library of Congress. G3701 S3345 1778 S5.

10. *Plan of Savannah and its Fortifications in 1782.* Incomplete and unfinished manuscript, 16½ by 10⅜. Library of Congress. G3701 S3345 1782 P52.

11. [*Savannah and Fortifications.*] Somewhat untutored, unfinished manuscript 17¾ by 14⅝. Two other copies in less completed form. Library of Congress. G3956 S37 17-- M3.

12. [*Savannah and Fortifications.*] Unfinished manuscript 5½ by 9. Clements Library. Brun 639.

13. [*Savannah and Fortifications.*] Careful, detailed, incomplete manuscript in color, 17 by 10. Library of Congress. G3701 S3345 1778 M3.

14. *Plan of Savannah And Its Environs in 1782.* Careful, but somewhat untutored manuscript 17¾ by 14½. Same hand as no. 15. Library of Congress. G3956 S37 1782 P5.

15. *Plan of Savannah & its Environs in 1782.* Careful, but somewhat untutored manuscript 17⅜ by 14½. By same hand as no. 14. Library of Congress. G3956 S37 1782 P51.

16. *Ft. Prevost in 1781.* Careful, unfinished manuscript 12¼ by 10½. Same hand as no. 17. Library of Congress. G3956 S37 1781 F6.

17. *Ft. Prevost in 1781.* Careful, incomplete manuscript 12¼ by 10½. Same hand as no. 16. Library of Congress. G3701 S3345 1781 P6.

18. *Ft. Prevost in 1782.* Careful, incomplete manuscript, 15⅜ by 12½. Library of Congress. G3701 S3345 1782 F6.

19. *Fort Prevost in 1782.* Careful, incomplete manuscript 15½ by 12½. Library of Congress. G3956 S37 1782 F6.

20. *Powder Magazine in Fort Prevost at Savannah 1780.* Careful, colored manuscript 1⅞ by 5¼. Library of Congress. G3956 S37 1780 P6.

21. *Powder Magazine in Fort Prevost at Savannah 1780.* Careful manuscript 3 by 5¼. Library of Congress. G3701 S3345 1780 P6.

137. FLORIDA

1. *St. Augustine and its Environs.* Careful, colored manuscript 17⅞ by 13¾. All forts identified. Library of Congress. Lowery Collection 646.

2. *Plan of the Town Harbour and Fort of St. Augustine.* Careful, colored manuscript 34½ by 29. Reminiscent of style of George Gauld. Hydrographic Department, Taunton. 11.

3. *Pensacola B. Entrance.* Careful manuscript 33 by 27, with distances and references. Reminiscent of style of James C. Smith c. 1768. Hydrographic Department, Taunton. A251/1.

4. *Pensacola B. Entrance.* Careful manuscript 24½ by 30. In style of James C. Smith. Hydrographic Department, Taunton. A251/2.

5. *A Plan of the Town of Pensacola 1767.* Careful, colored manuscript 10½ by 6¼. Library of Congress. Faden Collection no. 44.

6. *Plan of Fort at Pensacola.* Careful, part colored manuscript 18¾ by 14¼. British Museum. Royal United Services Institution Collection. A30/60.

7. *Plan of the Commanding Officer's Quarters at Pensacola.* Careful manuscript 19¼ by 13½. Reminiscent of hand of Elias Durnford. Removed from CO5/579. Public Record Office. MPG980.

8. *Plan of Fort George at Pensacola Built With Squard Timber: the Lines of Fascines & Sand: The S.W. side is two 24 Pounders, and the others 12 & 9 Pos.* Careful manuscript 14⅛ by 26⅜. In lower right "C. Towne 9th. October 1781 W W." Library of Congress.

9. [*Plan of Fort George.*] Careful manuscript 9 by 12⅝. Library of Congress.

10. *Plan of Fort George and Adjacent Works at Pensacola in West Florida.* Careful manuscript 17⅞ by 27¼. Library of Congress.

As noted previously, the contributions of the individual cartographers is the primary purpose of this volume, shared by the contributions of the anonymous draftsmen of the other manuscript maps.

Printed maps, the contribution of the map publishers, engravers, mathematicians, and geographical editors, while exceedingly important and interesting, are of secondary interest. The practitioners and businessmen accomplished their work in London, far from the distant and hazardous America. Their accomplishments have been the subject of numerous published studies.

Printed maps were separate publications, or were included in books, magazines, accounts and atlases. Many have obvious common origins, recognizable antecedents, or authority. Others present less obvious relationships. The larger maps varied from copies of original manuscripts, to compilations from secondary sources of varying degree of reliability. Some sources predated employment by one or two decades.

After the mid 18th. century, England was challenging the leadership of France in map production and cartographic development. Centered in London, the industry depended upon the increasing number of reports and surveys of explorers, mariners and the military. The number and abilities of engravers, mathematicians, printers, editors and publishers increased concomitantly. All of these were the result of England's commercial and maritime expansion.

Thomas Jefferys, primarily an engraver, was an outstanding figure. His publication of maps, atlases, pilots and other material relating to America increased rapidly after the mid century. He later dominated the field, expressing England's strategy in geographical terms. His position was enhanced by appointment as Geographer to the Prince of Wales, later George III. Entree to the resources of the military and important administrative officers gave him early knowledge and use of governmental reports, draughts, surveys and other material. Employing able geographical editors and specialized draughtsmen, his maps were accurate and carefully rendered. His *A General Topography of North America and the West Indies* of 1768 was an outstanding work. Robert Sayer gained control of part of Jefferys' trade about 1767 as the result of financial problems. Sayer became associated with John Bennett in 1770. An excellent and detailed study of the bankruptcy of Jefferys was published by J. B. Harley *(Imago Mundi XX, 27, 1966).*

William Faden, also an engraver, became associated with Jefferys sometime after 1767. The firm "Jefferys and Faden" continued at least to 1774, although Faden succeeded Jefferys on his death in 1771. Faden, an able engraver and enterprising publisher quickly attained an even greater degree of eminence and respect, becoming a dominant figure until retirement in 1823.

Faden continued to reproduce the earlier North American maps of Jefferys, and published an increasing number of new North American maps, particularly after the beginning of the Revolution. Many were reproductions of the works of military cartographers and surveyors, which came to his hand because of the magnitude of his publications and appointment as Geographer to His Majesty. The maps were printed and sold separately, or were collected and bound into *The North American Atlas.* These were variable, containing from 23 to 39 maps, and bear a title page dated 1777. They were volumes bound for the individual requirements of the customer, and include numbers of maps from other engravers and publishers. None of the several examined were identical in content. An account of his early career is included in a study by J. B. Harley and R. W. Stephenson (The William Faden Collection of American Maps; Library of Congress, forthcoming).

Faden was a dealer as well as engraver and publisher. He sold the products of his competitors, and those published abroad. A collection of letters to Faden, written between 1773 and 1784, give a somewhat one-sided view of his trade, but demonstrate its extent, which was carried on in spite of wars. The letters, from Lattré of Paris, Coviens and Mortier of Amsterdam, Julien of Paris, other dealers, and a wide range of individuals, were the subject of a study by George Kiss *Imago Mundi* IV, 75, 1965.

During the war, Faden published a number of excellent maps of separate campaigns and battles. Some were collected and bound as an *Atlas of the Battles of the American Revolution,* dated 1793, and including from 17 to 22 maps. Faden's catalog of 1822 carried 11 maps of the area of the present United States, but dating from the years of the war. The catalog also carries 33 maps of the military campaigns of the war in the present United States, and Quebec. A number of impressions of maps were made on paper dated at least as late as 1794.

A large number of the remaining battle maps were purchased by Bartlett & Welford, combined into another edition of *Atlas of Battles of the American Revolution,* and marketed in New York after 1845.

The most popular atlas of the Revolution was Sayer and Bennett's *The American Military Pocket Atlas,* dated London 1776, containing six maps. It was widely used by officers of all armies. A particular attraction was its small size, causing it to be called "The Holster Atlas." It was offered for sale by Hugh Gaine, New York printer and book seller, in an advertisement dated 24 August 1778. The content of the atlas remained unchanged.

Sayer and Bennett's *The American Military Pocket Atlas....* remained constant during its period of publication. Occasional copies are noted with additional maps, which appear to have been added after they left the hands of the publisher. In most copies, the maps are dated 1776, or before. Two copies may have maps issued later.

Other atlases were produced by Sayer and Bennett. *The American Atlas: or a Geographical Description of the Whole Continent of America* was published with dates of 1775, 1776 and 1782, and probably other years. It contained from 22 to 34 maps. *A General Atlas, Describing the Whole Universe* was published in 1780, and other years. It contained four or more American maps, which appeared in the other. The title pages featured heavily the honored and famous names of the more prominent geographic authorities. Maps of other publishers were included.

Other engravers and publishers contributed a varying number of maps to the aggregate production of Revolutionary War London. These, and the maps included in the atlases, have been divided on the basis of the publisher, in alphabetical order. As indicated previously, maps were produced individually, combined into atlases by the more enterprising dealer, and occasionally included in printed works as illustrative material.

138. JOHN ANDREWS AND ANDREW DURY

1. *A New Map of the British Colonies in North America Shewing the Seat of the Present War Taken from the best Surveys, Compared with and improved from Manuscripts of Several Noblemen and Gentlemen by John Andrews & Andrew Dury. London, Jan'y 16, 1777.* Printed map 29½ by 38.

139. JOHN ANDREWS AND JOHN HARRIS

1. Same title as Andrews and Dury no. 1. By John Andrews & John Harris, London. Jan'y 16th. 1781.

140. JOHN BEW

1. *A Map and Chart of those Parts of the Bay of Chesapeak York and James Rivers which are at present The Seat of War. London: J. Bew.* Printed map 14¼ by 9¼. Issued 30 November 1781, after the surrender at Yorktown, but prior to receipt of the news in England. Same map as no. 11, *The Political Magazine.*

141. CARINGTON BOWLES

1. *A Map of the most Inhabited part of New England containing the Provinces of Massachusetts Bay and New Hampshire with the Colonies of Connecticut And Rhode Island Divided into Counties and Townships;... Printed for Carington Bowles, at No. 69 in St. Pauls Church Yard London. Published 1st. Jan. 1771 [1775?]* Detailed printed map 19½ by 24. Originally issued about 1765 by John and Carington Bowles, reissued by Carington Bowles alone in 1771, and probably reissued in 1775.
2. *Bowles's Map Of The Seat of War in New England, Comprehending the Provinces of Massachusetts Bay, And New Hampshire: With the Colonies Of Connecticut And Rhode Island: Divided into their Townships; the best Authorities- London: Printed for Carington Bowles, No. 69 in St. Pauls Church Yard. 1776.* Detailed printed map 19⅝ by 24⅜. Alteration of the preceding plate.
3. *Bowles's New Pocket Map of the Most Inhabited Part of New England....* Detailed printed map 19½ by 24¼. Reissue of the plate used in the preceding two, about 1780.
4. *Bowles's New Map of North America and the West Indies Exhibiting the British Empire therein with its Limits according to the Definitive Treaty of Peace in 1763 As also The Dominions Possessed in That Quarter, by the Spaniards, the French & other European States, the whole Compiled from the Best Surveys and Authentic Memoirs which have appeared to the Present Year 1780. Printed for the Proprietor Carington Bowles. No. 69 St. Pauls Church Yard, London.* Printed map 45 by 40. Below cartouche "Published...1 Jan. 1778." Previous edition in 1763, later editions 2 Jan. 1783, 1796 and 1808.

142. JOHN BOWLES AND G. KEARSLEY

1. *Plan of the Attack on the Provincial Army on Long Island August 27th 1776 with the Draughts of New York Island, Staten Island, and the Adjacent Part of the Continent, By an Officer of the Army.* Printed map 13 by 14¼, published Oct. 24. 1776. In lower right "Printed for J. Bowles, at No. 13 Cornhill, G. Kearsley No. 46 Fleet Street."

143. GEORGE CAMERON

1. *A Map Of The Island of New York and Environs with the March of the British Troops Published and Sold by Geo. Cameron Engraver Todericks Wynd Edinr. 14th. Novr. 1776 Pr. 1 sh.* Printed map 12⅜ by 10⅝, inset "Plan of the City of New York."

144. ANDREW DURY

1. *A New Map of the British Colonies in North America....* See under John Andrews and Andrew Dury, also John Andrews and John Harris.
2. *A Map of Nova Scotia or Arcadia with the Islands of Cape Breton and St. John from actual surveys by Captn. Montresor, 1768.* Printed map 54½ by 39½. Insets, "A Plan of the town of Boston," and "A plan of Boston Harbor." Printed and sold by A. Dury in Dukes Court. In Faden's *The North American Atlas,* 1777. (Library of Congress copy A).
3. *A Plan of Boston, and its Environs shewing the true Situation of His Majesty's Army. And also Those of The Rebels Drawn by an Engineer at Boston. Octr 1775. Published...12th. March 1775 by Andrew Dury. Engraved by John Lodge.* Printed map 25½ by 18. In upper left, attribution to Richard Williams. See Richard Williams no. 2.
4. *A Map of the Province of New York, with part of Pennsylvania, and New England from an actual survey by Captain Montresor, Engineer 1775. Published June 10th. 1775 by A. Dury, Dukes Court. P. Andrews Sculp.* Printed map 36¼ by 56½. Insets, Continuation of Lake Champlain, Continuation of Connecticut River. See Montresor no. 30. In Faden's *The North American Atlas.* Second and third issues 1775. Another "Republished with great improvements. April 1st. 1777."
5. *A Plan of the City of New-York & its Environs to Greenwich on the North or Hudson's River, and to Crown Point on the East or Sound River.* Printed map 26¼ by 21. London: A. Dury 1776 "Survey'd in the Winter, 1775." Inset "Chart of the Entrance to New York from Sandy Hook." See Montresor no. 28. Actually surveyed by Montresor in December 1765, hurriedly for military reasons during the stamp act riots. It was first published in 1766, and was included in Jefferys' *The General Topography of North America.*
6. *A Plan Of The City of Philadelphia the Capital of Pennsylvania from an Actuel Survey By Benjamin Easburn, Surveyor General 1776. London, Published...4th. November 1776 By Andrew Dury. P. Andre Sculp.* Printed map 26 by 19¼. Inset "Chart of Delaware Bay and River by Mr. Fisher of Philadelphia." See under Easburn and under Fisher.
7. *A Chart of Delaware Bay and River...Andrew Dury, 30 November 1776.* Printed map 26¾ by 17½. In Faden's *The North American Atlas,* 1777.

145. WILLIAM FADEN

1. *The British Colonies in North America, engraved by William Faden MDCCLXXVII.* In Faden's *North American Atlas* 1777. Printed map 24½ by 20¼. Ten editions or issues, with title changes, to 1820. Seven subsequent editions to 1843 by Joseph Wyld, Faden's successor.
2. *A Plan of the City and Environs of Quebec, with its Siege and Blockade by the Americans from the 8th. of December 1775 to the 13th. of May 1776. London,...12 Septemr. 1776 by Wm. Faden.* Printed map 24¼ by 17½. In Faden's *The North American Atlas,* 1777.
3. *A Topographical Map of the Province of New Hampshire Surveyed agreeably to the Orders and Instructions Of The Right Honorable the Lords Commissioners For Trade And Plantations unto Samuel Holland Esqr. His Majesty's Surveyor General of Lands for the Northern District of North America by the following Gentlemen His Deputies Mr. Thomas Wright, Mr. George Sproule, Mr. James Grant, Mr. Thomas Wheeler & Mr. Charles Blaskowitz. London: Printed for William Faden...March 1st. 1784.* Printed map, two sheets, each 30¼ by 22¾.
4. *A Topographical Map of the State of New Hampshire surveyed under the Direction of Samuel Holland Esqr. Surveyor General of Lands for the Northern District of North America By the following Gentlemen His Deputies Mr. Thomas Wright, Mr. George Sproule, Mr. James Grant, Mr. Thomas Wheeler & Mr. Charles Blaskowitz. London. Printed for William Faden...March 1st. 1784.* Printed map 30¾ by 23¼. (other half missing?)
5. *Boston its environs and Harbour, with the Rebel's Works Raised against that Town in 1775 from the Observations of Lieut. Page of His Majesty's Corps of Engineers and from the plans of Capt. Montresor. Published by Wm. Faden...1st. Oct. 1777.* Printed map 24 by 17½, published with and without partial overlay. In Faden's *The North American Atlas,* 1777.

6. *A Plan of the Town of Boston with the Intrenchments, etc., of His Majesty's Forces in 1775, from the observations of Lieut. Page, of His Majesty's Corps of Engineers and from plans of other gentlemen. William Faden, Oct. 1, 1777.* Printed map 17½ by 11¾. Later edition 1778. In Faden's *Atlas of the Battles....*

7. *A Topographical Chart of the Bay of Narragansett in the Province of New England with all the Isles contained therein, among which Rhode Island and Connonicut have been particularly Surveyed. By Charles Blaskowitz. Wm. Faden, July 22d. 1777.* Printed map 24¾ by 36½. In Faden's *North American Atlas, 1777.*

8. *A Plan of the Town of Newport in Rhode Island, surveyed by Charles Blaskowitz. Willm. Faden...Septr. 14, 1777.* Printed map 14¼ by 13¼. In Faden's *The North American Atlas, 1777.*

9. *A Map of the Inhabited Part of Canada from the French Surveys with the Frontiers of New York and New England from the Large Survey by C. J. Sauthier. Wm. Faden, 1777.* Printed map 33½ by 22¼.

10. *A Map of the Province of New-York Reduced from a large Drawing of that Province compiled from Actual Surveys by order of His Excellency William Tryon Esqr. Captain General & Governor of the same By Claude Joseph Sauthier to which is added New-Jersey, from the Topographic Observations of C. J. Sauthier and B. Ratzer. William Faden, Aug. 1st. 1776.* Printed map 21¾ by 27.

11. *A Chorographical Map of the Province of New York in North America divided into Counties, Manors, Patents and Townships: compiled from actual surveys by Claude Joseph Sauthier. William Faden, Jan. 1st. 1779.* Printed map 53½ by 71.

12. *Plan of the Encampment and Position of the Army under His Excelly. Lt. General Burgoyne at Swords House on Hudson's River near Stillwater on Septr. 17th. with the Positions of that part of the Army engaged on the 19th. Septr. 1777 Drawn by W. C. Wilkinson Lt. 62d. Regt. Asst. Engr. Engraved by Wm. Faden. Feb. 1st. 1780.* Printed map 13¼ by 12½, with part overlay. In Burgoyne's *A State of the Expedition from Canada....*

13. *The Attack and Defeat of the American Fleet under Benedict Arnold by the King's Fleet commanded by Capt. Thos. Pringle upon Lake Champlain, the 11th. of October, 1776. From a Sketch taken by an Officer on the Spot. London, Decr. 3, 1776.* Printed map 16½ by 10. Editions with and without text. In Faden's *The North American Atlas, 1777.*

14. *A Topographical Map of Hudsons River, with the Channels, Depth of Water, Rocks, Shoals, &c and the Country adjacent from Sandy-Hook, New York and Bay to Fort Edward, also the Communication with Canada By Lake George and Lake Champlain, as high as Fort Chambly on Sorel River. By Claude Joseph Sauthier... William Faden, Oct. 1st. 1776.* Printed map 20¾ by 31¼. In Faden's *The North American Atlas, 1777.*

15. *A Topographical Map of the Northn Part Of New York Island, Exhibiting the Plan of Fort Washington, now Fort Knyphausen, With the Rebels Lines to the Southward, which were Formed by the Troops under the Command of The Rt. Honble. Earl Percy on the 16th. Novr. 1776, and Survey'd Immediately after by Order of his Lordship By Claude Joseph*

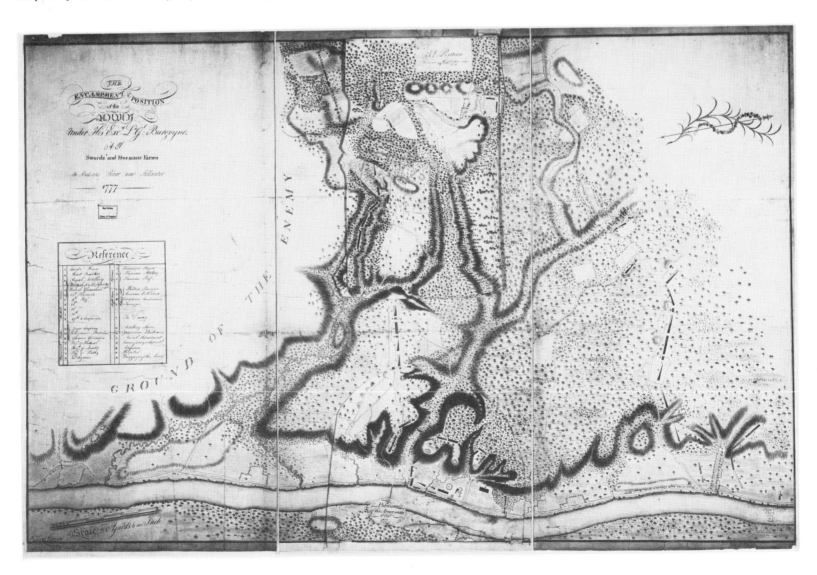

William Wilkinson's manuscript map of a Burgoyne position, see 118/1. For Faden engraved variations, see 118/2,3; 145/12.

Sauthier...Published by Permission of the Rt. Honble. the Commissioners of Trade & Plantations by Wm. Faden, 1777. London, March 1st. 1777. Printed map 10¼ by 18¼. In Faden's *The North American Atlas*, 1777.

16. *A Plan of New York Island; with part of Long Island, Staten Island & East New Jersey, with a particular description of the engagement on the Woody Heights of Long Island, between Flatbush and Brooklyn, on the 27th of August, 1776 between His Majesty's Forces, commanded by General Howe, and the Americans under Major General Putnam. Shewing also the landing of the British Army on New-York Island, and the Taking of the City of New-York, &c, on the 15th September...Engraved & Published...Octr 19th 1776 by Wm. Faden.* Printed map 16½ by 18¾. Five separate issues with the same date, and one more later. Each issued on small paper, or on a larger sheet with four columns of descriptive text below. In Faden's *The North American Atlas*, 1777.

17. *A Plan of the Operations of the King's Army, under the Command of General Sr. William Howe, K.B., in New York and East New Jersey, against the American Forces commanded by General Washington, from the 12th of October, to the 28th of November, 1776. Wherein is particularly distinguished the Engagement on the White Plains the 28th of October. By Claude Joseph Sauthier.* William Faden, London, Feby 25th. 1777. Printed map 19½ by 28½. Another issue shows British vessels off "Terry Town." In Faden's *The North American Atlas*.

18. *Plan of the Operations of General Washington against the King's Troops in New Jersey from 26th. of December 1776, to the 3rd. January 1777, by William Faden.* Published 15th April 1777. Printed map 15¼ by 11. Two issues with same date. In Faden's *North American Atlas*.

19. *The Province of Jersey divided into East and West commonly called the Jerseys.* Wm. Faden, London, Dec. 1, 1777. Engraved map 22¼ by 30½. See under Bernard Ratzer and Gerard Bancker. Second edition, Dec. 1, 1778. In Faden's *The North American Atlas*.

20. *A Plan of the City and Environs of Philadelphia Surveyed by N. Scull and G. Heap Engraved by Willm. Faden 1777.* March 12th. 1777. Printed map 17¾ by 24. Several issues. In Faden's *North American Atlas*.

21. *A Plan of the City and Environs of Philadelphia and Encampments of His Majesty's Forces under...Sir William Howe, K.B.* Wm. Faden, January 1st., 1779. Printed map 18½ by 20¼. In Faden's *Atlas of Battles of the American Revolution*.

22. *British Camp at Trudruffrin from the 18th to the 21st of September 1777, with the Attacks made by Major General Grey against the Rebels near White Horse Tavern.* Wm. Faden. July 1st 1778. Printed map 16¼ by 10. In Faden's *Atlas of Battles of the American Revolution*.

23. *The Course of Delaware River from Philadelphia to Chester Exhibiting the Several Works erected by the Rebels to defend its Passage with the Attacks made upon them by His Majesty's Land & Sea Forces.* Wm. Faden. Printed map 28¾ by 21. Inset Sketch of Fort Island. Published April 30, 1778, also 1 Jany 1785. In Faden's *Atlas of Battles of the American Revolution*.

24. *A Chart of Delaware Bay and River Containing a full & exact description of the Shores, Creeks, Harbours, Soundings, Shoals, Sands, and Bearings...from the Capes to Philadelphia. Taken from the Original Chart Published at Philadelphia by Joshua Fisher.* March 12, 1776. Printed map 26¾ by 18½. In Faden's *The North American Atlas*. Also issued with printed "Directions for Navigating Up Delaware-Bay..." by Capt. James Campbell, late R.N.

25. *A Plan Of The Attack Of Fort Sulivan near Charles Town in South Carolina, by a Squadron of His Majesty's Ships on the 28th June 1776, with the Disposition of the King's Land Forces, and the Encampments and Entrenchments of the Rebels....Augt. 10 1776 by Wm. Faden.* Printed map 14½ by 11. At least four states or issues. In Faden's *The North American Atlas*.

26. *Sketch of the Battle of Hobkirk's Hill, near Camden, on the 25th. of April 1781. Drawn by C. Vallancy, Capt. of the Vols. of Ireland.* London, Wm. Faden, Aug. 1, 1783. Printed map 11¾ by 17⅛. In Faden's *Atlas of Battles of the American Revolution*.

27. *A Map of South Carolina...Wm. Faden, June 1st. 1780.* Included in his *The North American Atlas*. See under Jefferys No. 3.

28. *The Bay of Espiritu Santo...St. Augustine...East Florida.* W. Faden [1777.] included in his *The North American Atlas*. See under Jefferys no. 5.

29. *A Plan of the Town, Bar, Harbour, and Environs of Charlestown in South Carolina, from the Surveys made in the Colony. Engraved by Wm. Faden, London, June 1st 1780.* Printed map 26⅝ by 19¾. Fort Sulivan now named Fort Moultry.

146. W. HAWKES

1. *The Country Twenty Five Miles round New York. Drawn by a Gentleman from that City. London. Published...1st. November 1776, by W. Hawkes.* Printed map 14¾ by 14½. Table of "Most interesting occurrances..." Issues also dated 21st. November, 1st. January 1777, and R. Sayer & J. Bennett 2 June 1777.

147. JEFFERYS AND FADEN

1. *A Sketch Of The Action Between The British Forces And The American Provincials on the Heights of the Peninsula of Charlestown, the 17th. of June 1775. Engraved by Jefferys & Faden, 1 Augt 1775.* Printed map 12 by 13³⁄₁₆.

2. *Plan of the City of New York, in North America: Surveyed in the Years 1766 & 1767. London: Published by Jefferys & Faden Jany. 12, 1776.* See Ratzer 2 and 3. Two issues with same date. In Faden's *The North American Atlas*.

3. *A Plan of Port Royal in South Carolina. Survey'd by Capn. John Gascoign. Engraved by Jefferys & Faden 1773.* Printed map 22¾ by 28. Editions by Sayer & Bennett 15 May 1776, and by Sayer 15 Jany 1791, Laurie & Whittle in 1794.

4. *A Plan of the River and Sound of D'awfoskee, in South Carolina. Survey'd by Captain John Gascoign. Engraved by Jefferys & Faden 1773.* Printed map 17¾ by 25. Edition by Jefferys & Faden in 1776, R. Sayer & J. Bennett 15th May 1776, Laurie & Whittle 12 May 1794.

148. THOMAS JEFFERYS

1. *A Map of the Most Inhabited Part of New England containing the Provinces of Massachusetts Bay and New Hampshire with the Colonies of Conecticut and Rhode Island. London, November 29th 1774 by Thomas Jefferys.* Printed map 38 by 40½. Inset plans of Boston and Boston Harbor. Editions or issues in 1755, republished with the same date about 1763 and 1768, and later by Laurie & Whittle in 1794. First issue edited by John Green. In Faden's *The North American Atlas*.

2. *An Accurate Map of The State and Province of New-Hampshire in New England, taken from Actual Surveys of all the Inhabited Part, and from the best information of what is uninhabited, together with the adjacent Countries, which exhibits the Theatre of this War in that Part of the World, by Col. Blanchard, and the Revd. Mr. Langdon.* Thos. Jefferys. Printed map 26¼ by 28, dated 21 Oct. 1761. Then dedicated to John Hancock at Boston April 22, 1784 in manuscript. In the description of New Hampshire, it is dated AD 1783. First published 1756. The 1761 issue was in Jefferys' *The General Topography of North America*, of 1768. Library of Congress. G3740 1784 B6, see also G3740 1761 B5.

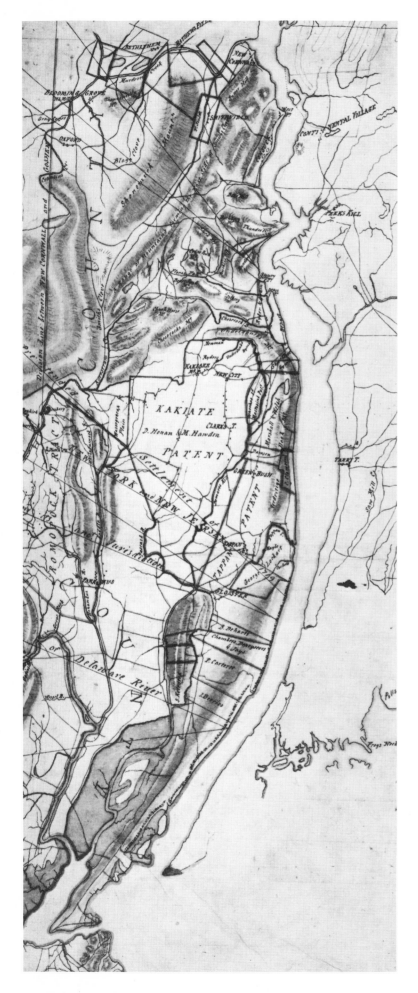

Bernard Ratzer's 1769 survey of Hudson River west shore, section, embodied into later maps. See 92/145;145/19.

3. *A Map of South Carolina and a part of Georgia containing the Whole Sea-Coast, all the Islands, Inlets, Rivers, Creeks, Parishes, Townships, Boroughs, Roads and Bridges. From surveys taken by the Hon. William Bull, Esq. Lt. Governor, Capt. Gascoign, Hugh Bryan Esq., and the author William DeBrahm.* Printed map 47¼ by 57. Initially engraved by Jefferys with date October 20, 1757, and included in his General Topography of North America, of 1768. Reissued by Wm. Faden...June 1st. 1780, included in his *The North American Atlas.*

4. *A Chart of the Entrance into St. Mary's River, taken by Captn. Fuller in November 1769.* Printed map 24 by 19¾. Insets of Amelia Island in East Florida, and the mouth of the Nassau River. London, 26 March 1770 by Thomas Jefferys, (Faden, 1776?) In Faden's *The North American Atlas*, 1777.

5. *The Bay of Espiritu Santo, and the Western Coast of East Florida. Plan of the Town of St. Augustine the Capital of East Florida.* Both on one page, respectively 10¼ by 8 and 11¼ by 8½. *T. Jefferys.* Printed map. Printed for W. Faden (1777?) In Faden's *The North American Atlas.*

149. ROBERT SAYER

1. *An Accurate Map of North America describing the British and Spanish Dominions according to the Definitive Treaty concluded at Paris, 10th Feb. 1763. Also all the West India Islands. By Eman. Bowen, Geogr. to His Majesty, and John Gibson, Engraver.* London: Printed for Robert Sayer, No. 53 Fleet Street 2d July 1775. Printed map 43½ by 37¼. In Jefferys' American Atlas, published by Sayer and Bennett. Initially published 1755, other issues 1763, 1772. Later issue dated 10th Jany 1777 with additional "corrected from Original Materials of Govern. Pownall, Member of Parliament, 1777." Other editions or issues 1777, 1779, 1783, 1786, 1794, and 1798.

3. *The Coast of West Florida and Louisiana. By Thos. Jefferys 1775.* Printed map 48¼ by 18½. "Printed for Robert Sayer 20th Feby 1775." In Faden's *The North American Atlas.*

4. *Course of the River Mississippi From the Balise to Fort Chartres, Taken on an Expedition to the Illinois in the latter end of the Year 1765 by Lieut. Ross of the 39th. Regiment. Improved from Surveys of the River made by the French. London, Robert Sayer, 1 June 1775.* Printed map 13 by 44. In Faden's *The North American Atlas*, 1777.

150. ROBERT SAYER AND JOHN BENNETT

1. *A Map of the British Empire in North America by Samuel Dunn, Mathematician. London, R. Sayer & J. Bennett, 10 Jany 1774.* Printed map 12 by 17½. Later issues August 17, 1776, October 9, 1783, and 10 June 1786 by Robert Sayer. In the Holster Atlas.

2. *A New and Correct Map of North America, with the West India Islands...corrected from the Original Materials of Governor Pownall...Printed for Robt. Sayer and Jn. Bennett...15th. Feb. 1777.* Printed map 43½ by 37¼. Insets of Baffin and Hudson's Bay and Passage by Land to California. In Faden's *The North American Atlas*. See Robert Sayer, map no. 1.

3. *A New Map of the Province of Quebec according to the Royal Proclamation of the 7th. of October 1763 from the French Surveys connected with those made after the War, By Captain Carver and other officers of his Majesty's Service. London, 16th Feb. 1776. Sayer & Bennett.* Printed map 52½ by 26¾. In Faden's *The North American Atlas*, 1777. Later issues by Robert Sayer, 1 Jan. 1788; and by Laurie & Whittle, 12 May 1794. See under Carver.

4. *A New Map of Nova Scotia and Cape Breton Island with the Adjacent Parts of New England and Canada. Compiled from a great number of actual Surveys and other Materials Regulated by*

many new Astronomical Observations of the Longitude as well as Latitude by Thomas Jefferys, Geographer To The King. Printed map 23¾ by 17¾. "Printed & Sold by R. Sayer & J. Bennett...15 June 1775." First issued 1755, and reissued in the same year. Numerous issues in 1775, later issues in 1783, under the name R. Sayer in 1786, and Laurie & Whittle in 1794. In Faden's *The North American Atlas.*

5. *A Map of the Most Inhabited Part of New England...By Thomas Jefferys.* Printed map 38 by 40. Sayer & Bennett, 1776. See Thomas Jefferys, map no. 1.

6. *Seat of War in New England by an American Volunteer, with the Marches of the several Corps sent by the Colonies towards Boston, with thé attack on Bunker Hill.* London, Sayer and Bennett, Sept. 2, 1775. Printed map 18 by 15½. Insets of Boston Harbor, Plan of Boston and Charlestown.

7. *A Plan of the Battle on Bunkers Hill. Fought on the 17th. of June 1775. By an officer on the spot.* Printed for R. Sayer & J. Bennett 27 Nov 1775. Printed map 13½ by 19. Description of the battle from Gen. Burgoyne's letter to his nephew Lord Stanley.

8. *A Survey of Lake Champlain including Lake George, Crown Point, and St. John...William Brasier, draughtsman 1762.* London, R. Sayer & J. Bennett, Aug. 5, 1776. Printed map 17 by 23¼. In Faden's *The North American Atlas*, and the *Holster Atlas*. Another issue in 1776 and 12 May 1794 by Laurie & Whittle. See under Brasier.

9. *The Seat of Action between the British and American Forces, or An Authentic Plan of the Western Part of Long Island with the Engagement of the 27th August 1776 between the King's Forces and the Americans containing also Staten Island, and the Environs of Amboy and New York, with the Course of Hudsons River, from Courtland the Great Magazine of the American Army, to Sandy Hook from the Surveys of Major Holland.* London, R. Sayer & J. Bennett, 22d Octr 1776. Printed map 15¼ by 17⅜. Inset of Road from Amboy to Philadelphia.

10. *A General Map of the Middle British Colonies in America. Containing Virginia, Maryland, The Delaware Counties, Pennsylvania and New Jersey.* London, R. Sayer & J. Bennett, 1776. Printed map 19 by 26¼. See under Lewis Evans. In the Holster Atlas.

11. *A Map of Pennsylvania Exhibiting not only the Improved Parts of that Province, but also its extensive frontiers, from the late map of W. Scull published in 1770.* London, printed for Robt. Sayer & J. Bennett 10 June 1775. Printed map 52½ by 26¾. In Jefferys' *The American Atlas* and Faden's *The North American Atlas.*

12. *A General Map of the Southern British Colonies in America comprehending North and South Carolina, Georgia, East and West Florida....from surveys...DeBrahm, Capt. Collet, Mouzon & others, By B. Romans.* London, Robt. Sayer & J. Bennett, 15 Octr. 1776. Printed map 18½ by 24¼. In the *Holster Atlas.*

13. *An Accurate Map of North and South Carolina, with their Indian Frontiers, Showing in A Distinct Manner, All the Mountains, Rivers, Swamps, Marshes, Bays, Creeks, Harbours, Sandbanks and Soundings on the Coasts, With The Roads And Indian Paths As Well As The Boundry Or Provincial Lines, The Several Townships And Other Divisions Of The Land In Both The Provinces, The Whole From Actual Surveys. By Henry Mouzon and Others.* Printed for Robt. Sayer and J. Bennett...May 30, 1775. Printed map 56 by 38, insets of Harbour of Port Royal and the Bar and Harbour of Charlestown. In various of Sayer & Bennett's *The American Atlas*, in Faden's *The North American Atlas.* Reissued by Laurie & Whittle in 1794.

14. *An Exact Plan of Charles-Town Bar and Harbour. From An Exact Survey.* London, Printed for Robt. Sayer and Jn. Bennett...July 17, 1776. Printed map 18 by 26¾. Another issue dated 31st. August 1776.

15. *A Plan of the Attack of Fort Sulivan, the Key of Charlestown in South Carolina on the 28th. of June 1776 By His Majesty's* Squadron Commanded by Sir Peter Parker By an Officer on the Spot. London, 7 Sept. 1776. Printed map 15¼ by 12½. Descriptive text below.

16. *A Plan of the Military Operations against Charlestown, the Army being Commanded by L.G. Sir Henry Clinton, K.B. and the Fleet by Vice-Admiral Arbuthnot, from an original drawing sent by an Officer in the Army.* 27 May 1780, London. Printed map.

17. *A Plan Of Port Royal In South Carolina, Surveyed By Captn. John Gascoign.* London, 15 May 1776. Printed map 27¾ by 22½. Included in Sayer & Bennett's *The North American Pilot*, 1777.

18. *A Plan of Cape Fear River from the Bar to Brunswick.* London, Robt. Sayer & J. Bennett, 1 July 1776. Printed map 13¼ by 20. In Faden's *The North American Atlas*, 1777.

19. *The Coast of West Florida and Louisiana. The Peninsula & Gulf of Florida, or Channel of Bahama, with the Bahama Islands. By Thomas Jefferys, Geographer to his Majesty.* Robt. Sayer & J. Bennett, 20 Feby 1775. Two printed maps on one sheet, 47½ by 18¼.

20. *A Complete Map of the West Indies, containing the Coasts of Florida, Louisiana, New Spain...by Samuel Dunn, Mathematician.* London, 15 Jany 1774. Printed map 12 by 17½. In the Holster Atlas.

151. ROBERT SAYER AND THOMAS JEFFERYS

1. *A Map of the most Inhabited part of Virginia Containing the whole Province of Maryland With Part of Pensilvania, New Jersey and North Carolina. Drawn by Joshua Fry & Peter Jefferson in 1751. To the Right Honourable, George Dunk, Earl of Halifax, First Lord Commissioner, and to the Rest of the Right Honourable and Honourable Commissioners for Trade and Plantations, this Map is most humbly Inscribed to their Lordships, By their Lordship's Most Obedient & most devoted humble Servt. Thos. Jefferys. 1775.* Printed map 46¾ by 28¼. Printed for Robert Sayer and Thos. Jefferys. First issued by Jefferys in 1751. Additional issues the same year, in 1755, in 176-?, 1775, and 1794. The 176-? issue was printed for Robert Sayer and Thos. Jefferys and the 1794 issue for Laurie & Whittle. See under Joshua Fry and under Peter Jefferson.

PRINTED MAPS IN MAGAZINES

Arranged by Magazine Title

Magazine maps of the military events in North America were those most widely circulated, and the most generally available to Britain's reading public.

Many of the maps are excellent, although generally copied from, or based upon, existing maps. Many were engraved by, or for, the principals who were making current maps for the regular and recognized publishers of maps and atlases. A few of the maps in magazines may have been the first published of contemporary events. Many were reproduced in a surprisingly short time after the event, if the dates of publication are correct.

The magazines or journals are arranged alphabetically, with the individual maps listed chronologically. Occasionally, maps had been omitted, or were inserted irregularly.

The maps in *The Universal Magazine* were of very high caliber, followed by those in *The Political Magazine*. While many of the editorial writers may have represented the views of the political opposition, there is frequently a tone of sympathy, or at least tolerance for the stand of the Americans. There are a few who were violently anti-Colonial. The accuracy and completeness of news coverage is particularly wide in Almon's *The Remembrancer....* It reproduces most of the official documents of both sides, and should be a convenient resource for the student.

A few of the maps appear to have been printed for the first time in these magazines. They were sometimes reproduced in books, or in America, without acknowledgement.

152. THE GENTLEMAN'S MAGAZINE AND HISTORICAL CHRONICLE

1. *A Plan of the Town, and Chart of the Harbour of Boston.* Printed map, 14 by 12. Opposite page 41, January 1775.
2. *A Map of 100 Miles Round Boston.* Printed map 9¼ by 8½. Opposite page 264, June 1775.
3. *Plan of the Redoubts and Intrenchment on the Heights of Charles Town (Commonly called Bunker's-Hill), opposite Boston, in New-England attacked and carried by his Majesty's Troops,* June 17, 1775. Small text diagram 3¾ by 3½. Page 416, September 1775.
4. *A New and Correct Plan of the Town of Boston.* Printed map 7½ by 10¼. Opposite page 493, October 1775.
5. *A Map of the Country round Philadelphia Including Part of New Jersey, New-York, Staten Island & Long Island.* Printed map 8¼ by 6½. Opposite page 396. September 1776.
6. *Sketch of the Country Illustrating the late Engagement in Long Island.* Printed map 12 by 7¾. Opposite page 452. October 1776.
7. *A Map of Connecticut and Rhode Island with Long Island Sound, &c.* Printed map 8¼ by 6¼. Opposite page 525, November 1776.
8. *Map of the Progress of his Majesty's Armies in New York during the late Campaign illustrating the accounts Published in the London Gazette.* Printed map 12 by 7¾. Opposite page 607, December 1776. Copied in Low's Almanac 1776 and Isaac Warren's Almanac 1777.
9. *A Map of Philadelphia and Parts Adjacent By N. Scull and G. Heap.* Printed map 11½ by 13¼. December 1777. Reproduced from the 1753 number.
10. *Map of Hudson's River with the adjacent Country.* Printed map 7⅞ by 11⅛. Opposite page 41, January 1778.
11. *A Chart of Delaware Bay And River from the Original By Mr. Fisher of Philadelphia in 1776.* Printed map 9¼ by 7. Opposite page 369, July 1779.

153. THE LONDON MAGAZINE OR GENTLEMAN'S MONTHLY INTELLIGENCER

1. *A Chart of the Coast of New England from Beverly to Scituate Harbour including the Ports of Boston and Salem.* Printed map with inset of the town of Boston, 7 by 9½. Opposite page 165, January 1774.
2. *A View of the Rivers Kenebec and Chaudiere with Colonel Arnold's Route to Quebec.* Printed map 4⅜ by 6⅞. Opposite page 48, September 1776.
3. *Seat of War in the Environs of Philadelphia By. Thos. Kitchin, Senr. Hydrographer to his Majesty.* Printed map 9½ by 7¼. Opposite page 587, December 1777.
4. *Part of the Counties of Charlotte and Albany in the Province of New York; being the Seat of War between the King's Forces under Lieut. Gen. Burgoyne and the Rebel Army. By Thos. Kitchin Senr. Hydrographer to his Majesty.* Printed map 7 by 9¼. Opposite page 51, February 1778.
5. *The Southern Part of the Province of New York: with Part of the adjoining Colonies. By Thos. Kitchin Senr. Hydrogr. to his Majesty.* Printed map 6¾ by 8⅛. Opposite page 99, March 1778.
6. *Map of New York I. with the adjacent Rocks and other remarkable Parts of Hell-Gate By Thos. Kitchin Senr. Hydrographer to his Majesty.* Printed map 6¾ by 9¼. Opposite page 147, April 1778. A view of Hellgate on the following page.
7. *A Map of the Colony of Rhode-Island: with the adjacent Parts of Connecticut, Massachusetts Bay, &c. By Thos. Kitchin Senr. Hydrographer to his Majesty.* Printed map 8⅞ by 6½. Opposite page 513, November 1778.
8. *A Map of such parts of Georgia and South Carolina as tend to illustrate the Progress and Operations of the British Army, &c. By Thos. Kitchin Senr.* Printed map 8¾ by 6⅝. Opposite page 224, May 1780.
9. *Map of the Province of West Florida By Thos. Kitchin Senr.* Printed map 9 by 7. Inset plan of Pensacola. Opposite page 240, May 1781.
10. *A Map of the Seat of War in the Southern Part of Virginia, North Carolina and Northern Part of South Carolina By Thos. Kitchin Senr. Hydrographer to his Majesty.* Printed map 13 by 10¼. Opposite page 292, June 1781.

154. THE REMEMBRANCER OR, IMPARTIAL REPOSITORY OF PUBLIC EVENTS
(Printed for J. Almon.)

1. *Boston and Environs.* Printed Map. August 1775.
2. *A Map 40 Miles about Boston.* Printed map with inset of the Town, and of the vicinity. In the second edition of *The Remembrancer....* 1775.
3. *A Map of Rhode-Island And Providence, with the Adjacent Country, from New London to Newbury, From the best Authorities.* London, Printed according to Act of Parliament for J. Almon, in Piccadilly, February 1st. 1777. Printed map 4 by 6⅜. Opposite page 260, 1777.
4. *A Map of the Seat of War in the Province of York, Jersey and Pennsylvania; with the Interior Country as far as Albany. From the best Authorities.* London Printed according to the ·Act of Parliament for J. Almon, in Piccadilly, March 1st., 1777. Printed map 4 by 6½. Opposite page 291, 1777.

155. THE POLITICAL MAGAZINE

The maps are engraved by John Lodge and John Bew.

1. *A Plan of Charles Town the Capital of South Carolina with the Harbour, Islands, and Forts; the Attack on Fort Sulivan by His Majesty's Ships under Sir Peter Parker, in 1776; the Position of the Land Forces, under General Clinton, and the Rebels Camp and Intrenchments, exactly delineated.* Printed map 11 by 5⅛. Opposite page 171, May 1780.

2. *A New and Correct Map of North America in which the Places of the Principal Engagements during the Present War are accurately Inserted.* Printed map 14⅝ by 10⅜. Opposite page 290, April 26, 1780.

3. *A New and Accurate Map of the Chief Parts of South Carolina and Georgia From the Best Authorities.* Printed map 14¼ by 10⅛. Opposite page 454, 30 June 1780.

4. *A New and Accurate Map of the Province of New York and Part of the Jerseys, New England and Canada, Shewing the Scenes of our Military Operations during the present War. Also the New Erected State of Vermont.* Printed map 10¼ by 14¼. Opposite page 670, October 31, 1780.

5. *A Accurate Map of Rhode Island Part of Connecticut and Massachusetts Shewing Admiral Arbuthnot's Station in Blocking up Admiral Ternay.* Printed map 14½ by 10⅛. Opposite page 692, November 30, 1780.

6. *A New and Accurate Map of North Carolina and Part of South Carolina with the Field of Battle between Earl Cornwallis and General Grant.* Printed map 14½ by 10¼. Opposite page 730, November 30, 1780.

7. *A New and Accurate Map of Virginia and Part of Maryland and Pennsylvania.* Printed map 14¼ by 10¼. Opposite page 786, 31 Dec. 1780.

156. THE POLITICAL MAGAZINE AND PARLIAMENTARY, NAVAL, MILITARY AND LITERARY JOURNAL

(*The Political Magazine* was changed to this title in January 1781, but was otherwise unaltered.)

8. *Cape Fear River with the Countries Adjacent and the Towns of Brunswick and Wilmington against which Lord Cornwallis detached a Part of his Army the 17th. of January last.* Printed map 7 by 9¼. Opposite page 163, March 31, 1781.

9. *A Map of East and West Florida Georgia and Louisiana, with the Islands of Cuba, Bahama, and the Countries Surrounding the Gulf of Mexico, with the Tract of the Spanish Galleons, and of our Fleets thro' the Straits of Florida from the Best Authorities.* Printed map 14 by 10¼. Opposite page 293, May 31, 1781.

10. *Western or Atlantic Ocean, with Part of Europe, Africa and America.* Printed map 20 by 15. Opposite page 568, September 1781.

11. *A Map and Chart of those Parts of the Bay of Chesapeak York and James Rivers which are at present the Seat of War.* Printed map 14¼ by 9½. Opposite page 624, 30 November 1781. See under Section 140, Bew No. 1.

12. *Chart and Plan of the Harbour of New York & the Couny Adjacent From Sandy Hook to Kingsbridge Comprehending The Whole of New York and Staten Island, and Part of Long Island & the Jersey Shore: And Shewing the Defences of New York Both by Land and Sea.* Printed map 9½ by 16½. Opposite page 657, Nov. 30, 1781.

13. *A Map of the Province of Massachusetts Bay, and Colony of Rhode Island, with Part of Connecticut, New Hampshire, and Vermont.* Printed map 13¾ by 10¼. Opposite page 171, April 1782.

14. *A New & Accurate Map of the Province of Canada in North America; from the latest and best Authorities.* Printed map 12¾ by 9½. Opposite page 440, 31 July 1782.

15. *A New and Accurate Chart of the Harbour of Boston in New*

Map of Arnold's 1776 expedition to Quebec, published in England four months after the operation. See 153/2.

England in North America. Printed map 6½ by 8¾. Opposite page 628, 30 Nov. 1782.

157. THE UNIVERSAL MAGAZINE OF KNOWLEDGE AND PLEASURE

(Containing News Letters Debates Poetry Musick Biography History Geography Voyages Criticism Translations Philosophy Mathematics Husbandry Gardening Cookery Chemistry Mechanicks Trade Navigation Architecture and other Arts and Sciences.)

1. *A New Plan of Boston Harbor from an Actual Survey.* Excellent, detailed printed map 13⅜ by 10⅚, inset of the Town of Boston. Opposite page 225, May 1774. A view of the city was in the March 1775 number.

2. *A New and Accurate Map of the present Seat of War in North America from a late survey.* Shows Massachusetts Bay area and Cape Cod. Printed map 14⅜ by 10¾. Opposite page 169, October 1775.

3. *An Accurate Map of the present Seat of War between Great Britain and her Colonies in North America. Engraved for the Universal Magazine May 1776.* Printed map 13½ by 10¼. Opposite page 169, October 1776.
4. *A Plan of the City and Environs of New York in North America.* Printed map 14¼ by 11. Opposite page 225, November 1776.
5. *A New and Accurate Map of the Present Seat of War in North America comprehending New Jersey, Philadelphia, Pennsylvania, New York &c.* Detailed map 10⅞ by 13¾. Opposite page 281, June 1777.
6. *A New and Accurate Map of the Province of Georgia in North America.* Printed map 10⅛ by 12⅛. Opposite page 169, April 1779.
7. *A New and Accurate Map of the Province of South Carolina in North America.* Printed map 10¼ by 12½. Opposite page 281, June 1779.
8. *A New and Accurate Map of North Carolina in North America.* Printed map 13⅜ by 9⅞. Opposite page 169, October 1779.
9. *A New and accurate Map of the Province of Virginia in North America.* Printed map 12¾ by 10½. Opposite page 281, December 1779.
10. *A New Map of the Province of Maryland in North America.* Printed map 12½ by 10⅜. Opposite page 57, February 1780.
11. *A New and accurate Map of the Province of Pennsylvania in North America, from the Best Authorities.* Printed map 12¼ by 10¼. Opposite page 169, April 1780.
12. *A New and Accurate Map of New Jersey from the best Authorities.* Excellent printed map 9¾ by 11⅞. Opposite page 281, June 1780.
13. *An accurate Map of New York in North America from a late Survey.* Printed map 10 by 12⅝. Opposite page 57, August 1780.
14. *A New and accurate Map of Connecticut and Rhode Island from the best Authorities.* Printed map 12⅞ by 9¾. Opposite page 169, October 1780.
15. *A New and accurate Map of the Colony of Massachusetts Bay in North America from a Late Survey.* Printed map 12¼ by 9¾. Opposite page 281, December 1780.
16. *An accurate Map of New Hampshire in New England, from a late Survey.* Printed map 10⅜ by 12. Opposite page 57, February 1781.
17. *A New and accurate Map of the Province of Nova Scotia In North American from the latest Observations.* Printed map 12½ by 10⅝. Opposite page 169, April 1781.
18. *A New and Accurate Map of Quebec and its Boundries.* Printed map 12 by 9¾. Opposite page 113, September 1781.

158. THE SCOT'S MAGAZINE

1. *Thirty-Miles Round Boston. By M. Armstrong Geo. 14th. Augt. 1775.* Printed map 10 by 10. Inset of Bunker Hill, and lists of the memorable occurances, engraved by A. Bell, opposite page 440.

159. THE TOWN AND COUNTRY MAGAZINE OR UNIVERSAL REPOSITORY OF KNOWLEDGE, INSTRUCTION AND ENTERTAINMENT.

1. *An accurate map of the Country round Boston in New England, published by A. Hamilton, Jr., near St. John's Gate, Jan. 16, 1776.* Printed map 11½ by 12½, area bounded by Plymouth, Groton and Providence. Possibly last map during British occupation of Boston.
2. *The West Indies and Gulf of Mexico from the latest Discoveries and Best Observations.* Printed map 13 by 8⅜. Opposite page 593, 1778.

160. T. WALKER'S HIBERNIAN MAGAZINE

1. *Exact Plan of General Gage's Lines on Boston Neck in America.* Printed map 8⅝ by 11¼. In 1776 volume. An almost identical map was published in Robert Aitkin's *Pennsylvania Magazine* of August 1775.

161. WESTMINSTER MAGAZINE, OR PANTHEON OF TASTES.

1. *The Present Seat of War in North America.* Printed map 11 by 9, August 1776.

PRINTED MAPS IN BOOKS

Arranged by Author

Printed maps were used to illustrate books published during the years covered by this study. As in the magazine maps, some were not current, or pertinent to the war or the political situation. Others were republications from magazines or atlases. In the years following the period of this study, there was an increasingly common tendency to employ eclectic inventions.

162. JAMES ADAIR

The History of the American Indians. London, 1775. *A Map of the American Indian Nations Adjoining to the Mississippi, West & East Florida, Georgia, S. & N. Carolina, Virginia, & c.* Printed map 12½ by 9½. "Jno. Lodge Sculp"

163. [EDMUND BURKE?]

An Impartial History of the War in America, Between Great Britain And Her Colonies. London, 1780; Carlisle, 1780. *A New Map of North America.* Printed map 17 by 21¾, in considerable detail.

164. JOHN BURGOYNE

A State of the Expedition from Canada, as laid before the House of Commons; with a Collection of Authentic Documents, and an addition of many circumstances which were prevented from appearing before the House by the prorogation of Parliament. London, 1780. Two editions with 5 and 6 maps.
1. *Map of the Country in which the Army of Lieut Gen Burgoyne acted in the Campaign of 1777. Drawn by Mr. Medcalfe & Engraved by Wm Faden. Feby. 1st. 1780.* Printed map 10¾ by 22¼.
2. *Plan of the Action at Huberton under Brigadier Genl. Frazer supported by Major Genl. Reidesel, on the 7th. July 1777. Drawn by P. Gerlach Deputy Quarter Master General. Engraved by Wm. Faden. Feby. 1st. 1780.* Printed map 13⅝ by 10¾.
3. *Position of the Detachment under Lieut. Coll. Baum at Walmscock near Bennington Shewing the Attacks of the Enemy on the 16th. August 1777. Drawn by Lieut. Durnford Engineer. Engraved by Wm. Faden 1780. Feby. 1st.* Printed map 13½ by 10⅝.
4. *Plan of the Encampment and Position of the Army under His Excelly. Lt. General Burgoyne at Swords House on Hudson's River near Stillwater on Septr. 17th. with the Positions of that part of the Army engaged on the 19th. Septr. 1777. Drawn by W.C. Wilkinson Lt. 62d. Regt. Asst. Engr. Engraved by Wm. Faden. Feby. 1st. 1780.* Printed map 13¼ by 12½. Partial overlay.
5. *Plan of the Encampment and Position of the Army at Braemus Heights on Hudson's River.* Printed map 13¼ by 12¼.

6. *Plan Of The Position which the Army under Lt. Genl. Burgoine took at Saratoga on the 10th. of September 1777, and in which it remained till The Convention was signed. Engraved by Wm. Faden. Feby. 1st. 1780.* Printed map 18½ by 8½.

165. MICHEL GUILLAUM ST. JEAN DE CRÈVECOEUR

Letters from an American Farmer, describing...the British Colonies in North America. London, 1782, and numerous other editions, usually without maps.
1. *Map Of the Island Of Nantucket.* Printed map 11 by 7¾, on page 122. References on facing page.
2. *Map of the Island of Martha's Vineyard with its Dependancies.* Printed map 10¼ by 8½, on page 160.

166. JOSEPH GALLOWAY

Letters to a Nobleman on the Conduct of the War in the Middle Colonies. London, 1779, and other editions.
1. *A Plan of the Operations of the British & Rebel Army in the Campaign 1777. J. Lodge Sculp.* Printed map 10 by 8¾. Inset of Mud Island Fort and Environs.

167. JOHN HALL

The History of the Civil War in America. Volume I, 1775-77. London, 1780, and another issue. Volume II was never published.
1. *Campaign of MDCCLXXVI.* Printed map 17½ by 21.
2. *Campaign of MDCCLXXVII.* Printed map 8½ by 9, on the same sheet as preceding.

168. ISRAEL MAUDUIT

Three Letters to Lt. Gen. Sir William Howe. London, 1781.
1. *Map of the New York Campaign.* Determined from Table of Contents only.

169. ISRAEL MAUDUIT

Three Letters of Lord Viscount Howe. London, 1780 and 1781.
1. Determined from Table of Contents only.

170. JAMES MURRAY

An Impartial History of the Present War in America. London and Newcastle, 1778-80, three volumes. Other editions.
1. *A New Map of North America.* Printed map 17 by 21¾.
2. *Plan of the Town of Boston with the Attack on Bunkers-Hill in the Peninsula of Charlestown the 17th. of June 1775.* Printed map 5¼ by 11¼.
3. *A New and Correct Map of the Country in which the Army under Lt. Gl. Burgoyne acted in 1777 shewing all the places where the principal actions happened, as taken by an Officer of Distinction.* Printed map 7⅝ by 9½.
4. *A Map of New Jersey, Pennsylvania, New York, Maryland & Virginia from the latest and best Surveys.* Printed map 9¼ by 7.

171. THOMAS L. O'BEIRNE

A Candid and Impartial Narrative Of The Transactions of The Fleet Under The Command Of Lord Howe, From The Arrival of The Toulon Squadron, On the Coast of America, To The Time of His Lordship's Departure For England, With Observations By An Officer Then Serving In The Fleet. London 1779.
1. *A Plan Of The Situation Of The Fleet Within Sandy Hook. Jno.*

Lodge Sculp. Printed map 14½ by 15¼. In the second edition, 1779.

172. OTHER MAPS

A few other maps, falling within the period of study, have been encountered. These do not apparently fall into any of the categories, and are included here.

1. *A Map of the Town and Harbour of Boston Drawn by a Captain in His Majesty's Navy.* Undistinguished printed map 14½ by 11½. "London. Published Feby 7th. 1776, and Sold at Spilsburys Print-Shop, Russel Court, Covent Garden." Massachusetts Historical Society.
2. *A Map of that part of Pennsylvania now the Principal seat of War in America, wherein may be seen the Situation of Philadelphia, Red Bank, Mud Island, & Germantown on a scale of an inch to a mile. From an actual Survey made by Nicholas Scull Surveyor of the Province of Pennsylvania. This Map was Engraved by L. Jackson. London 1777.* Printed map 11½ by 14⅞. Library of Congress. G3701 S3237 1777 S3.
3. *A Sketch of the Environs of Charlestown in South Carolina by Captain Geo. Sproule. Published 1st. June 1780.* Printed map, published as a separate, from DesBarres *The Atlantic Neptune.*
4. *Charles Town South Carolina with a Chart of the Bars & Harbour By R. Cowley. Jno. Lodge sculp. Published 1st of June 1780 By Fielding & Walker, Pater Noster Row.* Printed map 7½ by 7¼.

one mile

INDEX

To increase the utility of this volume, which is essentially an index in itself, section references have been substituted for page references. A number has been assigned to each map maker, or where this is not possible, to a geographical area, or other convenient classification.

Under these classifications, each map is assigned a number. For example, Adam Allen, the first map maker listed, is assigned number 1, and the maps under his heading are numbered 1, 2, 3, etc. Thus, in the index under the listing, Richmond, Va., there is shown 1/1, which indicates that Richmond is referred to in Allen's map number 1.

Other symbols used in the index are In, Bi, and Pg. These stand for introduction, biography of a particular map maker, and page number.

For assigned classification numbers, see Table of Contents.

Bouquet, Henry, In, 65/Bi.
Bouquet River, 19/8.
Bowen, Eman., 149/1.
Bowles and Kearsley, 142.
Bowles, Carington, 141.
Braddock, In.
Braemus Heights, 118/6, 164/5.
Brandywine, 2/12, 2/13, 95/16; 132/20, 132/21, 132/22, 132/23, 132/24.
Brasier, William, 12/Bi, 65/6, 65/7, 80/27, 89/Bi, 95/3, 150/8.
Breheam, 12/Bi.
Brentons Neck, R.I., 38/9.
Bristol Ferry, R.I., 26/2.
Bristol, Pa., 80/20.
Bronx, 130/55.
Bronx River, 130/56, 130/58, 130/60.
Brookhaven, N.Y., 59/10, 59/11.
Brookline, Mass., 87/1, 127/9, 127/10.
Brookland Ferry, 116/8.
Brooklyn, N.Y., 104/3, 107/5, 145/16.
Brown, John, 13/Bi.
Brown, Mrs. John Nicholas, In.
Brun, Christian, In.
Brunswick, N.J. (see New Brunswick, N.J.)
Brunswick, 150/18, 156/8.
Brunswick, N.C., 134/7, 134/8.
Brunswick, N.J., 131/27.
Bryan, Hugh, 109/1, 148/3.
Buchette, Joseph, 59/Bi.
Buck Tavern, Md., 2/8.
Bull, William, 28/Bi, 109/1, 148/3.
Bunker Hill, Battle of, 27/5.
Bunker Hill, Mass., 80/10, 80/11, 85/2, 85/7, 87/2, 127/29, 127/30, 127/31, 150/6, 150/7, 158/1, 170/2.
Burgoyne, John, In, 34/4, 145/12, 150/7, 164, 170/3.
Burke, Edmond, 163.
Burlington Bay, 19/24.
Burlington, N.J., 80/17, 80/20, 131/6, 131/35.
Burrard, Harry, In, 14/Bi.
Burrell's, 106/11, 106/34.
Burrington Hill, R.I., 128/22.
Buzzards Bay, Mass., 70/1.
Byran River, Conn., 105/1.

— C —

Calef, John, 15/Bi.
Calf Paster Pint, 117/1.
California, 150/2.
Cambridge, Mass., 27/2, 87/1, 95/6, 127/10, 127/11.
Camden, N.J., 131/39, 131/41.
Camden, S.C., 6/1, 7/12, 135/3, 135/4, 135/5, 145/26.
Camden, S.C., Battle of, 115/1.
Cameron, George, 143.
Campaign of MDCCLXXVI, 167/1.
Campaign of MDCCLXXVII, 167/2.
Campbell, In.
Campbell, Archibald, 136/3.
Campbell, Dougald (Dougal, Dugald), 16/Bi, 51/1, 57/44.
Campbell, James, 145/24.
Campbell, (Cambel), John, 17/Bi, 128/6.
Canada, 37/1, 80/Bi, 100/9, 125/1, 126/2, 145/9, 145/14, 150/4, 155/4, 156/14, 164.
Cannse, Rev. Mr., In.
Cape Anne, 11/4, 59/2.
Cape Blair, 46/2.
Cape Blaise, 46/2.
Cape Breton Island, 107/Bi, 144/2, 150/4.
Cape Canaveral, Fla., 63/4.

Cape Cod, Mass., 2/48, 157/2.
Cape Elizabeth, Me., 47/2, 116/3.
Cape Fear River, 150/18, 156/8.
Cape Henry, 2/51, 132/29, 133/14.
Carpenters Island, 80/22.
Carsons Tavern, Md., 2/8.
Carver, Johnathan, 18/Bi, 29/1, 33/1, 150/3.
Casco Bay, 116/2.
Gascoigne, Hugh, 28/Bi.
Castine Bay, Battle of, 125/2.
Castle, Wm., 80/5.
Cayo Largo, Fla., 46/7.
Cecil Church, 2/7, 132/25.
Chambers, William, 19/Bi.
Chandeleur Island, 46/14.
Chapman, T. A., 27/4.
Charleston, (Charlestown) S.C., 2/16, 11/15, 17/1, 17/2, 21/Bi, 22/1, 22/2, 40/1, 46/5, 66/1, 83/1, 95/13, 95/14, 97/1; 107/8, 135/8, 135/9, 135/11, 135/12, 135/13, 135/14, 135/15, 135/17, 135/18, 135/19, 135/20, 135/22, 135/23, 135/25, 135/27, 135/28, 135/30, 135/31, 145/25, 145/29, 150/15, 150/16, 155/1, 170/2, 172/3, 172/4.
Charlestown Neck, Mass., 127/37.
Charleston Neck, S.C. 95/14, 135/25, 135/29.
Charlestown, Mass., 27/4, 80/1, 80/2, 80/3, 80/4, 80/5, 80/8, 80/9, 80/10, 80/11, 85/1, 87/1, 120/1, 127/10, 127/29, 127/32, 127/33, 127/34, 127/35, 150/6, 152/3.
Charlestown, Peninsula of, 7/1, 61/1, 147/1.
Charlestown Point, Fort of, 127/36.
Charlestown, S.C. Harbor, 135/8, 135/16, 135/24, 150/13, 150/14.
Charlotte, N.Y., 153/4.
Chaudiere, 153/2.
Cheevers, T., 65/11.
Chelsea, Mass., 87/1.
Chesapeake Bay, 57/2, 57/3, 57/4, 104/4, 131/3, 132/26, 132/29, 132/30, 133/1, 133/2, 133/12, 140/1, 156/11.
Chester, Pa., 63/2, 132/9, 132/10, 132/11, 132/26, 145/23.
Chestnut Hill, Pa., 2/20.
Chief Little Carpenter, 109/Bi.
Churton, 24/Bi, 83/1.
Citadel Hill, Halifax, N.S., 7/8, 78/3.
Clements, William L., In.
Clinton, 20/Bi.
Clinton, Charles, 20/Bi.
Clinton, G., 20/Bi, 57/21.
Clinton, Henry, In, 21/Bi, 27/5, 57/Bi, 106/32, 108/Bi, 108/2, 130/80, 130/81.
Clinton, William Henry, 22/Bi.
Close, Abraham, 23/Bi.
Cohos River, 114/1.
Colchester Point, 19/23.
Collet, John Abraham, 24/Bi, 83/1, 97/1, 150/12.
Collins, John, 100/3.
Comit River, 65/3, 65/4.
Conanicut Island, R.I., 75/6, 128/31, 145/7.
Concord, Mass., 7/2, 27/3, 29/1, 75/1, 127/9, 127/12.
Connecticut, 57/48, 105/1, 129, 141/2, 148/1, 152/7, 153/7, 155/5, 156/13, 157/14.
Connecticut River, 126/2, 130/104, 144/4.
Cook, James, In, 59/Bi, 24/1, 83/1, 97/1.
Cornwallis, 108/5, 133/7.
Courtland, 150/9.
Covington Cove, R.I., 38/2.
Courtland, N.Y., 130/20.
Cowley, R., 172/4.
Cox, 25/Bi, 57/5.
Crevecoeur, Michel Guillaum St. Jean De, 165.
Crosswicks, N.J., 2/35, 57/10, 57/30, 106/4, 106/34.

Croton River, 111/1, 130/70.
Crown Point, N.Y., 11/1, 12/1, 12/2, 12/3, 12/4, 80/26, 80/27, 80/28, 130/98, 144/5, 150/8.
Crugar, John, 5/Bi.
Cuba, 156/9.
Cumberland Bay, 19/18.
Cumberland, Duke of, In.
Cumming, William P., In, 28/Bi.

— D —

Danbury, Conn., 80/12, 129/3.
D'Aubant, Abraham, 26/Bi.
D'Auvergne, P., 59/2.
D'awfoskee, S.C., 147/4.
De Berniere, Henry, 13/1, 13/2, 13/3, 27/Bi.
De Brahm, William, In, 24/1, 28/Bi, 59/Bi, 83/1, 97/Bi, 109/Bi, 109/1, 148/3, 150/12.
De Burriere, Henry, 27/4.
Deckers Ferry, Staten Island, N.Y., 77/1, 95/8.
DeCosta, 18/7, 29/Bi.
de Diemer, In.
Deer Island Haute, 107/1.
de Grasse, Count, 133/1.
DeLancey (Delancy) Oliver, 104/2, 107/Bi, 133/18.
Delaware, 35/Bi, 131/2, 131/3, 150/10.
Delaware Bay, 57/39, 104/4, 131/3, 132/26, 132/29, 132/30, 144/6, 144/7, 145/24, 152/11.
Delaware River, 2/28, 41/Bi, 57/39, 59/1, 63/2, 80/16, 80/22, 80/24, 80/25, 106/1, 113/1, 132/9, 132/10, 132/11, 144/6, 144/7, 145/23, 145/24, 152/11.
Delaware Valley, 132/7.
Demler, In.
Dennis, Anthony, 30/Bi, 57/5, 57/34, 57/37.
Derby, 2/23, 2/26.
Derby Creek, 106/1.
Des Barres, Joseph, F. W., In, 59/Bi, 172/3.
De Vorsey, Louis, 28/Bi.
Diascond, Va., 103/2.
Dixon, Matthew, 31/Bi, 116/8.
Dobb's Ferry, N.Y., 80/15, 95/15, 130/69, 130/76.
Dorchester Heights, Mass., 85/3, 127/38.
Dorchester, Mass., 27/1, 80/5, 87/1, 127/3, 127/39.
Dorchester Point, 127/40, 127/41.
Dumplin Point, R.I., 26/7.
Dunham, Azariah, 32/Bi, 57/15, 57/34, 57/36.
Dunmore, Earl of, 5/Bi.
Dunn, Samuel, 18/6, 33/Bi, 150/1, 150/20.
Duprey, Wilson G., In.
Durfee, Captain, 135/16.
Durnford, Elias, 34/Bi, 65/3, 65/4, 95/Bi, 137/7, 164/3.
Dury, Andrew, 35/Bi, 144.
Dutchess County, N.Y., 39/7.

— E —

Easburn, Benjamin, 35/Bi, 144/6.
East Ferry, 128/31.
Easton, 80/19.
Easton's Bar, 128/19.
Easton's Pond, R.I., 38/2.
East River, N.Y., 63/3, 80/28, 130/53, 144/5.
Ebenezer, Ga., 136/3.
Eden, William, 36/Bi.
Edgemaggia Reach, 107/1.
Elizabeth Islands, 116/2, 116/6.
Elizabeth, N.J., 57/43, 131/1, 131/19, 131/20.
Elizabeth River, Va., 106/8, 106/9, 106/23, 108/2, 108/3, 133/14.
Elizabethtown Point, N.J., 57/16, 57/43, 131/22.
Elk, 132/2, 132/3, 132/27, 132/28.

Elk River, Md., 2/30, 2/31, 57/4, 57/5, 63/1.
Erskine, Robert, 101/Bi.
Espiritu Santo, Bay of, Fla., 46/10, 145/28, 148/5.
Essex County, N.J., 57/22, 131/12.
Europe, 156/10.
Evans, Lewis, In, 37/Bi, 101/Bi, 150/10.
Evesham, N.J., 2/32.
Ewing, William S., In.

— F —

Faden, William, 5/Bi, 118/2, 118/5, 118/6, 132/21, 133/1, 164/1, 164/2, 164/3, 164/4, 164/6.
Fage, Edward, 38/Bi.
Fairfield County, Conn., 23/1, 39/3, 104/1.
Fair Haven, Mass., 2/49, 2/50.
Falmouth, Mass., 116/2.
Ferguson, Patrick, In, 39/Bi.
Fielding and Walker, 172/4.
Finnegan, Patrick, 40/Bi.
Fisher, Joshua, 41/Bi, 57/5, 57/39, 144/6, 145/24, 152/11.
Fishkill Creek, 130/70.
Fishkill River, 96/1.
Flagstaff Redout, S.I., N.Y., 130/10.
Flatbush, N.Y., 4/1, 116/8, 145/16.
Florida, 123/1, 137, 150/20, 156/9.
Florida, East, 24/1, 28/Bi, 46/5, 63/4, 91/2, 97/1, 97/3, 97/4, 97/6, 137/10, 145/28, 148/4, 148/5, 150/12, 156/9, 162.
Florida Keys, 46/7, 46/8, 46/9, 150/19.
Florida, West, 24/1, 46/2, 46/5, 46/12, 91/2, 97/1, 97/5, 97/6, 137/10, 145/28, 149/3, 150/12, 150/19, 153/9, 156/9, 162.
Fogland, R.I., 128/24, 128/25, 128/26.
Force, Peter, In.
Fort Annapolis, N.S., 7/11.
Fort Bristol Ferry, 128/29, 128/30.
Fort Brown, R.I., 26/3.
Fort Castine, 125/3.
Fort Chambly, 100/11, 145/14.
Fort Chartres, 149/4.
Fort Clinton, N.Y., 2/44, 57/45, 57/46, 59/5, 59/6, 59/7, 130/84, 130/85, 130/91.
Fort Constitution, 130/70.
Fort Cumberland, N.S., 7/7, 78/2.
Fort Defiance, N.Y., 50/1.
Fort Edward, 130/98.
Fort Edward, N.S., 7/6, 7/9, 95/4, 145/14.
Fort Fanning, R.I., 26/4.
Fort George, 69/1, 69/2.
Fort George, Fla., 137/8, 137/9, 137/10.
Fort George, N.Y., 5/1, 16/1, 16/2, 100/7, 100/8, 130/15.
Fort Griswold, Conn., 48/1, 73/1, 73/2, 129/2.
Fort Hill, 127/19.
Fort Howe, N.S., 7/10.
Fort Independence, N.Y., 108/Bi, 130/70, 130/82, 130/94.
Fort Island, 145/23.
Fort Johnson, N.C., 24/Bi, 24/1.
Fort Knyphausen, (see Fort Washington).
Fort Lafayette, N.Y., 2/45.
Fort Lee, N.J., 2/1, 130/44, 130/46, 131/6, 131/11.
Fort Made, 5/2.
Fort Massey, N.S., 78/3.
Fort Mercer (see Fort Red Bank)
Fort Mifflin, (Mud Fort) 11/14, 43/1, 80/23, 116/10, 132/12.
Fort Montgomery, N.Y., 2/44, 57/45, 57/46, 59/5, 59/6, 59/7, 130/82, 130/84, 130/85.
Fort Pitt, Pa., 65/6, 65/7, 65/8.
Fort Prevost, S.C., 136/16, 136/17, 136/18, 136/19, 136/20, 136/21.
Fort Red Bank, N.J., 131/40, 131/41, 132/11.

Fort Rutledge, 135/2.

Fort St. John, 19/1, 130/95.

Fort Sulivan, S.C., 22/1, 22/2, 66/1, 66/2, 66/3, 66/4, 95/19, 145/25, 145/29, 150/15, 155/1.

Fort Ticonderoga, N.Y., 12/5, 19/1.

Fort Tomony-Hill, 128/27, 128/28.

Fort Trumball, 57/48, 73/1, 73/2.

Fort Washington, N.Y. 95/7; 100/5; 100/12, 107/3, 130/40, 130/41, 130/42, 130/44, 145/15.

Forth, Lieutenant, 42/Bi, 116/8.

Four Brothers Islands, N.Y., 19/12, 19/21.

Fox Island, 107/1.

Fraser, Simon, 43/Bi.

Fredericton, N.B., 107/Bi.

Freehold, N.J., 2/38, 57/11, 57/12, 57/13, 57/14, 57/32, 106/5, 131/28, 131/33.

Freeman's Farms, N.Y., 118/1.

Fry, Joshua, 24/Bi, 44/Bi, 151/1.

Fuller, Capt., 148/4.

Fyers, William, 45/Bi.

Fylers Bay, 19/33.

— G —

Gage, Thomas, In, 46/3, 97/5.

Galloway, Joseph, 166.

Galveston Bay, Tex., 46/14.

Gardiner's Bay, 130/16.

Gascoign, Capt., 109/1, 147/4, 148/3, 150/17.

Gauld, George, In, 46/Bi, 97/6, 109/Bi, 137/2.

General Topography of North America, The (Jefferys), 144/5, 148/2.

Gentleman's Magazine and Historical Chronicle, The, 152.

Georgia, 2/1, 28/Bi, 46/5, 91/Bi, 97/6, 109/1, 121/5, 136, 148/3, 153/8, 155/3, 156/9, 157/6, 162/1.

Gerlach, P., 164/2.

Germaine, George, In, 15/1.

Germantown, Pa., 2/18, 2/19, 57/7, 132/14, 132/15, 132/16, 172/2.

Gibson, 149/1.

Gist, Mordecai, 106/33.

Gloucester Neck, Va., 103/3.

Gloucester Point, Va., 110/2.

Gloucester, Va., 57/50, 103/4, 108/5, 110/1, 133/1.

Goat Island, R.I., 26/1.

Gordon, Harry, In, 65/6, 65/7.

Gouldsborough Harbor, 11/2, 116/3.

Graham, Mr., In.

Grand Bahama Bank, 97/4.

Grant, 116/4, 116/5, 116/9.

Grant, James, In, 11/4, 47/Bi, 57/23, 107/1, 116/6, 145/3, 145/4.

Grant, Thomas, 116/1.

Gray, Alexander, 48/Bi.

Great Bridge, Va., 93/3, 106/8, 106/9, 106/23, 108/3.

Great Valley, Pa., 2/15.

Green, John, 148/1.

Greenwich, 80/28, 144/5.

Grey, Charles, In, 2/25.

Griswold, Conn., 57/48.

Groton, Conn., 73/1, 73/2, 159/1.

Guilford, N.C., 134/2, 134/3, 134/4.

Gulf Coast, 17/5.

Gulf of Mexico, 156/9, 159/1.

Gum Swamp, 6/1.

— H —

Hackensack, N.J., 57/20, 80/17.

Hackensack River, 131/13.

Hadden, James Murray, 49/Bi.

Haddonfield, N.J., 57/8, 57/28, 131/34.

Haldimand, Frederick, 46/3.

Hale, E. E., In.

Halifax, N.S., 7/4, 7/11, 11/Bi, 78/3, 78/4, 95/4.

Hall, C., 29/1.

Hall, John, 167.

Hamilton, A. Jr., 159/1.

Hammill, Daniel, 50/Bi.

Hammons, Samuel, 51/Bi, 16/3.

Hamond, Andrew Snape, 52/Bi, 113/1.

Hampton, Alsop, 53/Bi, 57/21.

Hampton Harbor, 11/4.

Hampton, Va., 133/9, 133/18.

Hancock's House, N.J., 106/3.

Harley, J.B., pg. 61

Harmar, Josiah, In.

Hartley, David, 54/Bi.

Haverstraw Bay, 93/2, 130/68.

Hawkes, W., 146.

Hayman, John, 55/Bi.

Hays, S., 56/Bi, 57/21.

Heap, G., 101/Bi, 145/20, 152/9.

Hells Gate, N.Y., 11/13, 75/9, 75/10, 130/53, 130/54, 153/6.

Hibernian Magazine, T. Walkers, 160.

Highlands, 80/19, 81/1.

Hills, I (same as John Hills), 57.

Hills, John, In, 57/Bi, 130/3.

Hobkirks Hill, S.C., 115/2, 145/26.

Hogback Island, 19/22.

Hogg, William, 58/1.

Hog Island, Mass., 80/5.

Holland, Samuel, In, 11/Bi, 11/2, 11/4, 24/1, 47/2, 57/45, 58/Bi, 59/Bi, 97/1, 107/Bi, 107/1, 107/2, 116/1, 116/2, 116/4, 116/6, 122/Bi, 125/4, 126/1, 127/1, 130/20, 145/3, 145/4, 150/9.

Holster Atlas, 150/1, 150/8, 150/10, 150/12, 150/20.

Honeyman's Hill, R.I., 38/2, 75/8.

Hoopers Town, N.J., 106/10.

Horn's Hook, N.Y., 2/46.

Howe, William, In, 7/3, 27/4, 100/4, 116/Bi, 127/33, 130/67, 132/21.

Howlands Bridge, R.I., 75/5, 128/21.

Howlands Neck, R.I., 108/1.

Howland's Point, R.I., 26/8.

Hubbard's House, 128/20.

Hubbill, Nathaniel, 60/Bi.

Huberton, 164/2.

Hudson Highlands, 130/77, 130/86, 130/87, 130/88.

Hudson River, (North River), 11/9, 39/4, 57/20, 57/46, 59/7, 63/3, 80/28, 81/1, 96/1; 97/Bi; 100/11, 118/1, 118/2, 118/3, 118/4, 118/5, 118/6, 130/3, 130/20, 130/37, 130/58, 130/69, 130/70, 130/71, 130/74, 130/75, 130/76, 130/82, 130/83, 144/5, 145/12, 145/14, 150/9, 152/10, 164/4, 164/5.

Hudson's Bay, 79/1, 150/2.

Humfrey, John, 61/Bi.

Hunter, James, 62/Bi.

Hunter, John, 63/Bi.

Hurd, Thomas, 64/Bi.

Hutchins, Thomas, In, 12/Bi, 12/5, 34/4, 65/Bi.

— I —

Iberville River, 65/1, 65/2, 65/3, 65/4, 65/5.

Illinois River, 65/11.

Imlaystown, N.J., 131/2.

Indian Country, 65/9, 65/10.

Ipswich, 11/4.

Iron Hill, 2/11.

Isaac Warren's Almanac, 152/8.

Island Point, 19/3, 19/10.

Morgan, Benjamin, 57/5, 57/17, 57/34, 57/35, 82/Bi.
Morgan, General, 106/32.
Moriches, 95/11, 95/12.
Morris House, 107/Bi.
Morristown, N.J., 80/18, 131/23.
Mosquito Inlet, Fla., 63/4.
Mount Holly, N.J., 2/33, 57/9, 57/29, 131/35.
Mouzon, Henry, Jr., In, 24/1, 28/Bi, 83/Bi, 97/1, 150/12, 150/13.
Mowat, Henry, 59/2.
Mud Island (Fort Mifflin) 2/29, 11/14, 80/22, 80/23, 80/24, 116/10, 132/9, 132/12, 166/1, 172/2.
Murray, James, 170.
Musingham, 65/10.

— N —

Nansemond River, 3/1, 133/14.
Nantucket, 2/48, 70/1, 70/2, 116/2, 116/6, 165/1.
Narraganseet, Bay of, R.I., 11/5, 11/6, 38/4, 38/7, 59/4, 116/6, 116/7, 117/1, 128/1, 145/7.
Narrows, N.Y., 130/6, 130/7.
Nassau River, 148/4.
Navesink, N.J., 57/5.
Needham, Mass., 27/3.
Neele, John, 15/1.
Neversink Hills, N.J., 8/1.
Newark Bay, 131/12, 131/13.
Newark, N.J., 131/12, 131/14.
New Bedford, Mass., 2/49, 2/50.
New Bridge, N.J., 80/17.
New Brunswick, N.J., 2/4, 57/25, 131/27.
Newbury, 154/3.
Newbury Harbor, 11/4.
New Castle, N.H., 11/3, 126/1.
Newcastle, Pa., 132/26.
New England, 37/1, 80/30, 100/9, 141/1, 141/2, 141/3, 144/4, 145/7, 145/8, 148/1, 148/2, 150/4, 150/5, 150/6, 153/1, 155/4.
New England Shore, 2/48, 58/1.
Newfoundland, 123/1.
New Garden, 2/10.
New Hampshire, 116/2, 126, 126/2, 130/104, 141/2, 145/3, 145/4, 148/1, 148/2, 156/13, 157/16.
New Haven, Conn., 60/1.
New Jersey, 2/40, 11/9, 20/Bi, 21/Bi, 44/1, 57/17, 57/34, 57/38, 57/39, 57/41, 71/1, 80/16, 92/4, 92/5, 104/2, 130/1, 130/19, 131, 131/1, 131/2, 131/3, 131/5, 131/6, 131/21, 131/38, 145/10, 145/18, 150/10, 151/1, 152/5, 154/4, 155/4, 156/12, 157/5, 157/12, 170/4.
New Jersey, East, 32/Bi, 57/5, 57/6, 57/15, 57/18, 57/20, 57/21, 57/22, 100/13, 131/4, 145/16, 145/17, 145/19.
New Jersey, West, 57/5, 57/6, 57/8, 145/19.
New Kent, Va., 103/2.
New London, Conn., 39/3, 57/48, 73/1, 73/2, 129/1, 154/3.
New Orleans, La., 46/11.
Newport, R.I., 11/Bi, 26/5, 26/6, 38/2, 38/3, 39/9, 100/1, 116/2, 116/6, 128/8, 128/9, 128/10, 128/11, 128/12, 128/16, 128/22, 145/8.
New Road, 19/31.
New Spain, 150/20.
New Windsor, N.Y., 130/71, 130/93.
New York, 11/1, 20/Bi, 21/Bi, 36/1, 57/21, 63/3, 80/13, 80/14, 80/28, 80/30, 92/4, 100/2, 100/3, 100/9, 100/10, 100/13, 100/14, 104/2, 130, 130/103, 130/104, 131/5, 131/6, 144/4, 145/9, 145/10, 145/11, 145/17, 146/1, 150/9, 152/5, 152/8, 153/4, 153/5, 153/6, 154/4, 155/4, 156/12, 157/5, 157/13, 168/1, 170/4
New York City, N.Y., 2/48, 92/1, 92/2, 92/3, 95/10, 100/6, 100/7, 116/9, 130/2, 130/4, 130/6, 130/7, 130/19, 130/20, 130/21,
130/22, 130/23, 130/24, 130/25, 130/26, 130/27, 130/28, 130/29, 130/30, 130/31, 130/32, 130/33, 130/34, 130/36, 130/37, 130/38, 130/39, 130/41, 130/43, 130/44, 130/45, 130/46, 130/47, 130/48, 130/53, 130/57, 144/5, 145/16, 147/2, 157/4.
New York Harbor, 8/1, 63/Bi, 100/11, 130/1, 145/14, 156/12.
New York, Island of, 2/46, 11/8, 11/9, 11/13, 16/1, 16/2, 75/2, 80/15, 100/5, 100/12, 112/3, 112/4, 112/5, 142/1, 143/1, 145/15, 145/16.
Niagara River, 74/1.
Nicole, Pierre, 84/Bi.
Noodle's Island, Mass., 80/5, 127/43.
Norfolk, Va., 93/3, 133/15, 133/16, 133/17.
Norman (The American Pilot), 59/Bi.
Norman's Woe, 11/4.
Norrington, Pa., 2/17.
North America, 18/1, 18/2, 18/3, 18/4, 18/6, 37/1, 39/2, 79/1, 80/Bi, 91/3, 123, 123/1, 138, 139/1, 141/4, 144/1, 145/1, 145/3, 149/1, 150/1, 150/2, 155/2, 156/10, 157/2, 157/3, 161/1, 163, 165, 170/1.
North American Atlas, The (Faden), 144/2, 144/4, 144/7, 145/1, 145/2, 145/5, 145/7, 145/8, 145/14, 145/15, 145/16, 145/17, 145/18, 145/19, 145/20, 144/24, 144/25, 145/27, 145/28, 147/2, 148/1, 148/3, 148/4, 148/5, 149/3, 149/4, 150/2, 150/3, 150/4, 150/8, 150/11, 150/13, 150/18.
North American Pilot, The, (Sayer & Bennett), 150/17.
North Carolina, 24/1, 44/1, 65/11, 83/1, 91/Bi, 134, 134/1, 134/6, 134/9, 150/12, 150/13, 151/1, 153/10, 155/6, 157/8, 162.
North Castle, Va., 106/7.
North Causeway, 128/31.
North Edisto Harbor, S.C., 135/22.
North Hero, Vt., 19/5.
North River, (Hudson River), 39/6, 80/16, 80/28, 130/59, 130/72, 130/81, 144/5.
Northumberland, Duke of, In.
Nova Scotia, 7/5, 78/1, 80/Bi, 95/4, 144/2, 150/4, 157/17.

— O —

O'Beirne, Thomas, 171.
Ocean County, N.J., 92/5.
Ogelthorpe, James, 109/Bi.
Ogunkett River, 47/2.
Ohio River, 37/1, 54/1, 65/6, 65/7, 65/10, 65/11.
Old Star, Staten Island, N.Y., 77/1.
Osburns, Va., 106/15, 106/16, 106/17, 106/18, 106/19, 106/34.
Oyster Bay, L.I., N.Y., 106/31.

— P —

Page, Thomas Hyde, 85/Bi, 80/33, 145/6.
Pamunkey River, 133/13.
Paoli, Pa., 132/17.
Parker, William, 86/Bi, 116/8, 131/10, 132/19.
Parson's Point, 19/32.
Passaic River, 131/13.
Passamaquody Bay, 11/2, 125/4.
Pauli, George, In.
Paulus Hook, N.J., 57/18, 57/19, 57/21, 57/40, 57/41, 57/42, 84/3, 84/4, 131/7, 131/8, 131/9, 131/10.
Peckham, Howard C., In.
Peekskill, N.Y., 39/4, 81/1, 130/72.
Pelham, Henry, 87/Bi.
Pemaquid River, 107/1.
Penfold, Peter A., In.
Pennsylvania, 44/1, 52/1, 57/5, 57/6, 57/39, 65/11, 80/30, 131/2, 131/3, 131/5, 132, 132/7, 132/8, 144/4, 150/10, 150/11, 151/1, 154/4, 155/7, 157/5, 157/11, 170/4, 172/2.
Penny Hill, N.J., 57/9, 57/29.
Penobscot, 15/1, 64/2.

Whitworth, Richard, 29/1.
Wightman, (Whiteman) George, 117/Bi.
Wilkinson, William Cumberland, 118/Bi, 145/12, 164/4.
Williamsburg, Va., 103/1, 106/12, 106/13, 106/24, 106/25, 133/9.
Williams, I. (see John), 57/37.
Williams, John, 57/5, 57/34, 119/Bi.
Williams, Richard, 120/Bi.
Willsborough Point, 19/11.
Wilmington, Del., 131/2.
Wilmington, N.C., 134/5, 134/6, 156/8.
Wilson, John, 2/46, 121/Bi.
Windmill Hill, R.I., 128/16, 128/17, 128/18.
Windmill Point, N.Y., 12/3, 49/2.
Windsor, 80/19.
Winter Hill, 127/42.

Winter Harbor, 47/2.
Wintersmith, In.
Woodward, David, In.
Woody Heights, L.I., N.Y., 145/16.
Wright, Thomas, 122/Bi, 145/3, 145/4.
Wyld, Joseph, 145/1.

— Y —

York Island, 107/3.
York River, 133/1, 133/9, 133/12, 133/13, 140/1, 156/11.
Yorktown, Va., 21/Bi, 55/1, 57/50, 108/5, 110/Bi, 110/1, 110/2, 133/1, 133/6, 133/8, 140/1.
Yorktown, Va., Siege of, 133/3, 133/4, 133/5.
Yazous River, 46/12, 65/5.